HOOKED & KNOTTED
RUGS

by Ethel Jane Beitler

LITTLE CRAFT BOOK SERIES

STERLING PUBLISHING CO., INC. NEW YORK
SAUNDERS OF TORONTO, Ltd., Don Mills, Canada

 London & Sydney

Little Craft Book Series

The author and publishers wish to extend their appreciation and indebtedness to the many people who contributed in various ways to this book: to the art students and faculty of Texas Tech University for the many ideas and designs they provided; to those who permitted their rugs and wall pieces to be photographed—Mrs. Mattie Smithee, Regal Rugs, Inc., and Cabin Crafts, Inc.; those who worked diligently on the photography—Kathy Hinson, Dr. Bill Lockhart, and Randy Miller; and to the editors and publishers of CREATE WITH YARN, Copyright © 1964, by International Textbook Company, for the use of the material they originally published.

Contents

Before You Begin

A particular craft may be generations old, but the design approach may be so entirely different from that of the past that it looks almost like a new, just-invented craft. Rug-hooking is a craft which flourished in New York and Canada during the early half of the 1800's and which reached its apparent height from 1870 to about 1890. After World Wars I and II, early hand-made rugs were bought by antique dealers and sold at very high prices. People had grown tired of machine-made products and again developed an interest in home crafts. A revival of crafts, especially those of hooking, stitchery and knotting, is now in full swing. Whereas originally, craftsmen hooked and knotted primarily floor rugs, today they also use these processes for making beautiful wall hangings.

For generations, commercial stamped patterns for making hooked rugs have been available on the market, but very little encouragement has been given to individuals to express their own imagination and to create works of art. This situation has certainly improved; in fact, most craftspeople prefer to design their own projects altogether. This book attempts to inspire you to design and then to make your own hooked and knotted rugs.

A hooked rug.

Hooking a Small Rug

The term "hooking" is actually a misnomer as far as most of today's hooking is concerned. The early rugs were literally hooked with a large crochet-type hook which was inserted into a woven foundation fabric and which brought the pile material to the surface in the form of a loop. The entire surface was covered with loops to make a compact, durable surface for a rug. In the early designs, the loops were usually made from old woollen garments which were cut into strips narrow enough to be pulled through the background fabric to form loops on the surface. Rug-hookers still use this method today, but, unless they hold or pull the loop underneath with their fingers, they do the majority of hooking with a punch-type needle which is adjustable to several different lengths of loops, varying from $\frac{1}{4}''$ to $1''$. Instead of old woollen garments, they use yarns because of the wide variety of weights and colors now available on the market, and also because of the ease of manipulating the punch-type needle.

In this book, the craft is referred to as "hooking" whether you use a punch needle or a hook. Commercial rugs with a similar pile are usually referred to as "tufted."

For your first project, make a small rug, perhaps 2' x 2', which you can hang on a wall to brighten an empty corner.

Frames

To hook a rug, you first need a solid, well built adjustable, non-adjustable or easel-type frame, depending on the size of your project.

Pieces of wood 2" x 2" from which you may cut areas out of the ends to interlock the pieces at right angles (see Illus. 1) make a sturdy frame, especially for a large hooked piece. The 2"-wood is rather heavy to handle, however, when you turn the frame back and forth to look at the hooked area when you are using a punch needle. Instead, you can cut and nail together a 3" x 2" or 3" piece of wood (see Illus. 2) like a box frame (no mitering at the corners is necessary). While you hook, suspend either of these types of frame between saw horses or between two card tables.

For this small rug, construct a frame from wood 1" x 1", which you nail together in a butt joint

Illus. 1. Fit four pieces of 2" × 2" wood with notched ends into each other for a large rug frame.

Illus. 2. You can make another type of rug frame if you nail four pieces of ¾" × 2" wood together in a butt joint as shown. Then reinforce with flat, prong-type braces.

and reinforce with metal corner braces as shown in Illus. 3.

You may sometimes use an adjustable frame similar to a quilting frame if you plan to make a very large hooked piece, because you will not be able to reach the middle of a box frame if it is wider than 30″ to 36″. If your rug is on a quilting frame, you can roll it so you are able to reach all parts.

Background Fabric

You are now ready to choose the background fabric for your first rug. Good quality burlap (hessian), firmly woven 2-ply monk's cloth, coarse linen, or upholstery fabric which has no rubberized backing, all make satisfactory background fabrics. Use burlap for this project. Buy enough so that you can make a 2′ x 2′ rug with enough

extra fabric to turn under about an inch before you attach the fabric to your frame and to leave another few inches unhooked for a hem. Stitch the edge of the material along the edge with a zig-zag stitch on the machine so the fabric will not ravel.

Now, stretch your backing securely on the frame and hold it in place with short, broad-headed tacks or staples (see Illus. 4). Before you staple, be sure the backing is taut enough to feel firm, but not so tight that the threads of the fabric will break when you push the hooking needle through it. Turn under at least 1″ of fabric to make a double thickness when you tack or staple it. Also, be certain that the fabric on the frame is straight with the weave. Staple two adjoining sides first. Next, staple the remaining corner, and then the middle of the last two sides before stapling the rest of the fabric.

Illus. 3. For a smaller rug frame, nail four pieces of 1″ × 1″ wood together in a butt joint and reinforce with metal corner braces as shown.

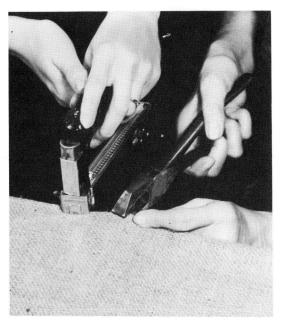

Illus. 4. Tack or staple the backing on to the frame. First, staple two adjoining sides; second, the remaining corner; next the middle of the last two sides, then the rest of the fabric.

If you plan to hook the entire surface (except a few inches of border to turn under for a hem), the fabric may be natural and undyed. However, if you want to have some of the background fabric show and wish to choose a color to harmonize with your yarns, remember that most burlap is not fast color. It is fine to use burlap to learn the process of hooking, but if you become a professional and are filling commissions which involve large amounts of money, your client will want a fabric which will not fade.

Sketch and Transfer a Design

The next step before you begin to hook is to choose a design. Start with a simple pattern—perhaps a circle, a triangle, a square, or even a small abstract motif. The cut-out shapes in Illus. 5 were inspired by tulips. The repeated shape is simple, with only a slight variation to add interest. For this first rug, you could hook only one tulip to fit your 2′ × 2′ piece of burlap. These tulips were cut from paper, artistically arranged, and then drawn around onto the burlap.

The abstract pattern in Illus. 6 is also a selection of cut-out paper shapes, traced round onto burlap (see Illus. 7). You might try hooking one part of this design for your first project.

Illus. 5. For your first project, choose a simple design. These tulip shapes were cut from pieces of colored construction paper.

7

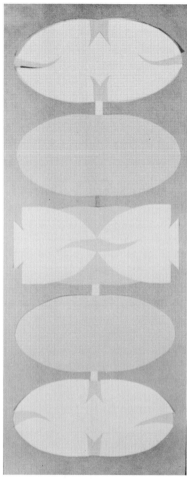

Whatever design you choose, sketch it directly on the burlap with chalk, crayon, grease pencil, or felt-tip pen (Illus. 8). If the fabric is dark enough for white chalk lines to show, sketch the design freehand. If you make mistakes, you can easily erase the chalk with nylon net. Repeat the chalk lines occasionally as they gradually rub off as your hand rubs over them while you are hooking. If you wish, you can go over the lines with crayon or felt-tip pen to make them more permanent.

In transferring your design to the burlap, keep in mind that most rug needles today are designed to punch the yarn through from the *back*, so the loops for the right side of the rug are underneath

Illus. 6. Cut abstract shapes and arrange them artistically on your backing.

Illus. 7. Then, trace round the shapes onto the burlap.

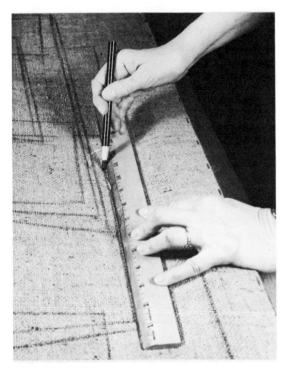

Illus. 8. Use grease pencil for light fabrics or white chalk for dark fabrics to sketch your design on the burlap.

In addition, there are various types of hooking needles available, and the one you decide to use also influences how you should draw the design. One type is the Columbia Minerva Deluxe Rug Needle, with two sizes of point for different sized yarns, which is adjustable to 10 different lengths of loops (see Illus. 9). You may purchase less expensive needles, but they make only one length

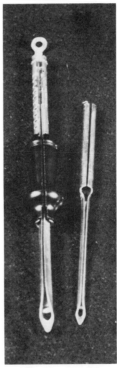

Illus. 9. The Columbia Minerva Deluxe Rug Needle comes with two sizes of needle and adjusts to 10 lengths of loops.

while you are working on the rug. This means that the design will be in reverse when you have completed it. Most geometric, abstract and non-objective designs are quite satisfactory in reverse, but you must reverse a design which should be seen from a particular angle *before* you put it on the burlap. If it does not really matter, as for the tulips or the abstract design in Illus. 6, then draw the design directly on the burlap.

9

of loop. The Susan Bates Rug Hook is more like a large crochet hook. You use it mainly with fabric strips hooked from the right side of the fabric, using your eye as a gauge in determining the length or height of loops (see Illus. 10).

If you plan to use a true hook, like the crochet hook, you should draw the design on the right side of the backing. If, on the other hand, you plan to use a punch-type needle, draw the design on the reverse or wrong side of the fabric. For this first rug, use a punch-type needle, and trace your design onto the back of your burlap.

Instead of drawing the design directly on the burlap, you may draw it on wrapping or tracing paper with a grease pencil or marking pencil (*not* wax crayon). Then turn over the paper, pin or tape it to the burlap and press with a hot iron to transfer the design to the burlap. It is generally easier to do this before you staple the fabric to the frame. The design must be straight with the weave of the fabric.

Winding the Yarn

Before you begin to hook your rug, you should choose and prepare your yarn. Today, most hooked rugs are made with 4-ply yarns, heavy rug yarns, or strips of woollen materials. For a wall hanging, you may use a variety of textures and weights of yarns, such as "thick and thin" (one yarn), Angora, eider-down, cow hair, goat hair, rayons and blends.

If you purchase the yarns in skeins, you should

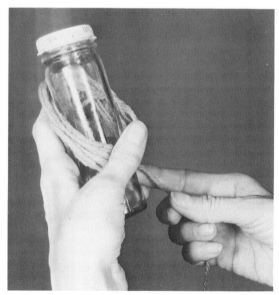

Illus. 11. Start winding the yarn in a diagonal direction.

Illus. 10. Two sizes of Susan Bates Rug Hooks.

10

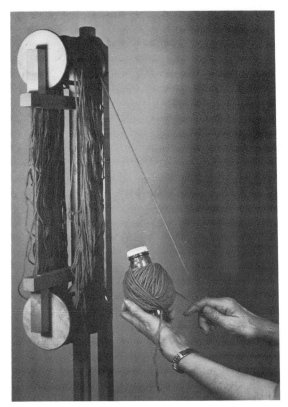

Illus. 12. Continue winding in a diagonal direction, constantly turning the ball.

yarn so the ball will not be hard when completely wound. A hard ball indicates that you have stretched the yarn. Start the winding by holding the beginning end so the yarn pulls from the middle. Sometimes you may want to have two strands of the same color in the needle. You can pull them from the same ball—from the inside and the outside—if you wind as shown in Illus. 12.

You also have the choice of cutting the fabrics

Illus. 13. A commercial strip cutter uses single-edge razor blades for knives.

wind them into balls. There are commercial yarn winders which you can buy, but you can make your own neat balls by winding the yarn, as your grandmother used to do, over your thumb, over a long, slender bottle (see Illus. 11), a thick dowel, or a cardboard paper-towel tube.

Whatever you use, keep a loose hold on the

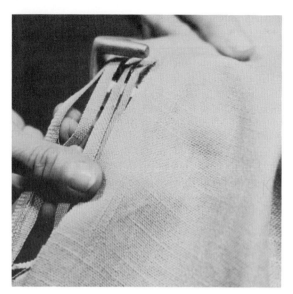

Illus. 14. You may adjust the cutter to produce several widths of fabric strips.

for hooking into strips with scissors or, more evenly, with a strip cutter which you can fasten to the edge of a work table and adjust to several widths of strips. Single-edge razor blades, the cutting tool, are inexpensive, easily replaceable cutters (see Illus. 13 and 14).

Illus. 15. This needle is adjusted to the longest loop. The open side of the needle must face the direction of the hooking.

Hooking

In Illus. 15, a punch-type needle has been threaded with two strands of 4-ply yarn. Note in Illus. 16 that the two strands threaded into the needle come from two balls of yarn. They *could* extend instead from the middle and the outside of just one ball. When you wish to have a gradation of hue or of dark and light, use two strands of yarn in the needle. You can then change one strand each time you wish to change the hue or tone. For instance, if you have three different color

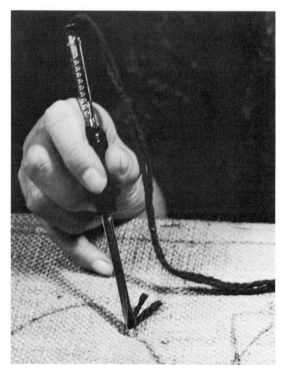

Place the open side of the needle so it faces the direction in which you plan to hook. Push the needle all the way through the fabric to the handle (see Illus. 17). Be sure to place the point of the needle *between* two threads in the weave of the burlap. Do not split threads.

In Illus. 18, the ends of yarn extend below the needle. Hold onto them as you pull the needle back up to the top surface of the fabric. Continue to hold them in place as you punch the needle into the fabric further along the lines of the design.

Illus. 16. A side view of the burlap on the frame shows the needle in the same position as in Illus. 15.

gradations of yarn, use two strands of, for example, color A, then a strand of color A and color B, then two strands of color B, then a strand of color B and color C, then two strands of color C. In this way, the change from color A to color C will not be too much of a sudden contrast.

After you decide on yarn colors, choose your desired loop length and lock the needle in place. (The needle in Illus. 15 was adjusted to the #1—longest—length of loop and was then locked in place.) Thread the yarn through the hole at the top and through the eye of the needle and pull it taut through the needle.

Illus. 17. Push the needle all the way through the fabric to the handle of the needle.

13

Illus. 18. A side view of Illus. 17. Push the needle all the way through to the handle. Hold the ends of the yarn as you pull the needle back to the surface.

Illus. 19. For the second insert, push the needle through the burlap skipping one, two or three threads. Push the needle all the way to the handle for each loop.

(You can trim the ends even with the loops when the rug is all hooked.) Note that you must push the needle all the way down to the handle for each loop. Pull the needle out of the burlap just enough so the point of the needle clears the burlap and insert it in the next space desired.

Illus. 20. Always bring the needle just to the surface before inserting it for the next loop.

Illus. 21. Several loops have been made. Try to keep the loops even.

Illus. 22. The finished loops are half the length of the gauge set above the handle of the needle.

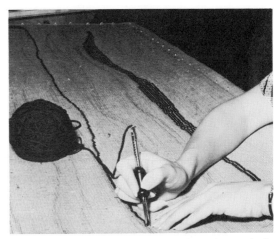

Illus. 23. Here, the yarn is too taut as it unwinds from the ball. The loops will be uneven or will pull out entirely when you pull out the needles.

For especially long loops, hold the loop underneath as you pull the needle back to the surface for the next loop. For "thick and thin" yarns, hold the yarn underneath for each loop as you pull the needle back to the surface of the burlap. Skip one, two, or three threads (see Illus. 19).

You may follow the straight weave of the fabric or the curves of your design (if, for instance, you are hooking the tulips or the abstract in Illus. 6)—this depends upon the effect and the lines of the design you desire. You need to hook short loops more closely together than long loops. In Illus. 21, several loops have already been made.

It is quite important that you have sufficient yarn unwound from the ball when inserting the needle. If you only unwind a small amount, there will be tension on the loops and they will either be shorter than desired, or they will pull out entirely (Illus. 23). Illus. 24 shows plenty of yarn unwound to relieve the tension.

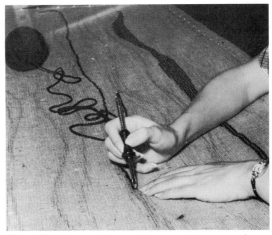

Illus. 24. To avoid tension on the yarn, have plenty of yarn unwound at all times.

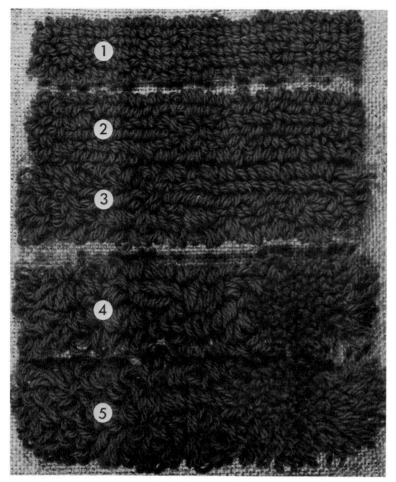

Illus. 25. Experiment in making various lengths of clipped and unclipped loops, in closeness of hooking and in combining colors. The loops here range from the shortest at 1 to the longest at 5. Notice particularly the texture you can achieve by clipping the loops.

This first rug is actually a trial piece. Experiment to determine the effect of different lengths of loops, clipped or unclipped, one, two or three strands in the needle. In Illus. 25, the Columbia Minerva Deluxe Rug Needle was used for some experiments.

If you use 4-ply yarn singly in the needle and hook in every other space in the burlap, leaving two rows of warp threads between each row of loops, at the #10 notch, the result is short loops as at 1. The #8 notch produced the loops at 2, slightly longer than those shown at 1. Here, two rows of warp threads were left between each row of loops. The #6 notch produced the loops at 3. The #4 notch was used at 4. The loops at the right-hand end of the rows are clipped to show variation in texture. The #2 notch produced the loops at 5. The loops at the right-hand end of the rows are also clipped to show the variation in texture.

When you come to the end of the yarn, or to the end of a desired color area, allow the end to extend through to the right side of the rug before you cut it off. When you re-thread the needle, insert it in the same hole that it came out of for the last loop. This means that the two ends come out of the same hole and give more even thickness of pile with no empty or thin spaces.

The beauty of a hooked rug depends not only upon the design, but also upon the way it is hooked, the length and evenness of the loops, whether the loops are clipped or unclipped, and the materials or combinations of materials you use. A beautiful texture is more important than a definite design. The basic design is important, of course, but you can enhance any design by the colors you use and the technique of hooking you apply. For this reason, especially, you should consider your first practice rug as an experiment in design, color and hooking techniques. Do not worry if it is not perfect.

Finishing the Rug or Wall Hanging

Finishing a rug or wall hanging after you have taken it off the frame is very important, just as is the finishing of seams on the inside of a garment: It is the mark of a good craftsman.

As you work, leave an unhooked border about 2″ wide all the way round your rug. You will turn this under for a hem after you take the rug off the frame. Before you turn the hem, however, cover the back of the loops with a liquid rubber (latex) backing, which you can purchase in shops or departments where floor coverings are sold, even though it is later difficult to sew through the rubber backing.

It is easier to apply the latex backing if you do it before you take your project off the frame. To apply the liquid to the back of a hooked piece which you have completely covered with loops, pour the latex on the back over an area about 12″ square and smooth it out with the edge of a piece of cardboard, a putty knife, or a plastic scraper.

Anchor the loops even if you are not planning to use the piece as a rug on the floor because you may wish to use a vacuum cleaner or a soft brush to clean a wall piece, and you could easily pull out the loops, especially clipped ones. In fact, in hooking the design, if you are not satisfied with a particular part, you can easily pull it out and fill the area in again in a different color, or with different length loops. Do not feel that once you have hooked an area you must leave it.

After the backing is dry, remove the rug from the frame, and turn under and stitch the unhooked border for a hem.

Now, find an empty wall space and hang up your first rug. If you are pleased with your tulip-shaped beginning, or with the section of the abstract or geometric design you hooked, you could go on to make a larger rug using the whole design, as in Illus. 5 or Illus. 6.

Designs for Hooking Projects

You are now familiar with the basic rug-hooking techniques. If you do not feel confident enough to attempt a large rug yet, continue experimenting with different backing fabrics, different yarns and yarn combinations, and different loop lengths.

At the start and as you learn, search for unusual, original ideas for designs. Works of art, such as abstract paintings that you see in museums, scenes from magazines, photographs (especially your own), advertising layouts, almost anything you see around you may lead you to develop an abstraction or design of your own. You do not have to copy other rugs or wall hangings for attractive designs. Keep in mind that to copy a design originated by someone else is to stand still. Your creation may or may not be a better design than one you would copy, but at least it means you are trying to do something on your own. It is best to start with a simple, original design and to use your taste and the manual skills you have already acquired or acquire as you work. Hundreds of simple, but effective and usable designs will come to you.

You can even hook a scene, a flower, or a leaf in any way you see it—not necessarily in its true proportions or coloration. Simplify, re-arrange and exaggerate lines, shapes, color, texture and space relationships first in your mind, and then on paper, or directly on your rug. Your design does not necessarily need to be identified by name as a horse, a building, or a tree. These objects, of course, are potential inspirations for designs, but you can also search in a wider area for ideas to express yourself. Everything you see can serve as a basis for original designs and new uses of materials.

Remember only that a rug is usually viewed from all sides and should, therefore, have no top or bottom. If you plan to hang your rug on the wall, however, the design may or may not have a top and bottom.

Illus. 26. Dried, cracked earth may be an inspiration for a quiet, linear design for a rug.

Suggestions

Illus. 26 is a photograph of dried, caked earth which shows a casual, irregular development of lines which vary in thickness as well as direction. Can you visualize a hooked rug with the grey areas as long, clipped loops, and the black lines as short, unclipped loops?

Illus. 27 was made by pulling a brush loaded with black water color over a wet surface. The paint spread and left irregular edges which could inspire you to make a rug with especially long, clipped pile.

Illus. 28 shows the start of a design for the rug shown in Illus. 29. Cut paper shapes of different

Illus. 27. Water colors or ink brushed onto wet paper blends and gives soft, fuzzy edges which could be a beautiful effect as a rug.

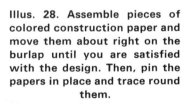

Illus. 28. Assemble pieces of colored construction paper and move them about right on the burlap until you are satisfied with the design. Then, pin the papers in place and trace round them.

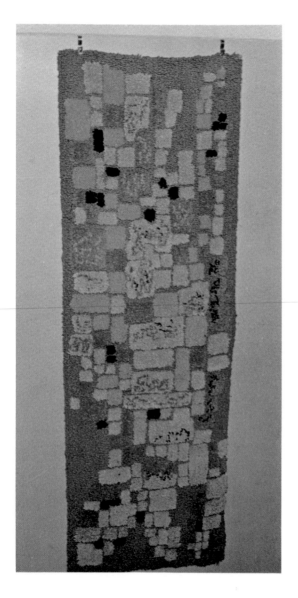

Illus. 29. "Green Acres" was the result of the design in Illus. 28 which was assembled from cut paper shapes.

Illus. 30. This striking, warm-hued rug was the the result of the dark and light experiments shown in Illus. 34.

Illus. 31. A photomicrograph of a drop of water inspired "The Forest."

Illus. 32. "Egyptian Desert" was inspired by a photomicrograph of copper crystals.

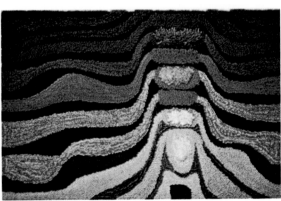

sizes, shapes and colors and experiment with their arrangement. Pin them in place while you draw lines round them preparatory to hooking the design. Illus. 29 shows the final design in the hooked rug. Note in Illus. 33, the reverse side of Illus. 29, that the shapes appear to be further apart than in Illus. 29. The longer, clipped loops in the squares and rectangles tend to lean over and fill in the space between the shapes, so the spaces between them are wider on purpose so the shapes do not appear to touch.

Illus. 34 shows three different paper arrangements of dark and light cut-outs of the same design. The rug shown in Illus. 30 is the result of these experiments. The color relationships are not exactly the same as those in any of the experiments, but at least they served as inspiration for the colors chosen for the rug.

Tempera paint experiments can also yield an endless variety of ideas. Illus. 35 was one such experiment which was chosen for the rug shown in Illus. 36.

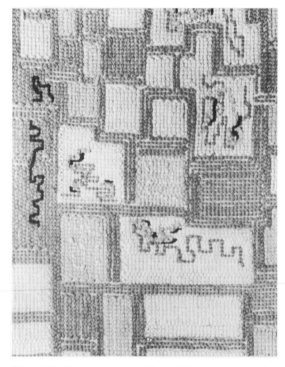

Illus. 33. The reverse of Illus. 29 shows that the spaces between the blocks are wider than they appear to be on the right side.

Illus. 34. The same design can appear quite different if you simply alter the arrangement of dark and light.

22

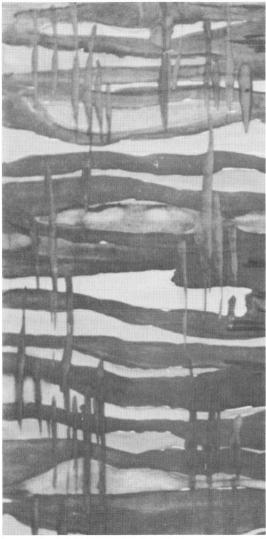

Illus. 35. Experiment with tempera paints until you create a painting you like well enough to imitate as a rug.

Illus. 36. Picture this rug, entitled "Dance of the Flames," in brilliant shades of red and orange with outstanding background areas of purple and royal blue. The design was taken from the tempera painting in Illus. 35.

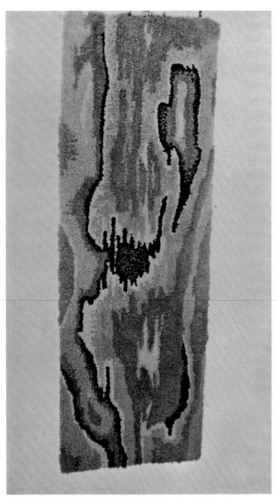

Illus. 37. "Grain-lines" was inspired by the ply-wood in Illus. 40.

Illus. 38. This is the attractive rug that resulted from the sketch of a cantaloupe cross-section in Illus. 41.

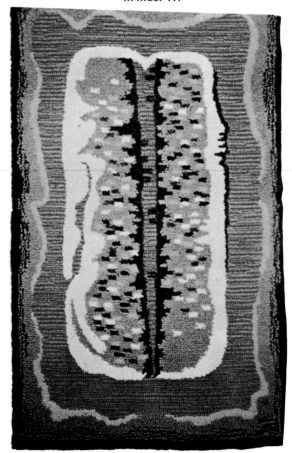

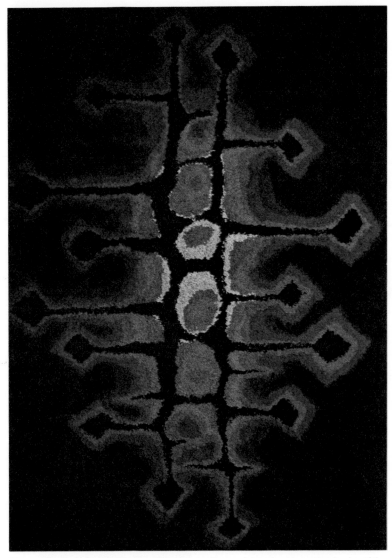

Illus. 39. A harmony of color and shape blend attractively in this wool hooked rug made with short, unclipped loops.

Illus. 40 shows a piece of plywood with an interesting grain-line design which is interpreted in the design of the rug shown in Illus. 37. The rough sketch shown in Illus. 41 was inspired by the seeds and pulp of a cantaloupe. Later, it was interpreted in the hooked rug in Illus. 38. Note the irregularity in the various parts of the design, rather than a strictly symmetrical treatment.

The rug in Illus. 42 was an experiment in the use of reverse values and simple circular shapes which you can draw round cups, saucers, and plates, or with a compass. Heavy eider-down yarn

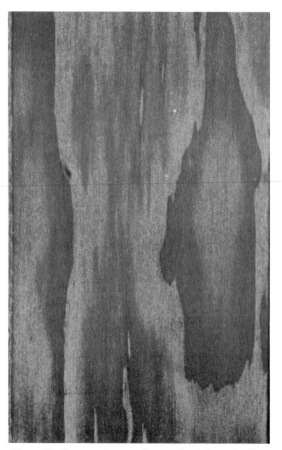

Illus. 40. Scrap pieces of wood with grain-lines may give you an unusual design idea.

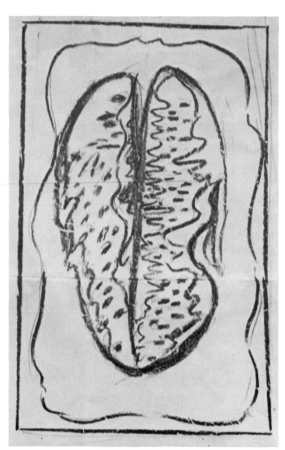

Illus. 41. The seeds and pulp in a cross-section of a cantaloupe inspired this rough sketch for a rug.

was used with the reverse tones executed in a reverse clipped and unclipped technique.

Photomicrographs of nature's wonders provide unlimited sources of ideas for designs. Illus. 32 was inspired by a photomicrograph of copper crystals. Illus. 31 was inspired by a drop of water. Perhaps an interesting hooked circular design might be inspired by the transverse (cross) section of a *Ranunculus* (Buttercup) root, shown in Illus. 43.

Sometimes, very precise and regular geometric shapes tend to give a more formal effect to a design (see Illus. 47). A design of this type, however, requires accurate hooking if you plan to leave the loops short and unclipped. Any unplanned variation of length of loops due to unskilled or careless craftsmanship can be very evident in the areas of solid colors. Note also, in Illus. 47, that some blocks are hooked horizontally and some vertically for variation in texture.

Many times, slices of rocks, such as the agate in Illus. 45, give interesting suggestions for a rug or wall hanging such as the one shown in Illus. 46.

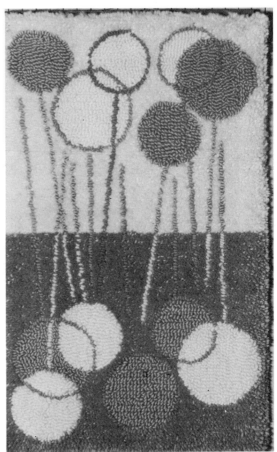

Illus. 42. These gay "Lollipops" were inspired by the simple shape of a child's delicacy.

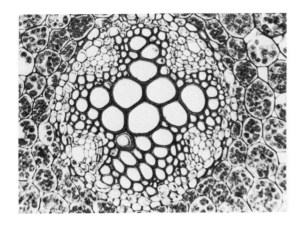

←
Illus. 43. You might design a rug with free-form circles of various sizes, patterned after this cross-section of a Buttercup root.

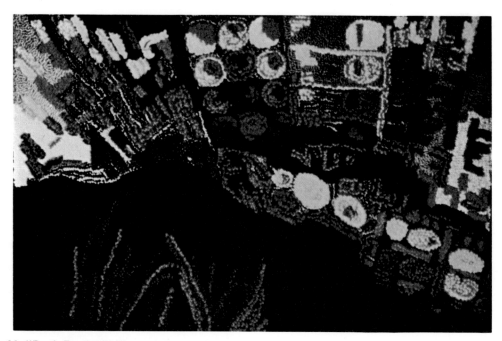

Illus. **44.** "Rock Festival" illustrates a method of filling in background space with curvilinear hooking. When hooking, simply follow the curved lines of your design instead of the straight weave of the fabric.

HOW THE DESTINATION CONTENT WORKS

Each destination includes a short introduction, an A–Z of practical information and recommended points of interest, split into 4 different categories:

• Highlights
• Accommodation
• Eating out
• What to do

You can view the location of every point of interest and save it by adding it to your Favourites. In the 'Around Me' section you can view all the points of interest within 5km.

HOW THE EBOOKS WORK

The eBooks are provided in EPUB file format. Please note that you will need an eBook reader installed on your device to open the file. Many devices come with this as standard, but you may still need to install one manually from Google Play.

The eBook content is identical to the content in the printed guide.

HOW TO DOWNLOAD THE WALKING EYE APP

1. Download the Walking Eye App from the App Store or Google Play.
2. Open the app and select the scanning function from the main menu.
3. Scan the QR code on this page – you will then be asked a security question to verify ownership of the book.
4. Once this has been verified, you will see your eBook and destination content in the purchased ebook and destination sections, where you will be able to download them.

Other destination apps and eBooks are available for purchase separately or are free with the purchase of the Insight Guide book.

Contents

THE BEST OF MOSCOW: TOP ATTRACTIONS

At a glance, everything you won't want to miss, from iconic cathedrals to palatial architecture and impressive art galleries to the city's best bathhouse.

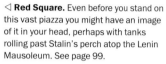

◁ **Red Square.** Even before you stand on this vast piazza you might have an image of it in your head, perhaps with tanks rolling past Stalin's perch atop the Lenin Mausoleum. See page 99.

▽ **The Kremlin.** Epicentre of Russian state power, this fortress once contained the original city. Patriarchs, tsars and Communist presidents ruled from here, as does Putin's regime today. See page 87.

▽ **Cathedral of Christ the Saviour.** Built to commemorate the defeat of Napoleon in 1812, this is Russia's largest cathedral. Destroyed by Stalin's dynamite, it was rebuilt in time for the new millennium. See page 129.

▽ **Pushkin Museum of Fine Arts.** One of Russia's best art museums boasts a collection of over half a million works, including everything from Egyptian papyrus to Picassos. See page 124.

△ **St Basil's Cathedral.** It's the building in Russia everyone outside the country recognises, and no one will believe you've been to Moscow if you don't post a selfie with this church in the background. See page 104.

▽ **Bolshoi Theatre.** Back from the dead after the building nearly collapsed, Russia's most illustrious stage once again reverberates to Slavic ballet and headline-making scandal. See page 115.

△ **Tretyakov Gallery.** The home of Russian art on the south side of the river, the highlight of the Tretyakov is the unrivalled collection of icons, including rare works by Rublyov. See page 188.

▽ **Novodevichy Convent.** One of the best preserved and most tranquil of Moscow's original convents was built in 1524 to celebrate a great military victory over the Poles and Lithuanians. See page 136.

◁ **Arbat.** Moscow's most celebrated street once drew artists and writers and now lures tourists and street performers to its pedestrianised length. See page 131.

▷ **Sandunovsky Baths.** Let yourself be pummelled, whipped and steamed at Moscow's most famous traditional bathhouse. Bathing is segregated and tea, beer and relaxed conversation are part of the cleansing process. See page 165.

THE BEST OF MOSCOW: EDITOR'S CHOICE

Setting priorities, saving money, unique attractions – here, at a glance, are our recommendations, plus some tips and pieces of etiquette to keep the scolding *babushki* at bay.

Mayakovskaya Metro station.

BEST QUIRKY SIGHTS

Museum of Unique Dolls. If eerie glass eyes and the vacant stares of old dolls freak you out, this may be a museum you'll want to avoid. See page 162.

Cabin of Peter the Great. Peter the Great seems to have liked living in humble cabins – he had one in St Petersburg and another at Kolomenskoye in Moscow. See page 198.

Tsaritsyno. Catherine the Great left this estate to rot as she didn't like the design, but these former ghostly ruins have been brought back to life. See page 199.

Perlov Tea Shop. A beautifully preserved, late 19th-century Chinese tea shop, created to impress a Chinese ambassador who never showed up. See page 173.

Grand Bridge at Tsaritsyno.

ONLY IN MOSCOW

Metro. Take a ride in Stalinist style on what must be the world's most ornate underground railway system. See page 120.

Fabergé eggs. The tsar's unique collection of priceless, original Fabergé eggs housed in the Kremlin is the last word in royal bling. See page 96.

Lenin's Mausoleum. Even two-and-a-half decades after the collapse of the USSR people still line up to view the first Communist leader's embalmed body. See page 103.

House-museums. It seems every street in Moscow has an apartment museum where a famous literary figure once resided. See pages 135 & 167.

Red Square. It's neither red nor square, but Russia's most famous piazza draws every tourist to its cobbles in the imposing shadow of the Kremlin. See page 99.

BEST CHURCHES

Dormition Cathedral, Kremlin. Once the cathedral used for the coronation of the tsars, this is still the Kremlin's finest house of worship.

Hotel Ukraina, one of the Seven Sisters.

See page 91.
Cathedral of Christ the Saviour. Russia's largest cathedral was rebuilt in the late 1990s after being absent from the Moscow skyline for almost seven decades. See page 129.
Church of the Intercession at Fili. A fantastic example of Russian Baroque, which somehow remained intact through the Soviet assault on religion. See page 154.
Church of St Nikolay the Wonderworker in Khamovniki. Built by a community of weavers, this ornate, gilded cathedral is one of the finest neighbourhood churches in the city. See page 135.

Church of St. Nikolay the Wonderworker, Khamovnik.

MOSCOW FOR FREE

Red Square. There's no ticket booth to tackle before that typical Moscow shot of you on the famous Red Square. See page 99.
Churches. Most of Moscow's churches are working places of worship and do not charge admission. See page 106.
Metro stations. OK, to see Moscow's elaborate underground palaces, aka metro stations, you need a ticket but you can ride all day for 50 roubles (£0.47/$0.66). See page 120.
City parks. Always free and great locations to people-watch as all of Moscow strolls, jogs and stumbles by. See pages 191 & 193.

Muzeon Sculpture Garden.

BEST SOVIET RELICS

Lenin's Mausoleum. Where else can you enjoy a private audience with a major world leader and be allowed to do all the talking? See page 103.
Museum of Cosmonautics. Relive the glory days of the Soviet space race at the Cosmonautics museum and see the first two (canine) astronauts to return from space: Belka and Strelka. See page 175.
Mayakovsky Museum. This whirlwind of a museum re-creates the heady optimism of the

Soviet Union's early days, which are often overlooked. See page 172.
Muzeon Sculpture Gardens. Following the Berlin Wall like dominoes, statues that once glorified the Soviet regime were pulled down. Now they are displayed here. See page 191.
Stalinist Skyscrapers. Stalin's architectural gift to posterity, these seven *vysotki* (high-rises), housing luxury apartments and hotels, still dominate the Moscow skyline. See page 181.

BEST SHOPPING

Vernisazh Izmailovsky Park. The old flea market in the eastern suburbs has become the city's premier location for souvenir shopping. See page 193.

GUM. The corridors of GUM are lined with the finest names in European fashion, jewellery and cosmetics. See page 102.

Okhotny Ryad Underground Mall. This standard mall experience is made unique by the ornamentation of Zurab Tsereteli, former Mayor Luzhkov's favoured artist. See page 119.

TsUM. Moscow's first department store and an old favourite of Chekhov and his family. See page 163.

Yeliseev's. Even during the darkest days of economic depression, the elaborately decorated counters of this food emporium were ready to serve. See page 159.

Petrovsky Passage. A smaller, more elite version of GUM, and especially popular with those looking for more intimate service – and even higher prices. See page 163.

Russian caviar.

Yeliseev's food hall.

BEST FOOD

Caviar. There are several types, and all taste best on fresh blini with a shot of chilled vodka to wash the taste down.

Black bread. Russia prides itself on the wholesome, hearty loaf, and the best is the heavy, rye-based *chyorny khleb.*

Georgian cuisine. Moscow's favourite ethnic food, despite the long-running tensions between the two countries.

Vodka. Russia's national drink is best enjoyed with plenty of *zakuski* (salads and pickles) with which to follow the shots.

MOSCOW FOR CHILDREN

Moscow Circus. The performing animals and gravity-defying acrobats of Russia's finest big top will amaze the kids. See page 165.

Detsky Mir. There doesn't seem to be a toy on earth that isn't stocked by Russia's premier toyshop, oddly situated opposite the former KGB headquarters. See page 169.

Moscow Zoo. The capital's zoo is not the cruel, underfunded place you might have heard about and provides an enjoyable afternoon for the little ones. See page 150.

Obraztsov Puppet Theatre. Experience the Eastern European tradition of excellent puppet theatre at this long-established stage. See page 167.

Victory Day in Victory Park.

PARKS AND GARDENS

Izmailovsky Park. One of the city's oldest green spaces and home to the Vernisazh market, with its souvenir-buying opportunities. See page 193.

Chistye prudy. A small but welcome area of city-centre greenery and one of the best places to try ice-skating in the sub-zero Russian winter. See page 173.

Gorky Park. Once a seedy funfair, the famous Gorky Park has been transformed into an ecofriendly recreational zone for joggers and picnickers. See page 191.

Victory Park. This themed park honours those who died in World War II, or the Great Patriotic War as Russians call it. See page 153.

Moscow Circus.

TRAVELLER'S TIPS

Dress appropriately for the season – Moscow's summers are as sweltering as its winters are nippy.

When visiting Moscow's churches women should cover their heads with a scarf, men shouldn't wear shorts or a hat.

Don't get involved in card games with strangers – it's a scam.

Despite what you may have heard, you have seven working days to register your visa in Moscow. Your hotel will probably do this for you anyway.

Haggling isn't a good idea these days.

Avoid the metro at rush hour (8–9am and 5–7pm) as the crush can be unbearable.

If you can, use the metro instead of

taxis. Always get your hotel to call you a taxi if you must use one and never hail a taxi in the street.

Avoid Moscow on 1–11 January and 1–9 May when many businesses shut and city folk escape to the country or somewhere warm.

Take care when crossing Moscow's crazy roads. Use underpasses.

Sightseers on a wet evening in Red Square.

Giant Russian dolls on display in AFIMALL City.

Novoslobodskaya Metro station.

Modern office blocks dwarf a small church in the business district at Belaya Ploshad.

A CAPITAL REBORN

While it still retains its legendary enigmatic aura, Moscow has re-wrapped itself in the familiar cloak of a grand European capital.

For generations in the West, Moscow has conjured up images of red stars and black limousines, grey apartment blocks and dowdy citizens, tanks on parade and tanks on the move, oligarchs and oil riches. While many of these old stereotypes linger, Moscow today is a vibrant European capital, lit by neon and filled with cafés, clubs and casinos. Once again graced by golden cupolas and pastel-coloured manor houses, its streets are crowded with beautiful young people in the latest fashions.

It is a city with something for everyone. For art-lovers, it has some of the world's finest collections of painting and sculpture, from European masterpieces to Russian avant-garde and monumental Socialist Realism, not to mention cutting-edge contemporary art. For music-lovers, there are magnificent 19th-century halls where the world's most celebrated musicians perform (at budget prices), along with sublime Orthodox church choirs. For lovers of the performing arts, local dance and theatre still define these arts throughout the world. For fans of architecture,

Kutuzovsky Avenue and the business district.

glorious cathedrals, palaces and emporia illustrate many styles, from the vaulted halls of medieval Muscovy through Classicism, *style moderne* and Constructivism.

Tretyakov Gallery.

Museums let visitors relive European history on battlefields, in palaces and in the homes of artists. Foodies can look forward to fabulous cuisine from across the former Soviet Union, accompanied by hearty local beers and flavoured vodkas. And for those who wish to step out of the hustle and bustle, there are quiet crooked streets shaded by ancient trees, where you can catch glimpses of fur-clad women slipping into courtyards, catch the scent of incense drifting from a brightly coloured parish church, or hear the doleful sound of a cow bell ringing on the breeze from a kitchen garden.

Moscow has reinvented itself, as it has done so many times before, after fire, invasion and shifts in power. It hasn't been an easy or smooth process. There is a gaudy jumble of epochs and styles, a sometimes-uneasy mix of rich and poor.

But that is the way Moscow has always been: flashy and dowdy, ancient and modern, Eastern and Western, elegant and kitsch, spiritual and vulgar, with twisting lanes and broad avenues, one street a cacophony of sound, the next so silent you can still hear the nightingales sing.

Fashionable Muscovite couple.

THE MUSCOVITES

In a billionaire's capital, where wealth is publicly paraded, daily life can still be very hard for the average citizen. Even so, the city remains the promised land for Russians from every corner of the country.

In any discussion of the country's wealth disparity, Russians will inevitably point out that 'Moscow is not Russia', a remark that brings the conversation to an end with nods and shrugs of agreement.

While parts of the country are economically depressed, Moscow stands out as a bustling bastion of opportunity and decadence. It is a city of frenetic consumerism, where streets are lined with expensive foreign cars, where posh restaurants and cafés spring up almost daily and where exclusive clubs are playgrounds for the country's richest and most beautiful. However, recently Western sanctions and economic woes have a taken a bit of the shine off things.

Like characters from a Chekhov play, millions of Russians dream of moving to the capital. Keenly aware of this, Moscow's authorities have kept in place a draconian, Soviet-era registration system to prevent the masses from flooding into the city. Unlike outer regions blighted by unemployment, there is plenty of work here, from building to banking, and it's the place to make a stellar career. It is, after all, the billionaire capital of the world. According to a survey published by the Credit Suisse investment bank in 2013, out of a declining national population of around 144 million, 35 percent of Russia's wealth is concentrated in the hands of just 110 people, most of whom either reside in, or made their fortunes in, Moscow.

If you've got it, flaunt it

Flaunting wealth in the form of luxury cars, clothes, eating out and entertainment is a favourite pastime among Moscow's rich, many

Celebrating the Day of Russia at Red Square.

of whom earned their fortunes in murky fashion during the violent, turbulent 1990s following the collapse of the Soviet Union. Hummers, Mercedes and Lexi are common sights on the perpetually jammed streets of central Moscow, as are burly men in expensive suits with ostentatiously dressed women in tow.

In the 1990s, many of Moscow's more deep-pocketed residents were Western expatriates who flocked to cash in on economic opportunities offered by the nascent capitalism of the Wild East. Consequently, foreigners were valued patrons of the city's most expensive clubs and restaurants, as were 'New Russians', a class of nouveau riche as notorious for their extravagantly bad taste as for their filthy lucre.

The rouble crash of 1998, however, sent many expats fleeing Moscow with their bank accounts all but wiped out, while millions of Russians were left to start from a financial Ground Zero. Buoyed by high world oil prices, the country's economy grew steadily until 2014, but recent troubles have put everything into reverse. Billionaires with their dollar and euro accounts in Luxembourg and Cyprus have survived unscathed but anyone holding roubles has seen their fortunes decimated.

The poverty gap

The wealth disparity between Moscow and the rest of the country is mirrored within the city itself, providing daily scenes worthy of the most exaggerated Soviet portrayals of victims of capitalism. It is not unusual to see the city's wealthiest residents strutting their stuff past drunks and beggars in states of extreme human degradation, begging for spare change or sprawled out unconscious awaiting removal to the drunk tank.

Russia's middle class

Between these economic extremes, however, a middle class has emerged, made up of small-business owners, employees in Western companies, marketing specialists, lawyers and middle-managers in an array of industries.

The steady economic growth of the early 2000s gave this social group the chance not only to make ends meet but to patronise mid-priced clubs, restaurants and fitness clubs, and take holidays abroad. Turkey, Egypt and Cyprus were popular destinations, due to bargain travel packages and the relative ease with which Russians could obtain visas for these countries.

However the middle classes have been hit hardest by Russia's recent economic nose-dive. The devaluation of the rouble has adversely affected the prices of foreign goods in the shops and a self-imposed ban on foreign food imports has meant less choice. Fewer Russians are taking holidays abroad, but a growing number of middle-class Russians are deciding to take permanent holidays, getting their families out of an increasingly unstable country to the safety of Europe. Property prices have also fallen, rendering some homes unsellable. Mortgages taken

Posing as a general for photos at Red Square.

out in euros during the days of plenty are now mostly unserviceable.

The ethnic mix

As the capital of a country with more than 130 ethnic groups, Moscow is hugely diverse. Many different nationalities came to the city in Soviet times, and, in spite of the tough registration systems, many others flocked and continue to flock to the capital following the collapse of the superpower. Officially, at least, the Soviet Union promoted the Friendship of Peoples, a phrase enshrined in the title of a Moscow university named after Patrice Lumumba, the first prime minister of the Democratic Republic of the Congo, who was assassinated in 1961. The Friendship of Peoples concept was also the inspiration for an enormous golden Soviet-era fountain at Moscow's All-Russia Exhibition Centre that features a giant wheat sheaf in a granite bowl surrounded by statues of young women in the national costumes of the Soviet Union's 16 republics.

Today, Moscow houses representatives of almost every ethnicity in the Russian Federation, as well as hundreds of thousands of migrants from former Soviet republics.

Moscow's official population hovers around 12.2 million, but unofficially the number is estimated to be as high as 15 million, including illegal migrants and commuters from the sprawling suburbs. A majority of Moscow residents are ethnic Russians, Tatars, Ukrainians and Belorussians, but Moscow also has large ethnic communities from the former Soviet Union's Central Asian and southern republics, including Kyrgyzstan, Moldova, Uzbekistan, Tajikistan, Armenia, Azerbaijan and Georgia. The Russian government estimates that between 500,000 and 800,000 immigrants live in Moscow, while more than 96,000 work permits are issued annually to foreign workers. A majority of these were issued to migrants from former Soviet republics, known in Russia as 'the near abroad' because of historical links, though tens of thousands were also issued to migrants from the 'far abroad', including Turkey, China and Vietnam.

Popular xenophobia

Internationalism and the Friendship of Peoples received much lip service in official Soviet policy, and Russia today still has the country's multiethnic make-up enshrined and honoured in its Constitution. But the influx of different ethnic groups has provided fodder for nationalistic politicians and xenophobic, Fascist organisations demanding that their country halt this 'invasion'.

In the ideological vacuum following the collapse of the Soviet Union, xenophobia has proved to be a violent, deadly and disturbingly popular doctrine, especially among young adherents to neo-Fascist groups. Beatings of non-Russians, particularly those with dark skin, have been common in the past decade or so, and the authorities have largely ignored the problem, despite several high-profile deaths by beatings from skinheads. The latest groups to be victimised have been Ukrainians, Georgians and Turks, citizens of countries that have stood up to Russia's aggressive foreign policy in recent years. Africans and Asians have also been the victims of racist attacks.

Many of the migrant workers from the 'near abroad' work for miserly wages at construction sites and sell produce at outdoor markets in order to send money home. Slowly, the authorities have begun to concede that these guest workers are beneficial to the local economy, but many Muscovites have trouble accepting this reality.

Arriving at Belorussky Train Station.

Construction of the Cathedral of the Archangel during the 14th century.

DECISIVE DATES

500 BC
First Neolithic settlements established in the region.

AD 500–1000
East Slavic tribe called Vjataichi occupies the area.

879
Death of Rurik, leader of the Varangians, or Vikings, after founding the empire of the Kievan Rus.

988
Prince Vladimir of Kiev accepts Orthodox Christianity.

1054
Death of Kievan ruler Yaroslav the Wise leads to division of Kievan Rus into multiple principalities.

1113–25
Vladimir Monomakh briefly reunites Kievan Rus for final time.

1147
First written mention of Moscow, by Prince Yuri Dolgoruky, considered the founder of Moscow.

1156
First wooden walls built around the Kremlin by Yuri Dolgoruky.

1237–8
Moscow plundered and burned by Tatar Batu Khan. Khans begin practice of appointing Moscow Grand Princes.

1340
Under Ivan Kalita, 'Moneybags', oak walls are built around the Kremlin, reinforced with stucco.

1366
White stone walls built around the Kremlin.

Statue of Yuriy Dolgoruki.

1380
Dmitry Donskoy defeats Tatars at the battle of Kulikovo Field.

1382
Tatars burn Moscow to the ground.

1427
Church of the Miraculous Icon of the Saviour completed, the earliest surviving architecture in the city.

1453
Turks take Constantinople, and Moscow claims the mantle of the 'true Church' of Eastern Orthodoxy.

1462–1505
Reign of Ivan III (the Great), who reconstructs the Kremlin and moves traders to Red Square. More importantly, he begins the process of uniting all Russian

The Kremlin during the reign of Ivan III.

principalities under the crown of Moscow. The Dormition Cathedral by Italian Aristotele Fioravanti is completed in 1479.

1480
Ivan III renounces the state's allegiance to the Tatar Khans.

1485–95
Current brick walls built around an enlarged Kremlin.

1493
Ivan III crowns himself Sovereign of All Russia. Moscow is its capital.

1508–16
Moat cut along the Kremlin walls on Red Square.

1533–84
Reign of Ivan the Terrible, who establishes a council of boyars.

1561
St Basil's Cathedral built to commemorate the routing of the Tatars in Kazan (1552) and Astrakhan (1556).

1563
First book printed in Moscow.

1585–93
The White City walls built (current Boulevard Ring).

1604–13
The 'Time of Troubles', in which the country searches for a strong leader and Poles occupy the city.

1612
Moscow liberated from the Poles by troops led by Minin, a butcher, and Prince Pozharsky.

1613
Mikhail Romanov elected tsar, ending the 'Time of Troubles' and beginning the Romanov dynasty.

1659
Wooden walls built around Earthen City (current Garden Ring Road).

1682–1725
Reign of Peter the Great.

1689
Peter's sister Sophia incarcerated at Novodevichy Convent after her attempt on the throne.

1702
First public theatre opened.

1703
Russia's first newspaper, *Vedomosti*, is printed.

The Arrest of Tsarevna Sophia, 1689.

1712
Peter the Great moves the capital to St Petersburg.

1755
Moscow University founded.

1780s
White City walls torn down.

1812
Moscow set alight and abandoned to thwart Napoleon's troops, who enter the city on 14 September. They retreat, suffering heavy losses, on 6 October.

1816–30
Earthen City walls torn down and Garden Ring Road built.

1819–22
Neglinnaya River forced underground and the Aleksandrovsky Gardens laid by the western Kremlin walls.

Tsar Alexander II at the Bolshoi Theatre, 1856.

1825
Bolshoi Theatre opens.

1861
Tsar Alexander II liberates the serfs.

1866
Moscow Conservatory founded.

1869
Tolstoy publishes *War and Peace.*

1882
First telephone system established in Moscow.

1883
First electric streetlights established.

1898
Moscow Art Theatre founded.

1902
Yaroslavl station completed by Fyodor Shekhtel, leading *style moderne* architect.

1905
Moscow torn apart by strikes and worker uprisings. Trans-Siberian Railway completed.

1912
Futurist Vladimir Mayakovsky publishes *A Slap in the Face of Public Taste.*

1914
Russia enters World War I.

1917
In February Tsar Nicholas II abdicates throne. Civil War begins. On 3 November Soviet power is proclaimed in Moscow.

1918
On 12 March the Soviet government is transferred to Moscow.

1922
Civil War ends. At the First All-Union Congress of Soviets, the USSR is established with Moscow as its capital.

1924
Lenin dies. Stalin rises to power.

1935
First metro line opens. The first General Plan for the reconstruction of Moscow is approved.

1941
On 22 June Nazi Germany invades the USSR and reaches Moscow.

1945
On 9 May Germany capitulates.

First World War propaganda poster for the Red Army, 1917.

1951
The Second General Plan for the reconstruction of Moscow is approved.

1953
Khrushchev comes to power after the death of Stalin.

1957
The 6th World Festival of Youth and Students is held in Moscow.

1980
The Summer Olympics are held in Moscow, but boycotted by the US after the invasion of Afghanistan.

1985
Mikhail Gorbachev becomes leader and declares a policy of '*perestroika, glasnost* and accelerated social and economic development'.

1989
Berlin Wall falls.

1991
Boris Yeltsin elected President of Russian Federation within the USSR. August coup of hardliners against Gorbachev. On 21 December the former Soviet republics declare the dissolution of the USSR and the establishment of the Commonwealth of Independent States. On 25 December Gorbachev resigns and the Soviet flag is lowered over the Kremlin.

1993
Russian Congress tries to unseat Yeltsin, but fails.

1996
Yuri Luzhkov elected mayor of Moscow with 95 percent of the vote; re-elected in 1999 and 2003.

1998
Default on government debts; rouble collapses.

2000
Prime Minister Vladimir Putin is elected President after Boris Yeltsin resigns. The rebuilt Cathedral of Christ the Saviour opens.

2002
129 hostages and 41 Chechen fighters die when Russian troops storm Palace of Culture theatre.

2004
Putin elected for second term with more than 71 percent of the vote.

2006
Russia temporarily cuts off the supply of gas to Ukraine because of a conflict over rising prices. Record low temperatures hit Moscow.

2014
Russia hosts the Winter Olympics, marred by Russia's reaction to a popular revolution in Ukraine. Russia subsequently annexes Crimea and stokes war in Ukraine's east. Moscow's population exceeds the 12 million mark.

2018
Moscow due to host the FIFA World Cup Finals.

Mayor of Moscow, Yuri Luzhkov, 2007.

MOSCOV

Moscow, 1683.

S: MICHEL

S: NICOLAS

CITY OF TUMULT

Built and rebuilt in the image of the ruling prince, tsar, general secretary and mayor, Moscow has grown from a small wooden settlement on a bluff between two rivers to a metropolis that rules the world's largest nation. Its past has been a glorious struggle between state and religion that has kept it in the spotlight on the world stage.

Come to me, brother, in Moscow ... These words – written by Prince Yuri Dolgoruky of Suzdal to his ally Prince Svyatoslav in 1147 – are the first known mention of the city that has charmed, terrified, awed and captivated the world for nearly 900 years. Archaeologists believe this fertile area of woods, bogs and rivers has been inhabited for much longer, perhaps as far back as the 5th century BC. Hence, the Prince didn't see the need to send any directions along with his invitation.

At the time the princes met to consolidate a base in the city, Moscow was just a small trading settlement in the vast Kievan Rus Empire, albeit a strategically placed one. This empire began in the 9th century when back a Viking (Varangian) leader named Rurik had consolidated western Russia and Ukraine with the capital in Kyiv (Kiev). In 988 Prince Vladimir of Kyiv accepted Christianity and baptised his subjects.

At its peak, Kievan Rus stretched from north of Lake Ladoga on the borders of Finland to the Caucasus on the Black Sea. When the Kievan ruler Yaroslav the Wise died in 1054, the kingdom was divided among his sons, and only briefly united under Vladimir Monomakh from 1113 to 1125 before it dissolved once more into internecine conflicts.

Suzdal, Vladimir, Novgorod, Chernigov, Tver, Rostov and other cities all became separate principalities, sometimes working together, sometimes vying for power.

The Tatar-Mongol Yoke

In 1156 Prince Yuri Dolgoruky, considered the founder of Moscow, built the first wooden walls

Construction of the Dormition Cathedral, 16th century.

around the Kremlin to enclose and protect the small settlement. But walls would not protect Moscow. In 1224 a Russian chronicler wrote: 'For our sins, unknown tribes came. No one knows who they are, nor whence they came, nor what their faith is, but they call them Tatars.' These Mongolian horsemen from the East appeared like a bolt from the blue, pillaged and plundered, and then reigned over Russia for almost 250 years. At the height of their conquest, their territory stretched from Poland to the Pacific Ocean and from the Arctic Ocean to the Persian Gulf. This period, called the Tatar-Mongol Yoke, began when Batu Khan attacked

Moscow in 1237; from then until the 15th century the khans appointed the Moscow grand princes, who were expected to pay tributes to them, by taking the Bolshaya Ordynka road from Moscow to the Golden Horde, the Tatar khanate set up by the Volga River and named after their glittering tents.

Russians still argue about the impact of the Tatar-Mongol Yoke on Russia. Some maintain it kept Russia fettered to Eastern traditions, away from the main trends of development in Western Europe. Others point out that the Tatars were relatively benign conquerors; the Church was left untouched (and paid no taxes), and judging by the Russian language, the Slavic people picked some skills from their Eastern overlords: the Russian words for customs, treasury, some monetary units and many other administrative concepts come from Mongolian.

In 1328 Ivan Kalita (called 'Moneybags' for his practice of skimming the other princes' tributes paid to the Tatars) was designated Grand Prince by the Khan. In 1340 he built sturdier oak walls around the Kremlin and reinforced them with stucco. Dmitry Donskoy started to build white stone walls in 1366, expanding the Kremlin's territory. In 1380 he defeated the

Dmitry Donskoy after defeating Khan Mamai, 1380.

> *Some in Russia are so convinced of Moscow's status as the Third Rome they have even claimed Russia's military interventions in Ukraine in recent years as a 'holy war'.*

Tatar Khan Mamai in Kulikovo Field on the Don, giving him the name Dmitry of the Don. The Tatars took revenge in 1382, burning the city to the ground once again, and launching damaging raids in 1451, 1455 and 1461 during the reign of Tsar Vasily II.

The 'Third Rome'

During the early centuries of the Moscow principality, the Church maintained contacts with religious leaders and councils in the West. Moves to return the Orthodox Church to Roman Catholicism were violently rejected by Vasily II, and when Constantinople, spiritual home of the Orthodox Church, fell to the Turks in 1453, Moscow claimed the mantle of the 'true Church'. A chronicler wrote: 'Two Romes have fallen, but the third stands. And a fourth there shall not be.'

Moscow was also loosening the grip of the Golden Horde (followers of Islam since the 14th century) by gathering the small principalities around it under its rule and assuming its mission as the leader of the Christian world. The idea of Moscow as the 'Third Rome' has held the imaginations of rulers and thinkers in Russia ever since, and has recently been felt more strongly under Putin.

Ivan III (Ivan the Great, r.1462–1505) is credited, along with his successor, Vasily III (r.1505–33), with 'the gathering of the Rus', the folding of the many Russian principalities under the rule of the Moscow Grand Prince, sometimes voluntarily, sometimes through violent struggle.

When Ivan III married Sophia Paleologue, niece of the last Byzantine emperor, Constantine XI, he cemented the tie that bound Moscow, the Third Rome, to the previous centres of the Orthodox Church. In 1480 Ivan III renounced allegiance to the Khan, and in 1493 he had himself crowned as the Sovereign of All Russia, adding the double-headed eagle of Byzantium to the image of St George as the ruling symbol. The prince among princes,

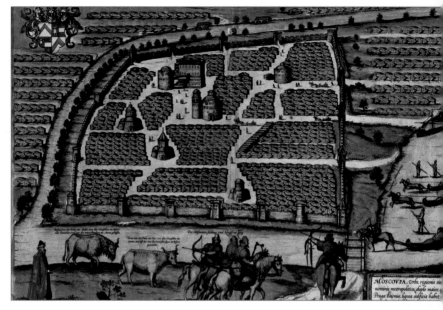

Map of 16th-century Moscow.

the Grand Prince, was now an autocrat, served by noblemen called boyars. As Moscow grew in importance, so did the Kremlin: Ivan III invited Italian builders to help construct enormous churches in Cathedral Square, expanded the territory of the Kremlin, surrounded it with high brick walls, and moved the traders out of the fortress to what is now Red Square. From 1508 to 1516 workers cut a moat 36 metres (120ft) wide and 12 metres (40ft) deep along the Kremlin walls on Red Square.

The first tsar

The city continued to grow and be fortified under Ivan IV, who has gone down in history as Ivan the Terrible (the Russian name really has the sense of awe-inspiring). He assumed the throne as a small child in 1533 and had himself crowned 'Tsar (the Russian for the Roman *caesar*) of All Russia' in 1547. The first period of his reign was relatively progressive and productive: Tsar Ivan oversaw the building of the Kitaigorod walls, established local governments, codified military service, formed the first *streltsy* (musketeer) regiments, and formed a council of

boyars that offered some rudimentary checks on unfettered autocratic power. He also successfully conquered the Tatar city of Kazan in 1552 and, four years later, the Golden Horde in Astrakhan, which he celebrated by commissioning the Cathedral of the Intercession by the Moat (St Basil's Cathedral) on Red Square.

In 1584 Ivan the Terrible died suddenly while preparing for a game of chess. The throne went

THE FIRST SECRET POLICE

After his beloved first wife Anastasia Romanova died, Ivan IV came unhinged. Suspecting his boyars of poisoning her, he left the city in 1564 and announced that he would step down from the throne. Fearful of being leaderless, the Muscovites begged him to return. He did, but on the condition that he be allowed to form a special force to protect him – the *oprichniki*. This force of 6,000, dressed in black and riding black steeds, carried out a reign of terror on boyars, citizens and towns – anyone the insane tsar accused of treachery. Later, in a fit of anger, he struck and killed his eldest son; this event is immortalised in a famous painting by Repin.

Polish invaders repelled from the Kremlin, 1612.

to his eldest surviving son, Fyodor, a religious but simple-minded man. The city of Moscow had grown, and during Fyodor's reign Kitai-gorod and Bely Gorod, the White City named after the stone it was built with, were enclosed with walls, forming a large arc stretching beyond the Kremlin, beginning and ending at the Moscow River and following what is now the Boulevard Ring. The walls were dotted with 27 towers, of which 10 were entrances, many elaborately decorated in tiers. Fyodor's main adviser was the boyar Boris Godunov, who mended the rifts caused by Ivan the Terrible. During Fyodor's reign the Church in Moscow became independent, with its own Patriarch in 1589.

The 'Time of Troubles'

When Fyodor died in 1598, there were no heirs – his brother Dmitry had been killed in the city of Uglich with his throat slit – so the council of boyars elected Boris Godunov, whose family was Tatar in origin. Before accepting the crown, he went to visit his sister, the tsar's widow, in Novodevichy Convent to ask her blessing, and when the people of Moscow turned up at the convent to beseech him, he accepted. But his reign was marred by crop failures and famines that took more than 100,000 lives in Moscow alone. Rumours swept the populace: Boris Godunov was responsible for Dmitry's death; the crop failures and famines were a sign of God's disfavour.

The Poles decided to profit from the instability in Moscow. In 1604 a young man claiming to be Dmitry invaded Russia with an army from Poland. Godunov died suddenly, and the false Dmitry was greeted as the true heir to the throne. The Poles took over the Kremlin, and another reign of terror began, ending with the false Dmitry being denounced, killed, burned and fired out of the Tsar Cannon in the direction of Poland. For another eight years the country went through a number of leaders (including another false Dmitry); armed bandits roamed the countryside; and the Poles launched waves of incursions. It wasn't until the volunteer army led by Minin and Pozharsky drove the Polish invaders from the Kremlin that peace returned. This period of chaos and lawlessness is called the 'Time of Troubles', and has remained a haunting memory for Russians. It is still invoked today to support a strong, even autocratic leader: Russians believe that history shows a strong hand is better than no hand at all, a fact Putin has used to his benefit.

The first Romanovs

In 1613 a gathering of boyars, clergy and ranking service gentry met to decide on a new leader. They finally agreed on a young boyar named Mikhail Romanov, the first in the dynasty that would not end until 1917 with the abdication of Tsar Nicholas II. Moscow in the 17th century enjoyed a period of relative calm. Around the Earthen City wooden walls were built along what is now Sadovoye Koltso (the Garden Ring Road), enclosing the small settlements of merchants and craftsmen that had grown outside the White City walls.

The city impressed foreign visitors as prosperous and grand, filled with churches, taverns and markets, its bearded and pious citizens clothed in long kaftans trimmed in fur. Markets were filled with the chatter of dozens of foreign languages. Noblewomen, however, did not appear on the streets; they were secluded in *terems* and left their houses only to attend church services and visit their families. Moscow was decidedly part of the East.

And then came the Romanov who would be called Peter the Great. When Tsar Fyodor III died in 1682, the council of boyars decided to bypass his feeble-minded son, Ivan V, and name his bright and active half-brother, Peter, as tsar. The conservative *streltsy* regiments rebelled, attacked the Kremlin and killed much of Peter's family. Peter's older sister Sophia whisked him off to the monastery at Sergeev Posad (see page 205), and eventually became regent of the two boy co-tsars. When Sophia seemed ready to grasp the throne for herself in 1689, she was incarcerated in the Novodevichy Convent.

Peter largely grew up on the outskirts of the capital, learning boat-building and trades, and playing war games with his 'toy regiments'. Curious and energetic, he set off to Europe incognito to study the crafts, arts, sciences and state institutions of his European neighbours, studying shipbuilding in London and Amsterdam. He rushed back to Russia in 1698 when it appeared Sophia had arranged yet another *streltsy* rebellion, executing thousands

of officers (some in view of Sophia's convent windows). Peter took control of Russia; he crowned himself emperor and began a series of reforms that would infuriate the Church (demanding that men cut off their beards, the Orthodox sign of piety), terrify the population (demanding that the kaftan be replaced by Western dress) and change Moscow forever. In 1703 he expanded Russia to the north, building a port in the boggy land straddling the Neva River. In 1712, he moved the court to this port – St Petersburg – and declared it the capital of the Russian Empire.

Moscow as second city

Moscow was no longer the epicentre of the Russian Empire. Tsars and tsarinas regularly came to Moscow for coronations, weddings and state visits, and built residences in the Kremlin and pleasure palaces outside the city. Some minor nobility remained, some retired to Moscow manors. But Moscow, with its winding streets and medieval walls and towers, was relegated to the Byzantine and Tatar past that Peter and his heirs wished to forget and overcome. For most of the next two centuries, the court, government, high culture and the arts would flourish in

Peter the Great at the founding of St. Petersburg, 1703.

Napoleon at the Battle of Borodino on August 26, 1812.

the Western-style city on the River Neva. Moscow flourished, too, but as the centre of the Orthodox Church and the capital of commerce. By the 1780s, the decrepit White City walls had been torn down and an elegant, tree-lined boulevard built in its place. Moscow may have been 'a big village', as the residents of St Petersburg called it, but it was not without grace and charm.

But another catastrophic invasion ruined the city once more – this time from the West.

In 1812 Napoleon attacked Russia with the largest army the world had ever seen, and after the indecisive battle of nearby Borodino (see below) moved into the capital. Governor General Rostopchin had ordered the city to be abandoned and set ablaze, destroying nearly three-quarters of the city's structures, and leaving little for the Grande Armée to live on. The French plundered the Kremlin's churches and palaces before they had to admit defeat.

THE BATTLEFIELD OF BORODINO

On 7 September 1812, Napoleon's armies and the Russian armies under General Kutuzov met on the battlefield near the village of Borodino 120km (75 miles) west of Moscow. It turned out to be one of the bloodiest battles of that war: the Russians lost 42,000 of their 112,000 men; the French lost 58,000 out of 130,000.

The next day Kutuzov retreated, allowing the French into Moscow, but Muscovites had torched and abandoned the capital, leaving the French to freeze in the harsh Russian winter with few provisions. Again, in 1941, a battle raged here for six days, as Russians held

off the German army's assault on the capital.

The battlefield of Borodino covers 1,000 sq km (400 sq miles) and includes fortifications of both 1812 and 1941 and an excellent museum *(Gosudarstvenny Borodinsky voenno-istorichesky muzey-zapovednik*; village of Borodino; suburban train from Belorussian station to Borodino Station and then by bus marked 'Borodino' or 'Poreche' to the museum stop). On the first Sunday in September, thousands of military-history enthusiasts don home-made, historically accurate French and Russian uniforms and enact the battle once more.

Moscow underwent an extraordinary renovation over the next decade. The wooden walls that protected the Earthen City were torn down to make what is now the Garden Ring Road. The moat that separated Red Square from the Kremlin was filled in and the Neglinnaya River put underground, so that the Aleksandrovsky Gardens could be laid on the western wall of the Kremlin. Stone houses and churches replaced wooden structures.

By the end of the 19th century Moscow shone once again. The merchant kings of this commercial capital funded the arts, theatre, music and dance. They built schools, hospitals, orphanages, train stations, clubs and churches. There was an explosion in the arts, as the poets of the Silver Age (so called because they followed the Golden Age of the realist prose writers in the mid-19th century) and the innovations of the Moscow Art Theatre thrilled the public.

Russia also exploded geographically over the 19th century, its borders extending from Afghanistan to China and even, for a time at least, Alaska and coastal California. The port city of Vladivostok opened up trade in Asia, and the Trans-Siberian Railway, completed in just 14 years in 1905, linked Europe with Russia's Far East for the first time. Russia's industrial development was rapid; by the turn of the century it was one of the fastest-growing economies in Europe.

But there were explosions of a different kind. The reforms of Alexander II, called the Tsar Liberator for emancipating serfs in 1861, did not go far enough. Absolute power remained in the hands of the tsar and his advisors; vast wealth and property were possessed and flaunted by a small aristocracy, while the poor barely managed to eke out a living in the countryside and cities. Writers and painters protested in their art; young revolutionaries protested with bombs, assassinations and uprisings. Alexander II was killed by a terrorist; his son Alexander III died unexpectedly in 1894.

The last tsar

Nicholas II, by all accounts a kind man but an utterly ineffectual ruler, inherited the throne at a critical time in the country's history. Had he possessed greater vision, or been more resolute, or made more concessions to the demands of the population, the course of Russian history might have been less brutal. He barely survived the uprisings of 1905, but with a few further political concessions, including the establishment of a parliament, the Duma, maintained the monarchy for a few more years.

The celebration of 300 years of the Romanov dynasty in 1913 was the last hurrah of the Russian monarchy. When Russia entered World War I in 1914, its overtaxed citizens were pressed further. Hungry and demoralised soldiers and sailors responded to new cries for change and revolution. In February 1917 the tsar abdicated the throne and a temporary government attempted to take charge. But it was too late. In October 1917 Vladimir Lenin, leader of the Bolsheviks, led a coup in St Petersburg. Most of the aristocracy that had not already fled the country now struggled to escape. Civil war rent the country, abetted by foreign powers helping the 'Whites' overcome the 'Reds', lest revolution burst over the borders. Fearing that the tsar and his family, held as prisoners in the Urals city of Yekaterinburg, would rally the opposition, Lenin ordered them killed. The Russian Empire was no more.

Nicholas II, the last tsar.

The capital of the USSR

In 1918 Lenin moved the new Bolshevik government to Moscow, although the city was only officially proclaimed the capital of the Soviet Union after the Civil War ended in 1922. Moscow's palaces and manor houses were expropriated and turned into communal apartments; dozens of families lived in partitioned rooms, sharing kitchens and bathrooms. Emptied of their sacred vessels and icons, churches were turned into warehouses, dormitories, offices and museums. War Communism – draconian methods to expropriate food from the peasants and keep the labour force at work – was nudging the beleaguered population towards rebellion once again; the Soviet authorities responded with the New Economic Policy (NEP). NEP permitted limited free markets of food and consumer goods, which brought the country and city back from the edge of starvation and desperation.

Lenin died in 1924. After an internal power struggle, he was succeeded by Joseph Stalin, a former seminary student who embraced the Revolution and power with a fervour that

Portrait of Vladimir Lenin, 1920.

verged on insanity. At least as paranoid as Ivan the Terrible, he consolidated his power through purges and repressions, imprisoning or executing purported 'enemies of the people', clearing villages of rich peasants and forcibly collectivising the rest. An estimated 8 million people were executed, sent to labour camps or died in prison; at the height of the Great Terror in 1937, at least 650,000 people were killed. Industrialisation, fuelled by convict labour, proceeded apace; the price was enormous, but the country began to recover from the devastation of revolution.

Moscow changed dramatically under Stalin. With the first General Plan for Reconstruction approved in 1935, the Sovietisation of the city began in earnest. The city's meandering lanes were cleared of houses, broad avenues laid, the famous markets of Sukharevka and Khitrovka closed and emptied, main streets widened and new highways built leading out of the city. What are now called 'Stalinist classical' apartment houses went up in the centre of the city for the Party faithful, the buildings trembling as the first metro line rumbled under the streets. Tenements and shanties fell, but so did churches, taverns, shops and palaces. Moscow was to become the Model Soviet City, designed more for parades of armaments and workers than for the comfort of its citizens.

The Great Patriotic War

Work halted abruptly on 22 June 1941 when Hitler launched an attack on the Soviet Union. Stalin was unprepared, having ignored the warnings of spies and diplomats, and insisting that the Non-Aggression Pact signed with Hitler in 1939 would hold. He ordered his commanders to 'ignore the provocations' from the German army and not return fire. By the time the order came to defend themselves, the majority of the armed forces' aircraft had been destroyed by Nazi bombs and entire divisions encircled. Many of Moscow's citizens and most of its artistic treasures were evacuated from the city. Although the city suffered from bombing raids, the advance of the Germans was halted at the outskirts of the city, not far from the main international airport today, in November 1941, and the city survived with only moderate damage. The country, however, was devastated: an estimated 20 million people died during what Russians call the Great Patriotic War.

A propaganda poster from 1952. The caption reads: 'Glory to the Great Stalin, the Architect of Communism!'

Large-scale reconstruction resumed only in the early 1950s when the great 'Stalinist skyscrapers' went up over the city, heralding, Muscovites hoped, a new era of prosperity and peace. Khrushchev, who came to power after Stalin's death in 1953, loosened some of the controls on the arts, denounced Stalin's atrocities, and promised Moscow's citizens that he would finally solve the 'housing problem' that dogged the city. New neighbourhoods were built of five-storey, yellow-brick apartment buildings: the apartments were small, but they were one-family dwellings, set in communities with stores and services. These buildings – called *khrushchevki* after their initiator – still dot the city. They have aged badly but are still inhabited – it's hard to believe today that they once represented a modicum of comfort to millions of Muscovites who had lived in communal apartments or worker's barracks.

Under Khrushchev and his successor, Leonid Brezhnev, the city centre was little changed; most of the construction went on at the edges of the city. Apartment buildings sprang up around Moscow that were taller, usually made of white-cement panels and sometimes decorated with mosaics or coloured stone. They were more spacious and comfortable than the *khrushchevki*, but monotonous in their similarity.

Sprawling estates

Moscow at the end of the Brezhnev era was a huge, sprawling city surrounded by housing estates. There were no slums, but neither were there ethnic neighbourhoods, business districts or private dwellings. There were few restaurants and clubs, and cultural life was staid, but entertainment was affordable and the streets were safe. The city and country had settled into a relatively predictable, stable monotony. There were no repressions or purges, but dissent in the arts or government was punished by imprisonment or exile. There were no large-scale wars, but the Cold War seemed destined to last indefinitely. After the triumphs of the Soviet weapons and space programmes in the 1940s–60s, there were no technological breakthroughs, but industry and agriculture produced the bare minimum to feed, clothe and house the population. Soviet power seemed unbreakable, the Soviet republics joined forever. There was nothing that hinted of the changes to come.

THE ART OF PROPAGANDA

The Revolution affected more than just politics, it nurtured some of the 20th century's greatest avant-garde artists until their work was thought less than ideal for the Party line.

The 1917 Revolution not only overthrew the social and political system in Russia – it revolutionised the arts. Avant-garde artists such as Kazimir Malevich, Alexander Rodchenko and Vasily Kandinsky, who were all sympathetic to the cause, suddenly found themselves in favour, heading art schools and studios.

Throughout the 1920s they splintered into many different unions and associations, such as *Komfut* (Communist Futurism), *Proletkult* (Proletarian Culture) and *Lef* (Left Front of the Arts). Often mutually antagonistic, they joined forces with the new Soviet government to proclaim, 'Long live the art of the Proletarian Revolution!' and 'Only Futurist art is the art of the proletariat now!'

These artists created cinema advertisements and public service posters, decorated agitprop (agitation and propaganda) trains that brought the message of Soviet power to the masses, and designed workers' clubs, books, china, workers' clothes and public monuments. The poet Vladimir Mayakovsky teamed up with artists Mikhail Cheremnysh and Ivan Malyutin to make witty cartoon posters on subjects ranging from personal hygiene to the evils of capitalism. The 'bourgeois' art of the upper class disappeared, and Moscow was filled with a new art for the new age: angular, expressive, jarring and in enthusiastic service to the new regime.

Propaganda poster from World War II, encouraging women to join in the battle against the invaders. The caption reads: 'Fascism - The Most Evil Enemy of Women.'

World War II propaganda poster, encouraging Russians to build more tanks and planes to win the war against Nazi Germany.

Propaganda campaigns during World War II were used to reminded people not to inadvertently give away state secrets.

A vintage poster by photographer Alexander Rodchenko (1925) shouts the need to to read. Many avant-garde artists embraced the new society, and work by Rodchenko was to define international poster and book design until the 1980s.

Communist political propaganda poster, encouraging the proletarian to unite and revolt against the bourgeoisie, by Vladimir Mayakovsky, 1920.

THE ROMANCE OF SOCIALIST REALISM

Romanticised depction of a socialist utopia by Alexey Ivanovich, 1950.

Radical innovation in the arts came to an end in 1934, when Andrey Zhdanov, secretary of the Communist Party of the USSR, made a speech to the First All-Union Congress of Soviet Writers that defined what art would be acceptable to the political leaders. Called 'Socialist Realism', it consisted of *ideynost* (ideology), *partiynost* (Party loyalty) and *narodnost* (national character, or rather the positive portrayal of the masses). This was first applied to literature and then to all the arts.

It called for a romanticised depiction of Soviet reality: kindly but authoritative leaders, healthy and prosperous workers, and peasants joyfully engaged in the great work of building the new Soviet state. Abstraction and critical realism were out. The image of a young woman at the wheel of a convertible tooling down a sun-dappled Moscow street was in.

Socialist Realism remained state policy until the 1980s, although its strictures were loosened in the post-war years. Some artists, temperamentally attracted to realism, created masterpieces; others churned out paintings of milkmaids and metalworkers for their Union of Artists contracts while privately experimenting with other genres. Today, there is a modest revival and appreciation for classics of Socialist Realism. It may be unsophisticated sentimentalism or slavish propaganda, but at least you can tell the girl from the goat.

Military propaganda portraying a highly idealised Soviet army.

Vladimir Putin gives his inaugral speech as the former president, Boris Yeltsin, looks on. May 7, 2000.

LAND OF THE FREE?

The break-up of the USSR was one of the defining events of the 20th century. Moscow, centre of power of the vast Soviet Empire, was at the eye of the storm that followed. For many citizens, optimism was soon superseded by bankruptcy and deprivation. Yet somehow they survived.

By the 1980s the USSR was in a period of stagnation: economic development, funded by high world prices for oil and gas and carried out on a wave of post-war enthusiasm, had slowed catastrophically. While the country was able to maintain most basic services – free education and medical care, pensions, transport and basic consumer goods – outside the major cities ration cards were issued for such necessities as meat, sugar, tea and coffee. Suburban trains leaving Moscow stations were called 'sausage expresses', filled with people hauling meat and staples they could no longer find even 100 miles from the metropolis.

Leonid Brezhnev died in 1982 and was quickly succeeded by two ancient and ailing party officials, Yuri Andropov (1982–4) and Konstantin Chemenko (1984–5). And then Mikhail Gorbachev, at age 54 the youngest General Secretary of the Communist Party since Stalin, was chosen to lead the country.

Protestors in the 1990s.

The lid pops off the boiling pot

Gorbachev immediately showed himself to be a different kind of Soviet leader. Determined to reform the ailing economy and moribund political system, he announced a policy of *glasnost* (public disclosure of economic and social issues), *perestroika* (restructuring of the economic and political system) and acceleration of social and economic advancement. He tried both to put an end to behaviour that inhibited economic growth (crackdowns on alcoholism and income from moonlighting) and to encourage a spirit of economic and political innovation, allowing co-operatives (small private enterprises) and joint ventures with foreign companies. In 1988 he supported an amendment to the Constitution that allowed real competition for seats in the Congress of People's Deputies, the first time that more than one candidate had stood in an election since 1917. What had once been a rubberstamp parliament became a real parliament, which elected Gorbachev to the newly created post of President of the Soviet Union in 1989.

But the process he unleashed proved impossible to control. Ethnic and economic tensions in Kazakhstan, Armenia, Georgia, Moldova and elsewhere erupted into uprisings and wars. The

Food lines in Moscow, 1991.

Baltic states of Latvia, Lithuania and Estonia demanded secession from the Union. Freedom to travel and access to foreign news and culture showed Soviet citizens how far their living standards lagged behind the developed world, and they took to the streets in demonstrations of hundreds of thousands, banging pots and demanding food and consumer goods in the stores. Spurred by the changes in the USSR and their own democratic movements, the citizens of Eastern and Central European countries rebelled at elections and on the streets. In November 1989 the Berlin Wall, the symbol of the Cold War, fell. By March 1991 the Warsaw Pact was dissolved. In this heady atmosphere of change, the republics of the Soviet Union declared various forms of 'sovereignty' within the Union. In Russia, still a constituent part of the USSR, a new Congress of People's Deputies first elected Boris Yeltsin its chairman in 1990 and then created the post of President, which Yeltsin won by a landslide in 1991.

This was a critical year. There was an untenable situation in the country: two centres of power, held by Gorbachev as President of the USSR and Yeltsin as President of the Russian Federation. Their competition, fuelled by personal animosity, competing visions of the country's development, a worsening economic situation, strikes and continuing wars in the republics, jerked the country between greater freedom and crackdowns. And the media, which had thrown off the strictures of censorship, showed everything – strikes, Congressional debates, corruption, poverty – all day, every day, to a fascinated nation.

In August 1991 a group of hardliners within the Communist Party staged a coup while Gorbachev was on holiday in Crimea. Boris Yeltsin and his government were not arrested and became the de facto leaders of the three-day resistance, eventually drawing the military to their side. The coup leaders capitulated on 21 August (one of them, the head of the KGB, shot his wife and then himself to avoid arrest), and Gorbachev returned to Moscow. But he returned to a different country. The Baltic states seceded from the Union, followed by virtually every other Soviet republic, most notably Ukraine.

While daily life did not immediately change (in fact, even the coup went unmarked in all but the largest cities), the USSR ceased to exist. In early December the leaders of Ukraine, Belarus and Russia – the three republics that had founded the Soviet Union – signed an agreement that established the Commonwealth of

> *In 1991 a one-room apartment cost 5,000 roubles; by 1993 a cup of strawberries cost 60,000 roubles.*

Independent States. It was then signed by the rest of the former republics (except the Baltic states and Georgia) on 21 December. On 25 December, Mikhail Gorbachev resigned as President of the Soviet Union. That evening, with little ceremony, the red Soviet flag was lowered over the Kremlin and the Russian tricolour was raised.

Towards a second coup

Boris Yeltsin inherited a country that was bankrupt, economically backward and corrupt, with a population of 145 million exhausted by six years of turmoil and deprivation. His 'shock therapy' to release fixed prices and jump-start the economy did put food and goods back in the shops, but at prices that were hundreds of times higher. Families lost their entire savings; factories closed or laid off workers; collective farms folded. Another state crisis was brewing, caused by internal dissent within the government reflecting both differing visions of the future and thirst for power – and facilitated by a state system that had been cobbled together in haste without clear lines of authority within the branches of government. The Russian Congress of People's Deputies took a turn to the right and attempted to wrest power from the presidency.

In a move still debated, in September 1993 Yeltsin defied the Constitution and disbanded Congress. The deputies retaliated by declaring Alexander Rutskoy, then vice-president, acting head of state. At the beginning of October, the Congress was well armed and barricaded in the White House. The leaders launched attacks on the Moscow Mayor's Office, the Ostankino TV Centre and a number of strategic sites throughout the city. The army and militia, also divided in its loyalties, did not immediately respond. Finally the army entered the city and tanks fired on the White House as the world watched. After two days of fighting, more than 140 were dead and nearly 1,000 wounded. The leaders of the second Russian coup surrendered. A new Constitution was quickly passed that focused power in the hands of the president. The White House was renovated by Turkish workers in record time, a tall fence was placed around it, and the country, once again, tried to put dissension behind it and move forward.

The wild '90s

There is probably not a soul in all of Russia who would disagree: the 1990s in Russia were hell. There was nothing in the country to facilitate or even permit private enterprise: no wholesale or retail distribution systems or infrastructure, inadequate financial institutions, insufficient transport and communications systems, no advertising and marketing resources, few office buildings, virtually no commercial space. Regulatory laws were contradictory or simply non-existent. The voucher system of privatisation, intended to give citizens a share of economic wealth, proved to be a sham; practically the entire industrial wealth of the country ended up in the hands of a few individuals. Fortunes were made overnight out of nothing. No one paid taxes. Pensions and salaries were not paid for months and even years.

The basic services in medical care and education deteriorated catastrophically. Street crime and prostitution soared. Drugs, casinos and HIV appeared, while high culture all but

Boris Yeltsin dancing on the Lenin Hills, May 1, 1996.

disappeared. Mafia groups divided up the economy and controlled sectors; protection rackets solved disputes through contract killings. People switched professions or invented new ones, like 'shuttling' to Turkey and China to buy goods they could sell at outdoor markets. War broke out in Chechnya. Pyramid schemes wiped out savings of unsuspecting investors for a second time. Media outlets owned by oligarchs played politics instead of reporting the news.

Although Yeltsin's approval ratings were 8 percent in January 1996, a skilfully run campaign and unabashed media support landed him 53 percent of the vote in July run-off elections. Then, in August 1998, the bubble finally burst: the government defaulted on its debts, causing the rouble to plummet from 6 to $1 to 25 to $1 virtually overnight. The freedom and democracy that people had longed for under the Soviet Union and fought for in the 1980s and early 1990s brought year after year of suffering and chaos.

Exchange value of the rouble against the euro and dollar.

And yet somehow under the outward manifestations of corruption, crime and confusion, people adapted, established businesses, taught in schools, made movies, built houses, graduated from universities, found jobs and muddled through. Somehow people began to build the foundations of a functioning political system and economy, however inadequate or malformed. Towards the end of the century, Russia was teetering but on her feet.

All the same, when the alcoholic Yeltsin surprised the nation on 31 December 1999 with his resignation, few rued the day. His time was over. If no one knew what to expect from Vladimir Putin, the former head of the FSB (the new name for the KGB) and prime minister for only a few months, people were ready to change.

The new millennium

Putin was elected president for the first time in 2000 with a very low 52 percent of the vote – his approval ratings since taking office have been consistently much higher. Apart from a period of four years between 2008 and 2012 when he was prime minister (a break from the presidency forced by the Constitution), he has been President of the Russian Federation for the last decade-and-a-half. Though credited with bringing relative stability and order to Russia, recent events have shown that his ambitions go beyond the country's borders. The annexation of Crimea, military intervention in Ukraine's eastern regions and Russia's involvement in Syria's civil war have brought the spotlight onto Russia's autocratic leader for all the wrong reasons. Despite his reputation abroad, Putin remains popular at home, mostly through total manipulation of the media, a massive propaganda campaign and the lack of a credible opposition. However, one of the pillars of his popularity, economic stability, has crumbled away under Western sanctions, a devaluation of the rouble and plunging oil prices. It remains to be seen whether the Russian people's patience will last.

The Russian capital today

The price was high, but Russia and its capital city of Moscow survived the turmoil of the 1990s. Under the stewardship of Mayor Yuri Luzhkov, building contracts may have been awarded with dubious objectivity, and reconstruction plans satisfy few – but Moscow has emerged as a bustling, modern European capital, the centre of the Russian government, culture and business.

But under the new facade, you can still find ghosts of the past: the quiet courtyard of a manor house; the statue of Lenin forever pointing to a bright future; the tiny parish church dwarfed by skyscrapers; the narrow lanes, winding down hills to the Moscow River, as placid today as it was nearly 900 years ago.

The Russian Federation

Russia has a complex political system – comprising government, a bicameral federal assembly, the federation council and the State Duma – but ultimatey, power lies with the president.

The Constitution of the Russian Federation, ratified in 1993, declares that the country is a multinational federation: a democratic, secular, federal state based on rule of law and a republican form of government, in which 'man, his rights and freedoms are the supreme value'. It consists of 89 constituent parts, called republics, regions *(oblasts)*, territories, cities of federal significance (similar to the District of Columbia in the US), one autonomous region and autonomous areas. It recognises private, state, municipal and other forms of ownership, including of land, and mandates ideological diversity.

Although the Constitution stipulates three main branches of government – executive, legislative and judicial – the power to make decisions and policy is concentrated in the executive branch. The president, elected by popular vote for up to two six-year terms, appoints the prime minister and Cabinet, determines the main foreign and domestic policies and can initiate legislation. The 89 constituent entities have been divided into seven large regional groups headed by a presidential envoy. A large Presidential Administration and Security Council wields considerable power and oversees much of the day-to-day running of the state.

The legislative branch, called the Federal Assembly *(Federalnoye Sobranie)*, is bicameral. The upper house, called the Federation Council *(Soviet Federatsii)*, is made up of appointed representatives from the 89 constituent parts of the Federation, and is largely tasked with issues related to relations between the constituent parts, although it also approves laws passed by the lower house, appoints judges to the higher courts, and can dismiss the president with a two-thirds majority vote. The lower house, called the State Duma *(Gosudarstvennaya duma)*, is the main law-making body in the country, and also approves the president's appointment of prime minister and other executive appointees. The Duma can give a vote of no confidence in the Cabinet, but in response the president may either dismiss the Cabinet or dissolve the Duma. The 450 seats in the Duma are filled by representatives from political parties that have won at least 7 percent of the vote.

Coat of arms on the Duma building.

As of 2016, 238 seats were held by Putin's United Russia, 92 by the Communist Party, 64 by A Just Russia and 56 by the Liberal Democratic Party of Russia (LDPR). As all four parties support President Putin there is little real discussion in the State Duma, and in recent years it has become little more than a rubber stamp as the president effectively rules by decree. The Russian government is increasingly being described as a 'regime' by the international press.

Café Pushkin.

Caviar at Volkhonka Mansion.

AT THE RUSSIAN TABLE: BEYOND BORSCHT AND BLINI

The popular belief is that most Russians survive on a diet of potatoes and beetroot supplemented with a few cucumbers and all washed down with vodka. It's an image that's soon shattered in Moscow.

Today in Moscow you can find almost every kind of food, and there are venues to suit every pocket, from street stalls selling *sloyki* (cheese-filled puff pastries) to elegant dining halls serving haute cuisine at prices that will make you gulp.

Russian cuisine was originally based on simple ingredients that could be farmed (or caught) in northern climes. In the 18th century it was strongly influenced by French cookery, which explains the penchant for thick meat sauces, complicated salads and the huge range of cream-filled *tortes*. Today, most restaurants offer a varied menu, from simple peasant soup to the most elegant French-influenced dessert.

Breakfast and snacks

At *zavtrak* (breakfast), start the day the Russian way with one of the varieties of *kasha* (porridge) or *syrniki*, thick pancakes made with *tvorog* (curd cheese) and *smetana* (sour cream) and served with jam. If you are still hungry, have some smoked fish and meats or fruit and *kefir* (Russian lassi). In the unlikely event that you need a mid-morning snack, head to a *kofeynaya* (coffee shop) or *gastronom* (grocery) for a *pirozhnoe* (pastry). *Khleb* (bread) is available from the *bulochnaya* (bakery). It is almost obligatory while in Russia to try *chyorny* or *rzhanoy* (black bread), a dense rye bread. Look for *Boroditsky*, a black bread dusted with dill.

Lunch and supper

Obed (lunch) is the largest meal of the day and consists of *zakuski* (starters) and *salaty* (salads), *sup* (soup), *vtoroye* (main course) and *sladkoe*

Georgian soup.

(dessert). In Moscow, more modest versions of the traditional heavy Russian lunch include the ubiquitous *biznes-lanch* (set-price business lunch). At home, the evening meal, *uzhin*, is often much lighter than a traditional lunch and comprises salads or *buterbrod* (open sandwiches). This is in contrast to celebratory dinners and meals in restaurants where guests sit at the table for hours, slowly making their way through plates of *zakuski* and main courses, all accompanied by vodka, toasts, stories, jokes and singing and dancing. And at the end of the meal, it is traditional to take *chay* (tea), usually with lemon and sugar, and, if you have room, a rich *tort* (cake).

Zakuski and salads

The glory of the Russian table are the *zakuski* appetisers that include salads, sliced smoked meats, smoked and salted fish, fresh and pickled vegetables, salted and marinated mushrooms and *pirozhki* (a yeast or puff pastry filled with meat, potatoes, mushrooms, sautéed cabbage or fish). Loading the table down with *zakuski* is part of traditional Russian hospitality and the main feature of the meal. Ingredients for salads include cucumbers and tomatoes (or radishes) seasoned with a dill and sour cream dressing. *Vinegret* is a salad of beetroot, potatoes, carrots and pickles. The classic Olivier salad is made of potatoes, onions, pickles and thin strips of meat, and is dressed with mayonnaise. For something lighter, try a fresh *kvashenaya kapusta* (sauerkraut), mixed with cranberries and carrots and drizzled with oil.

Russians are very good at preparing fish, and it is a main element to any feast. *Selyod*, pickled herring served with fresh onions and boiled potatoes, or *selyodka pod shuboi* – translated as 'salted herring in a fur coat' – made of beetroot, potatoes, boiled egg and sour cream, are included on most tables. Russian smoked fish is excellent (sturgeon, salmon, trout or cod), along with servings of *shproty* (sprats) or *ryba zalivnaya* (fish in aspic). If you're feeling flush when you're eating out, order blinis (pancakes) with *ikra* (caviar). The delicate bluish-grey, lightly salted Beluga caviar, *malossol*, is the finest. Other, less expensive caviar include *ossetra*, which has smaller grains and a stronger flavour, *sevruga*, which has even smaller grains and a strong, nutty

Steamed sturgeon.

taste, or *krasnaya ikra* (red salmon roe), which has large grains that pop in your mouth in an explosion of flavour. Meat starters include *studen* (or *kholodets*), veal or beef in aspic served with horseradish, and a variety of smoked meats and sausages. For vegetarians a classic hot appetiser is what Russians call *zhulen* (from the French *julienne*), which is a dish of sliced mushrooms in a white sauce topped with cheese and served in small pots bubbling straight from the oven.

Soups

The famous *borscht* (beetroot soup), actually a Ukrainian dish served with hot rolls called *pampushki* drizzled with garlic sauce, can be found in nearly all Russian restaurants. For a lighter soup, try *gribnoy*, made with fresh or dried field mushrooms; *ukha*, a simple fish soup made with potatoes, carrots and onions and sprinkled with dill; or *kurinaya lapsha*, a clear chicken broth served with noodles. *Shchi* (cabbage soup) is made with fresh cabbage or sauerkraut in broth and seasoned with a dollop of sour cream. *Pokhlebki* are hearty soups that nearly cross the line into stews, and can be made from meat, poultry or fish with onions, potatoes and carrots. The pride of Russian soups is the rich and piquant *solyanka*, made of mushrooms, fish or meat and seasoned with pickles, olives, capers and lemon and topped with sour cream. In summer, try cold *okroshka*, a light soup of *kvas* (a refreshing soft drink made from black bread) ladled over diced vegetables, or *svekolnik*, a clear beetroot soup served over a salad of potatoes, cucumbers and radishes dressed with sour cream and seasoned with dill or parsley.

Main dishes

After the glory of the starters and soups, traditional Russian main courses tend to be simpler and are usually a *myaso* (meat) escalope or grilled lamb or beef. You can also try beef Stroganov in a rich sour-cream sauce, or pre-Revolutionary dishes made of venison, boar, suckling pig, goose or duck. You may want to order *golubsty*, stuffed cabbage usually served in a tomato-based sauce, or *pelmeni*, the Russian version of ravioli served in a broth or baked under a hearty coat of sour cream.

You might also try *kutlety pozharsky*, cutlets made of minced and seasoned chicken, or chicken *tabaka*, a young chicken pressed and fried to crispness. *Treska, forel, karp, sterlyad* and *osetrina* (cod, trout, carp, starlet – a small sturgeon – and sturgeon) are traditionally baked in a white sauce or sour cream, fried in batter (*v klyare*) or grilled (sturgeon is especially good this way) and served with *tkemali* (a piquant sour-plum sauce). In most restaurants you make a separate order of *gamir* (garnish), which is usually a choice between baked or fried potatoes, rice or buckwheat (*grechka*).

If you can still manage a dessert, you might like to try *kisel*, a traditional soft jelly made of fruits and thickened with cornflour, or splurge on a Napoleon, which involves layers of puff pastry with a rich cream filling (so called because it was originally triangular and reminiscent of the traditional French three-cornered hat).

Table drinks

In general Russians have a huge capacity to drink alcohol, but they do also drink non-alcoholic drinks with their meals. *Mineralnaya voda* (mineral water), *mors* (fresh berries mixed with sugar and water) or *kompot* (a fruit drink made of simmered fresh or dried fruit and berries) are popular and widespread beverages. Starters

are traditionally accompanied by chilled vodka drunk straight: try one of the flavoured vodkas such as lemon or pepper and honey. The trick Russians use to stay on their feet is to take a mouthful of salad or appetiser immediately after the gulp of vodka. Russia also produces excellent *pivo* (beer).

Ethnic food

Apart from the usual international cuisines, Moscovites are mad for *Gruzinsky* (Georgian) food. The city has its fair share of places that sell delicious *shashlyk*, a kebab of marinated lamb, beef, chicken, seasoned minced meat or sturgeon grilled on skewers and served with a sour-plum or spicy tomato sauce. If you're eating in an ethnic restaurant, the meal includes an array of salads and starters: chicken *satsivi* (an onion-walnut sauce); *farshirovannye baklazhani* (aubergines stuffed with walnuts); *labia* (spicy, stewed beans); *basturma* (spicy dry-cured beef); *khachapuri* (puff pastry filled with a sharp cheese); and *khinkali* (dumplings filled with lamb served with fresh black pepper). Don't forget to order a carafe or two of excellent Georgian wine (see box).

Cooking shashliks at Noah's Arc Restaurant.

LITERATURE AND THE IMAGINATION

Literature from and about Moscow is perennially popular. From the pages of Muscovites' favourite books come the images of the city they love – an idealised place which can be more real to them than the busy streets themselves.

Anton Chekhov and Leo Tolstoy.

For some, Moscow is a city of brilliant musicians and singers; for others, it's a city of exquisite dance; for others still it's a city of avant-garde art or magnificent architecture. But for Muscovites, it's a city of literature: a city of poets and writers who lived in its houses, walked its streets and re-created their city in poetry and prose so well known and beloved that the boundaries between the imagined city and the real city have become hopelessly blurred.

Here Pushkin's Evgeny Onegin flew down a snow-covered Tverskaya ulitsa in a sleigh. Here Moscow's white stone walls turned red in Mayakovsky's poems of the Revolution. Here Tolstoy's Anna Karenina went to the horse races in the same place where the Hippodrome stands today, and the Rostov family of *War and Peace* lived in a manor house on Povarskaya ulitsa and walked along the little Arbat lanes.

The tour guides at the battle of Borodino panorama say that the question they are asked most frequently by both Russian and foreign guests is: 'Where did Pierre Bezukhov stand?' They say they are always a little sad when they remind visitors that Pierre was a character in a novel, as if they were telling a child that fairies don't exist.

The apartments and houses where writers lived have been lovingly preserved and are a wonderful introduction to Moscow. Even if you know little of Anton Chekhov, Leo Tolstoy or Marina Tsvetaeva, visit their homes. You'll see Moscow as it was in another era, with all the delightful details of home life: a basin for washing by a narrow bed; poems scribbled on a wall; knick-knacks in a curio cabinet. The older women who work in these apartment-museums know their long-gone housemates the way they know their neighbours in the next flat, and they will happily tell you all the family gossip: about playwright Anton Chekhov's marriage to the actress Olga Knipper (they disapprove; she wasn't kind enough to him); or how the Tolstoy children would slide down the staircase on pillows and slip out into the garden through the window (they consider them naughty, but charming).

They may also, if you ask, quote from memory page after page of prose and verse about Moscow, like this exalted description of the city by Mikhail Lermontov:

Moscow is not just a big city like thousands of others. Moscow is not a silent giant of cold stone

Reader at the Molodaya Gvardia (Young Guard) bookstore.

laid in symmetry. No! She has her own soul, her own life. Like in ancient Roman cemeteries, each of her stones preserves an inscription engraved by time and destiny, an inscription that is indecipherable to the masses, but rich with meaning and filled with thoughts, feelings and inspiration for the scholar, the patriot, the poet. Like an ocean, she has her own language, a language that is powerful and sonorous, sacred and prayerful.

Although the poet Anna Akhmatova was most closely associated with St Petersburg, she visited Moscow frequently (staying with friends in Zamoskvoreche) and wrote in 1963:

Everything in Moscow is saturated with verse,
Riddled with rhyme through and through ...

And it's absolutely true. All of Moscow has been captured on the page, from the majesty of the Kremlin walls in Lermontov's poetry to the huts and hovels of Khitrovka in Gorky's *The Lower Depths;* from the swish of silk dresses at a ball in Tolstoy's novels to the madness of Satan's flight over the city in Bulgakov's *The Master and Margarita;* from the foibles of the merchant class in Ostrovsky's plays to the bewitching romance of the Arbat lanes in the songs of Okudzhava; from the red flags of the 1905 uprising in Bryusov's verse to the crooked lanes and little houses of the old Moscow that Tsvetaeva knew and loved.

Moscow – in Russian *Moskva*, a feminine noun – is always 'she', and is often personified by Russian writers. When Moscow was captured by the French in 1812, the poet Dolgorukov wrote:

Mother-Moscow has scores of sons ...
Russia, you are enslaved when Moscow is held captive!

And Lermontov wrote:

Moscow! Moscow! I love you like a son,
As only a Russian can love – powerfully, passionately and tenderly!
I love the sacred shimmer of your grey strands,
And the Kremlin: crenellated and imperturbable.

Of course, writers were not always so high-flown when they wrote about Moscow.

The Ukrainian Nikolay Gogol wrote:

Moscow is a woman and Petersburg a man ... Petersburg is a tidy man, a typical German who regards everything with a calculating eye. If he should decide to give a party, he'll look in his wallet first. Moscow is Russian nobility, and if the nobility decide to party, they will party until they drop and won't worry if it costs more than they have in their pockets. Moscow doesn't like to do anything halfway.

Nicolas Gogol (1809–1852).

Marina Tsvetaeva (1892–1941).

Unchanged vision

You have only to look at Moscow's wealthier citizens today to see how little the city has changed over the centuries: there is nothing halfway about their ostentatious lifestyles.

Or read this passage from Alexander Pushkin's novel in verse, *Evgeny Onegin*, when the hero rides along Tverskaya ulitsa:

Watch booths flash past, and old women,
Street urchins, shops and lampposts,
Palaces, flowerbeds, monasteries,

Asians, sleighs, kitchen gardens,
Merchants, hovels, peasant men,
Towers, boulevards, Cossacks,
Chemists and fashion shops,
Balconies and lions on the gates,
And flocks of jackdaws atop church crosses.

If you changed 'watch booths' to 'traffic police booths' and 'street urchins' to 'smartphone-wielding teenagers', you'd have Tverskaya ulitsa today in all its bright confusion. Only the sleighs, hovels and kitchen gardens have

---

MOSCOW'S TOP FIVE FICTION

To get into the Moscow mood, dip into a classic of Russian literature, best enjoyed curled up on a snowy winter's night, in front of a roaring fire with a glass of tea.

Evgeny Onegin by Alexander Pushkin. A novel in verse written in the early 19th century that follows its cynical hero from the glitter of high society to the comfort of village life, from a fatal duel to love found and lost.

War and Peace by Leo Tolstoy. Immerse yourself in Tolstoy's complex world of Moscow families before, during and after Napoleon's invasion of 1812: a profound examination of individuals' roles in the making of history, and

the quest for love and happiness.

Woe from Wit by Alexander Griboyedov. A comic play about a homesick Russian nobleman who returns to Moscow after touring Europe to find the pettiness and hypocrisy of Russian high society and a yearning for freedom.

Master and Margarita by Mikhail Bulgakov. The devil and his band descend upon Moscow in the 1930s, as the Master writes his story of Christ and Pontius Pilate.

The Elagin Affair and Other Stories by Ivan Bunin. Moscow at the turn of the 20th century by the first Russian to win the Nobel Prize for literature.

disappeared into the past.

Of course, some fictional depictions of Moscow were never confused with reality. A favourite pastime of some Muscovites is finding all the places mentioned in Bulgakov's novel *The Master and Margarita*, when Satan and his devils descend upon the city (a chillingly apt description of Moscow during the political purges and repressions of the 1930s). Many are certain that Satan's Ball is really a description of a party held by the US ambassador in Spaso House:

In the next hall, there were no columns, but instead walls of red, pink and milk-white roses on one side and a wall of Japanese double camellias on the other. Between the two walls, fountains were already shooting up fizz, and champagne pooled and bubbled in three basins ...

Satan might not have been there, but the description matches the ambassador's residence perfectly.

In the poems about their city Muscovites love best, Moscow is 'white stone and gold crowned' by thousands of cupolas glittering in the sunlight against blue skies. Sometimes in Marina Tsvetaeva's poetry, the city is violently, vividly alive:

In my Moscow cupolas are blazing,

A mural of the writer Mikhail Bulgakov.

In my Moscow bells are pealing ...

But for other poets – and in other times – it was a quiet city, where narrow little streets were meant for dreamy contemplation. Andrey Bely wrote of the tangle of streets around Arbat:

Such unforgettable strolls,
Such unforgettable dreams,
Along the crooked lanes of
Moscow ...

A half-century later Bulat Okudzhava wrote his 'Song About Arbat', a haunting tune that virtually everyone in the country can sing by heart. Okudzhava's Arbat is a homeland, a destiny, a religion:

You flow like a river. Such a strange name!
Your asphalt is clear like water.
Oh, Arbat, my Arbat, You are my destiny.
You are my joy, you are my sorrow.

All of Moscow's joys and its many sorrows, its extravagance and piety, its grandeur and folly have been reflected through the ages on the pages of novels and in volumes of poetry. These books make excellent travel companions, providing intimate insights into the city. And as you explore the city, every once in a while step off today's streets and slip into the courtyards of the imagination, where Moscow's poets and writers dreamed other cities and other times.

FAIRY TALES AND MAGIC

Advertisements for magicians and fortune tellers fill the classified section of Moscow's most popular newspapers. This may seem mere superstition to most visitors, but it stems from a long tradition of fantasy and wizardry.

A fortune teller at work.

Move over, Harry Potter. Long before small British wizards were donning invisibility capes and casting spells, Russian magicians were putting on 'invisibility caps' or holding 'invisibility bones' to move about their villages unseen, or using their 'set tablecloth' to bring food and drink whenever they needed it. Not to mention using their magic wands to open doors and transform the village gossip into the form of a cat.

Spirits and sprites

Russia has a rich tradition of folk magic and fairy tales. Even today, everyone from lovelorn schoolgirls to Cabinet ministers consults respected practitioners of the white (benevolent) and black (evil) magical arts, a throwback to the days of the shaman and the Slavs' once animalistic religion.

When something goes awry in your hotel room, the staff might mutter that it's a *domovoy* (house sprite) making mischief. The solution? A glass of vodka and chunk of bread in the corner of the room usually placates them. In the woods, always the setting for supernatural goings-on, the troublemakers are usually the *lesnie* (wood spirits) or the *vodyanie* (water spirits) ready to lure the unsuspecting into their underwater world. The most dangerous spirits of the woods are the *rusalki:* beautiful women whose songs lure men below the waters.

Helping hands

If you need help with a nasty spirit or the evil eye, you can call in *volshebniki* (wizards), *vedmy* (witches), *kudesniki* (warlocks who cast spells), *kolduny* (wizards of a dark nature), *magy* (magicians) or even *chernoknizhniki* ('men of the black book', who practise the Black Arts). If you need help with an incantation (to rekindle your spouse's passion or cure an ingrown toenail), you can call on a *sheptun* (a whisperer of spells). If you can't find your car keys, call an *otgadnik* (someone who specialises in finding lost or stolen possessions). If you want to see what's really going on in your life, ask a *gadalka* (fortune teller) or someone who calls herself 'the all-seeing.' During the Christmas holidays young women put a gold ring in a glass of water and move a candle around it to create images within the circle, or let a candle drip in the water and divine the future in the shape of the wax. For centuries unmarried women have done this to see if the new year will bring them a husband. You can read about Tatiana and Olga conjuring in similar fashion in *Evgeny Onegin*, the verse novel by Alexander Pushkin.

Fairy tales

Russian children grow up on fairy tales in which fearful creatures roam the earth, but good almost always prevails in the end. They are terrified of Baba Yaga, a nasty old witch who lives in a house on chicken legs that turns around to lure children to their deaths. This is the same Hut on Chicken Legs the artists built at Abramtsevo for their children, although no witch cackled from the carved windows in the artists' colony (see page 208).

Equally terrifying to small people is Gorynych the Dragon, a winged beast with three fire-breathing heads. Or Koshey the immortal, a skinny old dark wizard who can only be defeated when the hero finds his death on the tip of a pin, which is hidden in an egg, in a duck, in a hare, in a trunk hanging from an enormous oak tree. Another nasty fellow is Karabas-Barabas, the cruel director of a puppet theatre in *The Golden Key* by Aleksey Tolstoy. The Golden Key is worth finding: it opens the door to the Land of Happiness.

A benevolent magical being is the Firebird, whose feathers are flame red. She brings happiness to anyone who catches her – the Firebird has become the national symbol of rarely attainable joy. One of the heroes who searched for and found her is Ivan the Fool. In *The Little Hunchbacked Horse*, Ivan, the youngest brother of a large family, is inept but kind, and ultimately succeeds in carrying out the impossible tasks set before him. Transformed into a handsome lad, he marries the beautiful maiden and – of course – lives happily ever after.

In the tale of *Sadko*, a poor musician plays his *gusli* (dulcimer) by the banks of a lake, and a water sprite rewards him by telling him the story of a golden fish, who restores youth to anyone who can catch and eat it. Sadko succeeds in doing this and is rewarded with gifts from the local merchants. In another tale, the wicked stepmother sends her stepdaughter to her death in the woods on a cold winter night, but when Morozko (Old Man Winter) asks if she is cold, she is too polite to complain. He makes a fire to keep her warm and

sends her home with riches. Most satisfyingly, the wicked stepmother sends her own nasty daughter back into the woods at night to gain her mother riches but the girl complains to Morozko and is punished by freezing to death.

Some tales tell of fleeting happiness. In *Snegurochka (The Snow Maiden)*, an old couple long for a child, so they make a maiden out of snow. She comes to life and is joyful in the winter but becomes sad as the days grow longer and the sun shines more brightly. One evening she goes into the woods to pick flowers with the village girls who make a bonfire to jump through. When the Snow Maiden jumps through the flames she melts and disappears in a cloud of white mist.

Today you can find beautifully illustrated books of Russian fairy tales (look for reproductions with illustrations by *style moderne* artist Ivan Bilibin). Or choose your favourite tale and find a scene from it decorating a lacquer box made in the towns of Palekh, Mstera, Fedoskino and Kholui. And should you find yourself in need of a wizard or a fortune teller, advertisements can be found in many local newspapers.

An illustration of Baba Yaga.

MOSCOW ON STAGE

The performing arts have a long tradition of excellence, fostered in the Soviet period when innovation was frowned on. Now, creative talent is breaking out, but it is still the established works that musicians, actors, dancers and singers perform best.

Dancers at the Kremlin Palace of Congresses.

Moscow's performing arts are among the finest in the world. Every evening you can choose between dozens of operas, ballets, concerts and plays featuring some of the world's finest performers. Tickets are still reasonably priced, and some performances are worth seeking out just to see the magnificent venues in which they take place.

Ballet and dance

Performed in the capital since the 1730s, Russian classical ballet emerged in its full glory at the end of the 19th century. Its inspiration was Marius Petipa (1818–1910), a French choreographer considered to be 'the father of classical ballet', who lived and worked in Russia as choreographer-in-chief of the Imperial Theatre for more than 50 years, staging ballets that are now part of repertories throughout the world. After Petipa came Mikhail Fokin (1880–1942), who scandalised audiences with his daring costumes and productions, and Sergey Diaghelev (1872–1929), whose *Russian Seasons* with Nijinsky debuted in Paris in 1909 and changed dance forever.

A period of experimentation continued for a few years after the 1917 Revolution, until, like the other arts, dance fell prey to the dictates of Socialist Realism, and some of the country's finest dancers defected to the West. However, dance training remained at an extraordinarily high level, and ballet experts maintain there is still nothing in the world like the delicacy and technical perfection of Russian dancers.

The best troupes in Moscow are the Bolshoi Ballet at the Bolshoi Theatre, founded in 1776, and the Kremlin Palace of Congresses, though their prima ballerinas are often on loan to touring companies and other world theatres. The Moskva Russian Chamber Ballet has two troupes that perform both traditional and modern ballets on several stages throughout the city, and the New Ballet has a small permanent stage where they perform dance pieces that include ballet, pantomime and drama.

The Kinetic Theatre, a modern dance troupe led by Alexander Pepelyaev, is often on tour, but is worth seeing at various venues around the city when it is in town. And don't forget folk dance: the Moiseyev troupe is the best and often

Opera at the Stanislavski and Nemirovich-Danchenko Moscow Academic Music Theatre.

performs in the capital. Visiting folk-dance troupes from across the Russian Federation and former USSR also come to Moscow on tour; check local listings and theatre kiosks.

Opera

Russians' love of opera is deeply rooted. By the late 18th century the Medoks Theatre in Moscow was performing a repertory of more than 400 operas, ballets and dramas, including many Russian operas by composers such as Mikhail Sokolovsky and Vasily Pashkevich. The greatest period in Russian opera was the late 19th century, when Tchaikovsky taught at the Conservatory, and his operas, ballets and symphonic music premiered on Moscow's stages. Once the imperial monopoly on opera troupes was lifted in 1882, several private opera houses opened that rivalled the Bolshoi in artistry.

Today you can see both traditional productions and original stagings. While European opera is performed frequently, the great Russian operas by Glinka, Mussorgsky, Borodin and Tchaikovsky provide an authentic evening out, and there is nothing like Moscow for lavish sets, often including live animals, top-notch choruses and great booming Russian basses – they are trained to sing several notes lower than in the West.

The Bolshoi performs a repertory heavy in traditional opera, and their foray into modern opera in 2005 in a performance of *Rosenthal's Children* with a libretto by the controversial author Vladimir Sorokin resulted in demonstrations and even a parliamentary inquiry, which may further inhibit experimentation. The Gelikon Opera House has two small stages where their troupes perform traditional operas in unusual productions and a variety of lesser-known Russian and foreign operas. The New *(Novaya)* Opera performs a mixed repertory in a beautifully renovated hall. The Moscow Chamber Musical Theatre, led by Boris Pokrovsky, puts on interesting, albeit rather obscure, chamber pieces, such as Dmitry Shostakovich's first opera, *The Nose*. The Moscow Operetta Theatre stages light opera and musicals, such as *My Fair Lady*, in Russian.

Impresarios have attempted to break out of the repertory tradition with stage musicals that perform every night, usually on the stage of one of the city's Soviet-era Houses of Culture. The experiment, which brought *Cats* to the Moscow stage, has had mixed results.

Great Hall of the Moscow Conservatory.

Macbeth at the Moscow Art Theatre.

Classical music venues

Until the late 18th century, Moscow's musical culture lagged behind the court-supported theatres and troupes in St Petersburg. It wasn't until music began to be printed at the University Printing House in 1772 that it became more accessible; and by the end of the century a vibrant scene had emerged. In the early 19th century, one of the most popular concert instruments was the guitar, and music was played as frequently in the city's literary salons as in its concert halls. With the founding of the Conservatory in 1866, performance and training were established on the highest level of professionalism, so that by the end of the 19th century there were dozens of concert halls and schools, including a school for women and academies for liturgical music and bell-ringing.

Musical life changed radically after the Revolution. Although Moscow grew as the centre of musical culture in the 1920s, in 1932 the Composers' Union was founded to apply the strictures of Socialist Realism. In a famous article denouncing Dmitry Shostakovich called 'Muddle instead of music', the state made clear that 'formalism', which meant any kind of

THEATRE IN MOSCOW

Theatre has thrived in the city since the late 18th century. After a little over a century of academic and mannered performances, Stanislavsky and Nemirovich-Danchenko changed the world of Russian drama with their Moscow Art Theatre (MKhAT), and avant-garde writers, directors and actors changed it once again in the first decades of the 20th century. Throughout the Soviet period actor training was on a par with anything across the globe, producing several generations of brilliant actors – even if Soviet political and artistic conservatism severely limited the theatres' repertories. After a dip in the early post-Soviet period, when funding was hard to find, theatre life has perked up, with fine productions in the classical repertory theatres like the Sovremennik, Lenkom, Theatre on Malaya Bronnaya, and the Moscow Art Theatre. The Taganka Theatre is no longer the cutting edge of drama that it was during the 1980s, but it still puts on interesting productions. The Maly Theatre is the most conservative theatre, and the place to see Ostrovsky's plays; for innovation, try the Fomenko Studio Theatre. If you don't understand Russian, try seeing a play you know well, by Chekhov or Shakespeare, for example. Seeing the seagull-decorated curtain at the old Moscow Art Theatre is worth the price of admission alone.

innovative music, was not to be tolerated. It was only after Stalin's death that composers breathed more freely, and only in the 1990s that innovation was celebrated once again.

The finest auditorium for classical music is the Great Hall of the Moscow Conservatory; the acoustics are sublime, and the performances are usually the best in the city. The Conservatory has two other spaces, the Small Hall and the Rachmaninov Hall, that offer chamber concerts and performances by soloists, often young performers just starting out. The Tchaikovsky Concert Hall is home to the Moscow State Academic Philharmonic, and the venue of the Moscow Symphony Orchestra and a variety of musical and dance performances. The newest music hall is the Moscow International House of Music, which hosts a variety of festivals and performers; it is worth getting tickets to any performance that includes the hall's magnificent organ. Some of the best of Moscow's concerts are held in unexpected places. During the summer the Arkhangelskoye, Tsaritsyno (see page 199) and Ostankino (see page 176) estates host chamber concerts in their elegant halls. When you visit small 'house museums', enquire about concerts: the apartments where Chaliapin, Aleksey Tolstoy, Chekhov, Skriabin and other notables lived are now the venue of chamber concerts throughout the year. Sometimes the performers are young or not top calibre, but you can hear excellent performances of little-played works, such as 20th-century or Baroque music, that don't draw large audiences, and the ambience in small halls a few steps from where Chekhov wrote his short stories or Skriabin composed his music is divine. Larger museums, such as the Tretyakov Gallery, the Pushkin Museum of Fine Arts and the Pushkin Literary Museum, also hold concerts in their halls, where you can listen to music surrounded by the world's finest works of art.

Popular music

The first jazz bands appeared in Moscow in 1922 and were, rather surprisingly, hugely popular throughout Soviet times. They still enjoy a fanatical following, and more than a dozen clubs perform jazz regularly. One of the best was the legendary Sinaya Ptitsa (Blue Bird), which occupied the same location for more than 40 years but which sadly closed in 2010. Others such as Forte, Le Club and the Jazz Art Club, have taken up the baton, providing high-quality sessions most nights.

Of course these days the Russian capital attracts big-name acts from the world of international rock and pop, with huge concerts held in football stadiums and arenas, though no longer on the scale of some of the events held in the late 1980s when Western bands sometimes drew audiences of a million people to monster outdoor festivals. Search the listings pages of *The Moscow Times* to see who is in town.

For children of every age

If you have bad childhood associations with sad elephants and frightening sideshows, the Moscow Circus may help change your view of the Big Top. Either on the old stage on Tsvetnoy bulvar or the new stage on prospekt Vernadskovo, the shows are filled with dozens of exuberant short acts, from trapeze artists to trained yaks, at a level of artistry that makes it seem like another art form. If you don't object to performing animals, try the circus at Durov's Circle, where performers range from rats to a hippo, or the odd House of Cats, where the trainers have convinced felines to perform tricks and routines without blinking at the shouts and applause of the audience. The Obraztsov Puppet Theatre is another delight that requires little knowledge of Russian.

The Yuri Kuklachev Cat Theatre.

A bishop during an orthodox liturgy at the High Monastery of St Peter.

UNRAVELLING THE RUSSIAN ORTHODOX CHURCH

At the heart of Moscow's culture is its historic role as the seat of the Russian Orthodox Church. The religious past and the significance of its contemporary symbols are explored here by William Craft Brumfield, a leading scholar of the Russian Church and its architecture.

The art of the Russian Orthodox Church is one of the great achievements of Russian culture. Any visit to Moscow can be enhanced by viewing and learning about this art. Most churches are open throughout the day and may be visited for contemplation of Russia's cultural and spiritual legacy in sacred art.

Moscow has many religions and faiths, and all have their places of worship. Catholic and Protestant churches, synagogues, mosques and other prayer houses coexist and contribute to the city's vibrant urban mix. By far the major religious presence, however, is the Russian Orthodox Church, headed by Patriarch Kirill. From the time of the acceptance of Orthodox Christianity by Prince Vladimir of Kiev in 988, the Orthodox Church has remained the leading religious presence among the eastern Slavs and has had a profound impact not only on Russian religious life, but also on the arts, on society – indeed, on virtually every aspect of Muscovite and Russian culture. Although relations between Moscow and the Orthodox Church have at times been troubled (to say the least), the extent of Moscow's power has rested in no small measure on the Church.

Following the fragmentation of Kievan Rus and the invasion by Mongol Tatars in 1237, Moscow began its gradual, methodical rise to power among the ruins left by the Mongols. In 1325 the leading Church prelate, Metropolitan Peter of Vladimir, made the Moscow Kremlin his de facto residence and, the following year, under Ivan Kalita, or 'Moneybags', the foundation was laid for the Kremlin's first stone cathedral, dedicated to the Dormition of the Mother

Lighting a candle during the Palm Sunday liturgy.

of God. With the patriarchate established in the Kremlin, the increasingly militant Orthodox Church, which had long accepted the authority of the Mongol Horde, played a major part in rallying Russian forces around the banner of Moscow in a crusade against the Tatars.

In Constantinople, it was not just the Turks who threatened the independence of the Byzantine Church. In 1439 it finally agreed to unite with the Roman Catholic Church (the Union of Florence) on terms that reflected doctrinal concessions and an acceptance of the authority of the Pope. Isidore, the Metropolitan of Russia and an appointee of Constantinople, supported the union, but a number of the accompanying Russian delegates in Florence refused. This faction succeeded in rejecting the union and in expelling Isidore from Russia. By repudiation of the authority of the Patriarch in Constantinople, the Russian Church had become autocephalous. The fall of Constantinople to the Turks in 1453 further increased the isolation of Russian Orthodoxy, and reinforced the mission of Muscovy as defender of the Orthodox faith. This sense of Moscow as the sole independent Orthodox power was consolidated during the reign of Ivan III (1462–1505), who supported a major rebuilding of the Kremlin cathedrals and walls, hiring a number of Italian architects, among whom the most notable was Aristotle Fioravanti, who undertook the rebuilding of the Cathedral of the Dormition in the Kremlin.

Structure and meaning

Although Fioravanti fundamentally rebuilt the Dormition Cathedral from the foundation trenches to the cupolas, its general form follows a pattern inherited from Byzantine culture and indicative of the relation between structure and meaning in the design of the church. The

Midnight Mass at the Cathedral of Christ the Saviour.

A meeting in Cuba in early 2016 between Patriarch Kirill and Pope Francis was the first such get-together between the heads of the Russian Orthodox and Catholic churches for a millennium.

Dormition Cathedral has five cupolas, but whether a church has one or many, the main cupola is always placed above a cylinder – also known as a drum – at the centre of the church. The holy of holies is the apse sanctuary with the altar, which is situated at the east end of the structure. The main altar of a church is dedicated to a sacred figure or event in the calendar, such as the Dormition of the Mother of God. It is this consecration that gives a church its name. Thus every church dedication has its date in the religious calendar, and the day allotted to this dedication is also that church's main festival day. The Dormition Cathedral displays in grand form the Russian Orthodox practice of painting the walls and ceiling vaults with scenes from the Bible and the lives of the saints. The interior of the main dome traditionally has an image of Christ Pantocrator (Ruler of All), while above the altar the apse is devoted to an image of Mary Mother of God standing in a pose that indicates a blessing extended to the worshippers. The altar is screened from the laity by an icon stand, or iconostasis. This is the general pattern of meaning that integrates building and sacred image in Russian Orthodox churches.

The design of most parish churches in Moscow is a modification of the earlier, rectangular structures exemplified by the Kremlin cathedrals. During the expansion of church construction for Moscow's parishes in the 17th century, there evolved a new form known as the 'ship'. In this plan the church consists of a cuboid main structure with an extension (the apse) for the altar at the east end, a low vestibule (*trapeza*) attached to the west, and, attached to the vestibule, a bell tower culminating in a 'tent' (conical) tower. The bell tower in the west can be seen as the 'prow' of the ship, providing a counterpoint to the 'sails', represented by the usual five cupolas, which are often gilded or decorated with bright metal stars. From the 17th century, hundreds of such churches were built throughout Russia.

Iconostasis at the Cathedral of the Transfiguration, Novospassky Monastery.

Entering the church

Despite the apparently endless variety of artistic detail, the plan underlying each church is readily comprehensible. The entrance is in most cases from the west, usually through a passage on the ground floor of the bell tower. (In some churches the bell tower itself will have an altar, or chapel, above the entrance.) Proper attire and behaviour are expected from anyone entering an active church, and this includes acceptable head covering for women (a scarf), modest dress (often ignored) and uncovered heads and long trousers for men. You may get away with taking photographs but you should never touch icons.

Passing through the main portal, you will enter the space of the vestibule, which typically is dimly lit and aglow with the light of votive candles. To the side of the entrance is a counter where devotional literature and votive candles are sold. The vestibule also usually contains its subsidiary altars, where baptisms and memorial services are held. Each of these altars has its own dedication to a sacred figure or church holiday, and each has its own icon screen. In addition to the altars, the vestibule can have separate icons placed against the wall or pillars, with a stand for votive candles.

In most churches the passage from the vestibule, with relatively low ceiling vaults, to the main space of the church produces a dramatic impression. Once again, structure provides insight into sacred meaning in the central part of the temple, with its brighter illumination, its rows of wall-paintings and the high vaults that rise above the richly carved and painted icon screen. It is with the icon screen that the visual message of the church achieves its greatest concentration. The icons serve as a conduit of spiritual power and meaning from the realm of the divine.

Reading the icons

In the early medieval period the icons in front of the altar presumably stood in a single row or a low configuration, thus allowing worshippers to see the image of Mary Mother of God (Theotokos) rising from the apse. But probably by the 15th century the Russian Church had developed a complex ranking of icons that placed the world of faith in an immediately visible hierarchy. And while the multitude of images may overwhelm the first-time visitor, the system underlying the iconostasis is readily accessible. At the centre of the first row (known

Fragment of Andrei Rublev's fresco, 'The Last Judgement', at Assumption Cathedral.

as the Local Row) are the Royal Gates, the passage used by the priests between the main part of the church and the altar. The top of the Royal Gates contains a depiction of the Annunciation (the Archangel Gabriel announcing to Mary the conception of Christ), beneath which are four panels – one for each of the Evangelists, Matthew, Mark, Luke and John. The space above the Royal Gates will often have a representation of the Last Supper.

OLD BELIEVERS

In the 17th century, Patriarch Nikon approved changes to Russian Orthodox liturgical texts and practices. Today the changes seem minor: a different way of spelling Jesus and making the sign of the cross with three fingers, not two. But millions of Russian Christians rejected the changes as a break with sacred tradition, and the church split, with the Old Believers persecuted by Church and state. The Old Believers also divided; some lived outside society, much like the Amish in the US; others, like the Ryabunshinsky banking family and Morozov textile magnates, lived within society, but with a tradition of industriousness that made them immensely rich. Remote communities of Old Believers can still be found in Siberia.

The images of the Local Row are among the largest in the iconostasis. The central Royal Gates are flanked by icons of Christ the Saviour (on the viewer's right) and Mary Mother of God. The Local Row also contains the icon of the saint or holiday to which the church is dedicated. This dedicatory icon is located to the right of the Royal Gates.

In some cases the church is dedicated to a miraculous icon, such as the Kazan Icon of the Mother of God, which is a particularly revered image of Mary and the Christ Child. Visitors are often confused by the presence of a 'Kazan Church' on Red Square. Kazan, after all, is a distant city on the Volga River. In fact, this is the shortened, popular Russian name for churches dedicated to the Theotokos of Kazan, or Kazan Icon of the Mother of God.

The Local Row is completed with other icons that are of special importance to the local parish. Each side of the Local Row has an additional door. The one on the north side (to the viewer's left) leads to the *prothesis*, which is used for the preparation of the sacraments. The one on the south side leads to the *diakonikon*, used by the deacons for the preparation of vestments.

The second row of the icon screen is known as the Deesis ('prayer' or 'supplication') Row, which is the most significant part of the icon screen in theological terms. At its centre is an image of Christ enthroned, with Mary Mother of God at his right hand (the viewer's left) and John the Baptist on his left. Beyond Mary stand the Archangel Michael and Apostle Peter, while the Archangel Gabriel and Apostle Paul are at the side of John the Baptist. The Deesis Row concludes on either side with figures of prelates and Church fathers, whose number can vary with the size of the iconostasis. The heads of all the figures in this row are bowed towards Christ in a posture of reverence and supplication (hence the name 'Deesis'). The icons are particularly elongated, thus increasing the height and the number of figures portrayed in prayer to the central figure of Christ.

In most churches the third row of the icon screen is the Festival Row, although in a few cases the position of the Deesis and Festival rows is switched. The Festival Row is distinguished by the fact that all of the icons within it are of square format, in contrast to the elongated, rectangular icons in the other rows. This row contains depictions of the 12 major festivals of the Russian Orthodox Church. Most of these are celebrated on fixed days in the Church calendar and are known as Immovable Feasts. Those related to Easter, however, do not have fixed dates and are known as Movable Feasts. It should be noted that the Russian Orthodox Church adheres to the Julian calendar, which is 13 days behind the Gregorian calendar generally in use throughout the world (hence Christmas and Easter are celebrated 13 days after the rest of the Christian world).

The fourth row is dedicated to the Old Testament Prophets, such as Isaiah, Jeremiah, Ezekiel and Daniel. The centre of Prophets' Row is usually occupied by an image of Mary Mother of God holding the Christ Child in the form known as 'the Sign' (*znamenie*). In the Russian Orthodox Church this central figure is interpreted as the ultimate goal of Old Testament prophecy.

The fifth row (sometimes absent in smaller churches) contains icons of the Old Testament Patriarchs from the Book of Genesis, and usually includes Adam, Seth, Noah, Abraham, Isaac and Jacob. The centre of this row can be occupied by an image of God the Father, or by a depiction of the Old Testament Trinity, the three angels that visited Abraham on the Plains of Mamre. This icon is particularly revered as a prophecy of the miraculous birth of Christ. If the church is dedicated to the Trinity, this icon will also be found in the Local Row.

The culminating point of the icon screen is a painted crucifix with an image of Christ. (In some churches the figure of Christ above the iconostasis is carved, although the Orthodox Church frowns upon sculpted images.) A similar, free-standing crucifix can often be found in the church, to the left of the iconostasis.

Wall and ceiling frescoes

The interior walls of most Russian Orthodox churches are covered with wall-paintings, usually in the fresco technique, that amplify the depictions of the sacred world. These are arranged in rows of scenes rising to the ceiling vaults. Although certain important scenes from the life of Christ are virtually mandatory, the choice of scenes will depend on the dedication of the church itself. In large churches with piers or columns these structural elements will also be painted with images of saints and archangels. The west wall of the main space of the church is reserved for a depiction of the Last Judgement.

Oklad Cover for the Holy Trinity icon by Andrei Rublev.

ARCHITECTURE

The glistening onion domes of Moscow's skyline symbolise the city, but they are just part of a monumental heritage. Walking the streets, you will find a vibrant mix of styles from neoclassical to the fabulous examples of *style moderne*, Russian Revival and Constructivism.

Cathedral of the Dormition in the Kremlin.

The architecture of Moscow has its origins in the architectural traditions of the medieval state of Kievan Rus. These traditions were themselves derived from the Byzantine Empire and, in particular, the Eastern Orthodox Church, which became the accepted religion in 988.

Little more than a log fort and trading settlement on the site of the Kremlin, Moscow was quickly rebuilt after being burned down during the Mongol invasion of 1237, and gradually increased its territory. But enduring stone buildings were not constructed until the 15th century. The earliest surviving architectural monument is the Cathedral of the Icon of the Saviour Not Made by Hands, located within the Saviour-Andronikov Monastery. Built at some point between 1410 and 1427, the church was endowed by a Moscow merchant family, the Yermolins, and was the most ornamental to be found throughout Muscovy at that time.

Italian masters

Although this and other limestone churches indicate a modest architectural revival during the first half of the 15th century, it was not until the latter part of the century that major monuments began to appear in the Kremlin under the direction of Italian masters brought in during the long and successful reign of Ivan III (the Great). The first was the Dormition Cathedral (1475–9) by Aristotle Fioravanti, who introduced both a rigorously geometric plan and technical improvements such as deep foundation trenches with oak pilings, strong brick for the vaulting and iron tie-rods. The interior, devoid of a choir gallery and with round columns, is spacious and well lit.

Brick soon displaced limestone for most masonry construction. Aleviz Novyi used it in his Cathedral of the Archangel Michael (1505–9), which had a number of Italianate elements. Italian influence also appeared in Marco Ruffo and Pietro Solario's design of the Faceted Palace (1487–91), and in the Kremlin walls and towers (1485–1516) built by Antonio Fryazin, Marco Ryazin, Solari and others. (The distinctive Kremlin tower spires were added by Russian builders in the 17th century.) The dominant element of the Kremlin, the Ivan the Great Bell Tower, was constructed in two stages, the lower two tiers in 1505–8 by Bon Fryazin and the upper tier with cupola in 1599–1600, during the reign of Boris Godunov.

During the 16th century, Moscow's brick-tower churches, designed as votive offerings, displayed boldly inventive designs and a continued Italian influence. The first of these great monuments is the Church of the Ascension at Kolomenskoye, commissioned by Vasily III in 1529 as a votive offering for the birth of his heir, Ivan IV. The church is of unprecedented height, culminating in an elongated brick conical roof (the shatyor, or 'tent' roof) rather than the traditional cupolas.

The distinctive impression of the Church of the Ascension was intensified by its site on a steep bank above the Moscow River with a dramatic view of the princely domains. Its location in the middle of a compound of wooden structures, including a large palace of haphazard form (burned down in 1571 and twice rebuilt), created an ensemble whose silhouette was richer than today's surviving masonry monuments that stand in isolation.

The walls of the Church of the Ascension, which rest on massive brick vaults reinforced with iron tie-rods, are between 2.5 and 3 metres (8–10ft) thick, and are further supported by the buttressing effect of the cruciform plan. The raised terrace, originally without a roof, girding the lower part of the church is reached by three staircases, each with a perpendicular turn that would have increased the visual drama of ritual processions. The main block of the tower, edged with massive pilasters, leads upwards to three tiers of pointed *kokoshniki* (decorated arches) whose design is echoed in the cornice of the octagon. From this point the 'tent' ascends, with eight facets delineated by limestone ribs. The tower concludes with an octagonal lantern, a cupola and, at 58 metres (190ft), a cross.

The chapel-churches

Within two decades of the completion of the Church of the Ascension at Kolomenskoye, Vasily III's heir, Ivan IV (r.1533–84), had commissioned another dynastic votive structure, the Church of the Decapitation of John the Baptist, at the nearby village of Dyakovo. The symmetrical arrangement of small churches around the central tower here – all resting on the same base – is the most intriguing feature of the church.

Following the example of his father, Ivan and his clerics dedicated the separate altars as an affirmation of the personal relation between the tsar and the deity. These ancillary chapel-churches are part of a highly integrated design that reproduces the central tower form at the four corners of a square base. This concept would soon be elaborated upon at the best-known of Russian churches, the Cathedral of the Intercession on the Moat, known as St Basil's.

Located on Red Square, the Cathedral of the Intercession (1555–61) has come to epitomise the extravagance of the Moscow imagination. The notorious character of Ivan IV (the Terrible), who built the Cathedral to commemorate his taking of the Tatar city of Kazan in 1552, and the savagery of the latter part of his reign have fostered the notion of a structure devoid of restraint or reason. Yet the builders, traditionally identified as Barma and Postnik Yakovlev from the city of Pskov (although research now indicates it may have been just one person), created a coherent, logical plan. The Cathedral of the Intercession consists of a central tower dedicated to the Intercession

Church of the Decapitation of Saint John in Dyakovo.

St Basil's Cathedral.

of the Mother of God and flanked by ancillary, free-standing churches, each with its own dedication – in an alternating pattern of major and minor forms: major at the compass points and minor on the diagonal. The four octagonal churches at the compass points repeat the octagonal motif at the base of the plan and in the drum and 'tent' roof of the central tower. The four smaller churches are cuboid, surmounted by a cupola and round drum raised on three tiers of *kokoshniki*. The height of their onion domes is measured to complement those of the alternating, larger churches.

Within this interplay of tower forms, the silhouette of the Cathedral gives remarkably different impressions of its shape, depending on the approach and perspective of the viewer. Like much great architecture, the Cathedral includes a calculated distortion: the central tower is not in the geometric centre of the plan but is shifted substantially westwards to allow the addition of an apse with the main altar. To accommodate this shift, the small churches on the west side are reduced to a size only large enough to contain a few worshippers. Thus, seen from the north or south, the Cathedral has

a dual centre: that of the tower itself and that of the structure as a whole.

Romanov revival

Although the end of the 16th century witnessed the expansion of Moscow's monasteries and fortresses, other construction declined, as an exhausted country tried to recover from the depredations of Ivan's reign, only to be followed in 1604 with an interregnum known as the 'Time of Troubles', which led to chaos throughout the land. With the establishment of the Romanov dynasty in 1613, the country began a recovery that was reflected in a marked increase in church construction during the long reign of Aleksey Mikhailovich (1645–76). Of the many Moscow churches that date from this period, the most notable is the Church of the Trinity in Nikitniki, located in the commercial district known as Kitai-gorod. Endowed by the wealthy merchant Grigory Nikitnikov, the Trinity Church exemplifies the elaborate exterior decoration favoured by merchant patrons. Relatively modest in size, the church consists of a central cube decorated with carved limestone window surrounds *(nalichnik)*, rows of *kokoshniki*, and five cupolas, four

Kokoshnik: an arch that is a decorative element on church exteriors; the original meaning is a headdress that was traditionally worn by Russian women. Zakomara: an arched gable, an element of construction and decoration in older Russian churches.

of which are purely decorative; they admit no light. After its completion in 1634, over the next two decades the original structure acquired two chapels, attached at the northeast and southeast and an enclosed gallery leading to a bell tower with a 'tent' roof on the northwest corner. This is the earliest example of the placement of a bell tower within the church ensemble – a practice that would become generally accepted in parish architecture during the 17th century.

Indeed, despite its decorative effusions, 17th-century church architecture achieved a measure of stability through the evolution of a basic plan known as the 'ship', consisting of a cuboid main structure with a low spacious apse for the altar at the east end, a low vestibule *(trapeza)* attached to the west, and, attached to the vestibule, a bell tower culminating in a 'tent' tower. This tower provided a counterpoint to the 'sails' of the ship – its five cupolas, usually gilded or decorated with bright metal stars. An excellent example of this design is the Church of St Nicholas the Wonderworker in Khamovniki but this is only one of dozens of such churches throughout Moscow.

As Russia experienced increased contact with the West during the latter half of the 17th century, the influence of Ukrainian, Polish and Central European architecture appeared in churches commissioned primarily by the Naryshkin and Sheremetev families on estates in and around Moscow. Notable examples of the 'Naryshkin Baroque' style, such as the Church of the Intercession at Fili (1690–9) and the Church of the Trinity at Troitskoye-Lykovo (1698–1703), show a revival of the tower form often elevated above a quatrefoil terrace. The 17th century also witnessed the use of brick for residences *(palaty)*, a number of which are still preserved in areas of central Moscow such as Kitai-gorod and the Kremlin itself.

The assimilation of Western architectural styles increased dramatically with the reign of Peter the Great. Of course the founding of St Petersburg in 1703 meant that most construction activity was shifted to what would soon become the new Russian capital, but new approaches to architecture also reached Moscow. A curious example is the Church of the Archangel Gabriel (1701–7), also known as the Menshikov Tower.

Neoclassical estates

During the reign of Catherine the Great, neo-classicism appeared in the design not only of numerous churches but also of houses and other institutions built by the nobility and wealthy merchants. Talented serf builders erected many of the grand estate houses, and the most prominent neoclassical architects in Moscow were Matvey Kazakov, Rodion Kazakov and Vasily Bazhenov. During Catherine's reign, period styles such as Gothic Revival entered the work of Bazhenov and Matvey Kazakov.

In the 1770s–80s Bazhenov and Kazakov were also involved in the building of a 'Moorish' Gothic Revival imperial estate at Tsaritsyno, but Catherine abandoned the project.

After the fire of 1812, damaged landmarks such as Bazhenov's Pashkov House and Kazakov's

Neoclassical façade in Moscow.

Moscow University – both facing the west wall of the Kremlin – were rebuilt, while new houses appeared in the Empire style as interpreted by Dominco Gilardi, Osip Bove and Afanasy Grigoriev. Many of these neoclassical buildings still grace sections of central Moscow.

During the 1830s the waning influence of neoclassicism made way for various historicist styles, such as Konstantin Ton's Great Kremlin Palace (1838–49) and his Cathedral of Christ the Saviour (1818–58; destroyed in 1931; rebuilt in the 1990s). Secular architecture in the latter half of the 19th century was largely an eclectic combination of various periods in Western architecture. Eclectic decorative styles were applied profusely to the facades of apartment houses and commercial buildings.

Russian Revival and *style moderne*

By the 1870s there arose a new national style based on decorative elements from 16th- and 17th-century Muscovy, as well as on motifs from folk art and traditional wooden architecture. Major examples of this Russian Revival style in Moscow include the Historical Museum (1874–83), built on the north side of Red Square to a design by Vladimir Shervud, the

Sergei Maliutin's Pertsov apartment house.

adjacent Moscow City Hall (Duma, 1890–2), built by Dmitry Chichagov, and the Upper Trading Rows (now the GUM department store, 1889–93), by Alexander Pomerantsev.

The Russian Revival style also characterised many mansions and apartment buildings, and its influence continued through the early 1900s in the 'neo-Russian' component of *style moderne*, Russia's Art Nouveau. Painters such as Viktor Vasnetsov, who created the entrance building at the Tretyakov Gallery (*c*.1905) and Sergey Malyutin, who designed the Pertsov apartment house (1905–7) opposite the Cathedral of Christ the Saviour, were particularly active in using traditional Russian decorative arts as part of a new architectural aesthetic.

Style moderne displayed a number of stylistic tendencies in Russian architecture at the turn of the 20th century. Its primary emphasis was on the innovative use of materials such as glass, iron and glazed brick in designs that were both functional and receptive to the applied arts. The style flourished above all in Moscow, where its main patrons came from the merchant elite. Its leading practitioner, Fyodor Shekhtel, is known for such landmarks as Yaroslavl station (1902), the house for Stepan Pavlovich Ryabushinsky (1900–2; now the Gorky Museum) and his modernist design for the mansion of Alexandra Derozhinskaya (1901; now the Australian Embassy residence). Other leading modernist architects of the period include Lev Kekushev, Adolf Erikhson and William Walcot. All three were involved in the prolonged construction of one of the largest and most significant *style moderne* buildings in Moscow: the Hotel Metropol (1899–1905). Like Shekhtel, both Kekushev and Walcot designed houses in the modern style for wealthy clients. These houses still adorn the central part of Moscow, and many of them are now used as embassies.

By the end of the 1900s, *style moderne* had yielded to or merged with a modernised form of neoclassicism. In Moscow this neoclassical revival is best represented by the work of Roman Klein, who designed the Museum of Fine Arts (1897–1912; now the Pushkin Museum) and the Muir and Mirrielees emporium (1906–8; now known as TsUM). The latter was the first modern department store in Moscow and its functional frame was clad in Gothic revival elements. Although less prolific

The Rusakov Workers' Club, built in 1929, is a notable example of Constructivist architecture.

than Klein, other architects designed in a more austere variant of the neoclassical revival for major office buildings that still function in Moscow's traditional commercial centre.

Utopia and the Constructivists

The economic chaos engendered in Russia by World War I, the 1917 Revolution and the ensuing Civil War proved catastrophic for building activity. However, with the limited recovery of the economy in the 1920s, bold new designs, often utopian in concept, brought Russia to the attention of modern architects throughout the world. Constructivism, the most productive modernist movement, included architects such as Moysey Ginzburg, Ilya Golosov, Grigory Barkhin, Aleksey Shchusev and the Vesnin brothers Leonid, Viktor and Alexander. Their work set a standard for streamlined, functional design in Moscow's administrative and apartment buildings, as well as in social institutions such as workers' clubs. Unfortunately, many of these buildings stand in a state of disrepair that belies their importance to the international modern movement. Another modernist architect active during the same period, but not a part of Constructivism, was Konstantin Melnikov, creator of designs for workers' clubs,

transport structures and exposition pavilions. During the 1930s more conservative trends asserted themselves, as designs inspired by neoclassical, Renaissance and historicist models received the approval of the Communist leadership. Moscow's most prominent architectural traditionalists during the 1930s were Ivan Zholtovsky and the versatile Aleksey Shchusev.

After World War II, architectural design became still more firmly locked in traditional, often highly ornate eclectic styles epitomised by the post-war skyscrapers that still define the cityscape, from Moscow State University to the apartment building on Kotelnicheskaya Embankment. After the death of Stalin in 1953, pressing social needs – above all in housing – led to the development of 'micro-regions' composed of standardised apartment blocks with prefabricated components. Most Muscovites live in such regions, served by an extensive transport system linked by the unparalleled Moscow metro. Many underground stations are significant works of architectural design.

With the demise of Communism, entrepreneurial developers and the revival of private architectural practices are changing the face of Moscow. However design tends to be 'off the shelf' and of little architectural value.

Cathedral of Christ the Saviour and the city skyline.

The Hall of Remembrance and Sorrow in the Museum of the Great Patriotic War.

Inside GUM, the State Department Store on Red Square.

The Kremlin walls tower above footpaths in the Alexandrovsky Garden.

INTRODUCTION

A detailed guide to the entire city with the principal sites clearly cross-referenced by number to the maps.

The attractions of Moscow's city centre are haphazardly scattered. Regardless of which part of the city you choose to explore, you are sure to find world-class art museums; quirky 'house-museums' preserving the lives of legendary writers, actors and theatre directors in period formaldehyde; historic churches and monasteries; first-rate theatres; and shops crammed with everything from caviar to Cadillacs.

This wide dispersion of attractions is the result of the vision that Soviet planners had for the city. Pre-Revolutionary neighbourhoods, with their crooked medieval streets and historic buildings, were bisected or destroyed by the authorities, who craved broad, straight boulevards built to accommodate tanks more than private cars, and believed society functioned better in high-rise apartment blocks than along café-lined streets.

Moscow State University.

Only the heart of the city still falls into self-contained sections: the Kremlin, with its astounding cathedrals and museums packed with imperial treasures; Red Square and Kitai-gorod, the most ancient trading area of the city with magnificent merchants houses; and Theatre and Manege squares, which include some of the city's finest theatres, hotels, shops and exhibition spaces.

Mosaic at Sergiev Posad.

The area to the southeast of the Kremlin (see page 123) is a must-see for lovers of art, with four major museums – including the Pushkin Museum of Fine Art with its extraordinary collection of European masterpieces – and Moscow's most celebrated street, the Old Arbat. Two more excellent museums, the Old and New Tretyakov Galleries, which have brilliant collections of Russian art, lie south beyond the Moscow River.

Be sure to stroll up Tverskaya ulitsa, Moscow's main drag, and slip into courtyards to see what treasures have remained from centuries past or what flashy nightclub has just opened (or closed). To the north, revisit the Soviet past at the Museum of Cosmonauts.

Wherever you go you'll see that Moscow has undergone a remarkable transformation over the last 25 years. New neighbourhoods may not yet have taken hold, but since communal flats have become individually owned, society has returned to its natural, European home – the café-lined street.

Moscow

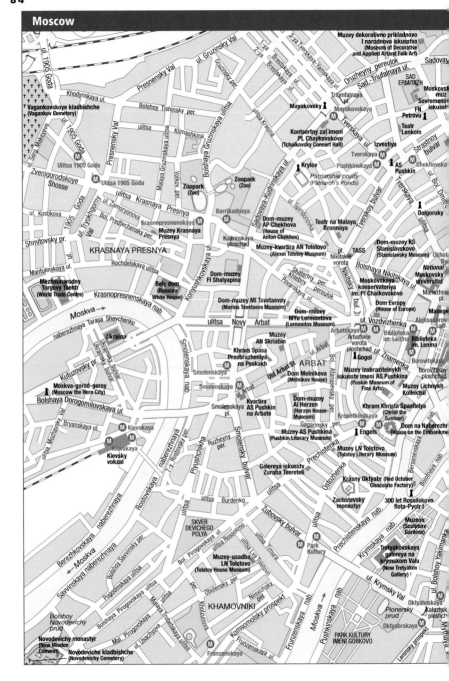

Muzey dekorativno prikladnovo
I naródnovo iskusstva
(Museum of Decorative
and Applied Artand Folk Art)

ul. Gruzinsky Val
ul. Gruzinsky

3-ya Tverskaya-Yamskaya ul.
2-ya Brestskaya ul.
1-ya Brestskaya ul.

Oruzheyny pereulok

Sadovay

SAD
ERMITAZH

Presnensky Val

Khodynskaya ul.

Bolshoy Tishinsky per.

ulitsa Krasina

Bolshaya Gruzinskaya ulitsa

Triumfalnaya
pl.

Sad.-Triumfalnaya ul.

Mayakovsky

Mayakovskaya

Moskovsi
muz
Sovremenn
iskusst

† † †
† † † †
† † † †
Vagankovskoye kladbishche
(Vagankov Cemetery)
† † † †
† † † †

ul. 1905 Goda

Presnensky Val

Malaya Gruzinskaya ulitsa

Klimashkina

Kontsertny zal imeni
Pl Chaykovskovo
(Tchaikovsky Concert Hall)

Tverskaya ul.

Petrovu

Teatr
Lenkom

ul. Serg Makeyeva

Ulitsa 1905 Goda

Volkov Per.

Krylov

Izvestiya

Strastnoy
bulvar

Chekhovska

Zvenigorodskoye
Shosse

Ulitsa 1905 Goda

Bolshaya Gruzinskaya ulitsa

Pushkinskaya

Pushkinskaya

AS
Pushkin

ul. Bol. Dmitr

ul. Kostikova

ulitsa Krasnaya Presnya

Zoopark
(Zoo)

Zoopark
(Zoo)

Patriarshie prudy
(Patriarch's Ponds)

Tverskaya ul.

ul. 1905 Goda

Bol. Predtechensky per.

Barrikadnaya

Sadovaya-Kudrinskaya ulitsa

Spiridonovka

Dolgoruky

Shmitovsky pr.

ul. Tryokhgorny Val

1905

ulitsa Zamoryonova

Krasnopresnenskaya

Muzey Krasnaya
Presnya

Kudrinskaya
ploschad

Dom-muzey
AP Chekhova
(House of
Anton Chekhov)

Teatr na Malaya
Bronnaya

Malaya Bronnaya

Mantulinskaya ul.

KRASNAYA PRESNYA

Rochdelskaya ulitsa

Muzey-kvartira AN Tolstovo
(Alexei Tolstoy Museum)

pl.
Nikitskie
vorota

TASS

Dom-muzey KS
Stanislavskovo
(Stanislavsky Museum)

Okhot
R

Mezhdunarodny
Torgovy Tsentr
(World Trade Centre)

Konyushkovskaya ulitsa

Bely dom
(Russian
White House)

Dom-muzey
FI Shalyapina

Skatertny per.
Khlebny
pereulok

Povarskaya ul.

Bolshaya Nikitskaya ul.

Moskovskaya
konservatoriya
im. Pl Chaikovskovo

National

Moskovsky
universitat

Manezhn
pl.

Moskva

naberezhnaya Tarasa Shevchenko

Krasnopresnenskaya nab.

Dom-muzey
MI Tsvetaevoy
(Marina Tsvetaeva Museum)

ulitsa Novy Arbat

Dom-muzey
MYu Lermontova
(Lermontov Museum)

Dom-muzey
(House of Europe)

Dom Evropy

ul. Vozdvizhenka

Aleksandrov
Sad

Kutuzovsky pr.

Krasnaya
Ukrainsky bulvar

Ukraina

Muzey
AN Skriabin

Novy
Arbat

Arbatskaya

ARBAT

Arbatskaya
vorota
ploshchad

Arbatskie
vorota
ploshchad im. Lenina

Biblioteka
im. Lenina

Biblioteka
im. Lenina

Borovitskay

Smolenskaya nab.

Khram Spasa
Preobrazheniya
na Peskakh

Smolenskaya

Old Arbat St

Dom Melnikova
(Melnikov House)

Bol. Afanasyevsky per.

Muzey izobrazitelnykh
iskusstv imeni AS Pushkina
(Puskin Museum of
Fine Arts)

Borovitskaya

Borovitsk
ploshcha

Moskva-gorod-geroy
(Moscow the Hero City)

Bolshaya Dorogomilovskaya ul.

Smolenskaya

ul. Arbat

Kvartira
AS Pushkin
na Arbate

Dom-muzey
Al Herzen
(Herzen House-
Museum)

Gagarinsky

Kropotkinskaya

Muzey Lichnykh
Kollektsii

Khram Khrista Spasitelya
(Christ the
Saviour)

Dom na Naberezhn
(House on the Embankme

Bryanskaya ul.

ul. Mozhaysky Val

Kievskaya

Kievskaya

Kievsky
vokzal

Rostovskaya naberezhnaya

Plyushchikha

Ruzheyny per.

Smolensky bulvar

Muzey AS Pushkina
(Pushkin Literary Museum)

Engels

Prechistenka

Muzey LN Tolstovo
(Tolstoy Literary Museum)

Bersenevskaya nab.

Bolshaya nab.

Krasny Oktyabr (Red October
Chocolate Factory)

Berezhkovskaya naberezhnaya

Savvinskaya naberezhnaya

Bolshaya Savvinsky per.

Pogodinskaya ulitsa

ulitsa Burdenko

Zubovsky bulvar

Ostozhenka

Galereya iskusstv
Zuraba Tsereteli

Zachatevsky
monastyr

300 let Rossiiskovo
flota-Pyotr I

Prechistenskaya nab.

Muzeon
(Sculpture
Gardens)

Moskva

SKVER
DEVICHEGO
POLYA

Bol. Pirogovskaya ul.

ulitsa Rossolimo

ulitsa Timura

ulitsa Lva Tolstovo

Park
Kultury

Muzey-usadba
LN Tolstovo
(Tolstoy House Museum)

Krymsky Val

Tretyakóvskaya
galereya na
krymskom Valu
(New Tretyakov
Gallery)

ul. Krymsky Val

ul. Bolshaya Yakimanka

Malaya Pirogovskaya ulitsa

Oksana

Nesvizhsky per.

Kholzunova

Komsomolsky prospekt

Moskva

Pushkinskaya nab.

Oktyabrskaya

Pionersky
prud

Kaluzhsk
ploshch

Mytnaya

Bolshoy
Novodevichy
prud

Malaya Pirogovskaya ulitsa

Mal. Pirogovsky per.

ul. Usachova

KHAMOVNIKI

Frunzenskaya nab.

PARK KULTURY
IMENI GORKOVO

Oktyabrskaya

Leninsky prospekt

Novodevichy monastyr
(New Miaden
Convent)

Novodeviche kladbishche
(Novodevichy Cemetery)

Frunzenskaya

Frunzenskaya ul.

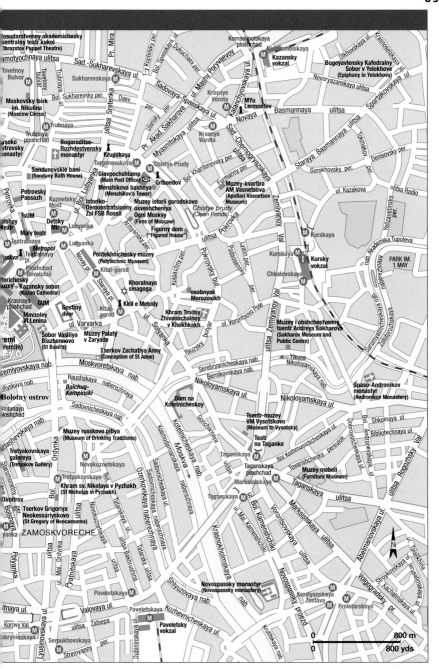

Gosudarstvenny akademichesky sentralny teatr kukol Obraztsov (Puppet Theatre)

Pr. Mira

Sad.-Sukharevskaya ulitsa

Komsomolskaya ploshchad

Kazansky vokzal

Bogoyavlensky Kafedralny Sobor v Yelokhove (Epiphany in Yelokhove)

Novoryazanskaya ulitsa

amotyovitaya ulitsa

Tsvetnoy Bulvar

Tsvetnoy bulvar

Trubnaya ul.

Sukharevskaya ulitsa

Bol. Sukharevsky per.

Sadovaya-Spasskaya ul.

Krasnye Vorota

MYu Lermontov

Basmannaya ulitsa

Spartakovskaya ulitsa

Moskovsky tsirk im. Nikulina (Moscow Circus)

Sretenka

ulitsa

Daev per.

Mashy Poryvaevoy

Kalanchovskaya ulitsa

Novaya

Tokmakov per.

Trubnaya ploshchad

Trubnaya

Pr. Akad. Sakharova

Sad.-Chernogryazskaya ulitsa

Staraya Basmannaya ulitsa

Gorokhovsky per.

Denisovsky per.

ysoko etrovsky onastyr

Bogoroditse-Rozhdestvensky monastyr

Krupskaya

Turgenevskaya

Myasnitskaya ulitsa

Krasnye Vorota

Zemlyanov

ul. Kazakova

ulitsa Radio

Elizavetinsky per.

Petrovka

Sandunovskie bani (Sanduny Bath House)

Petrovsky Passazh

Kuznetsky Most

Bol. Lubyanka

Glavpochtamp (Main Post Office)

Chistye Prudy

Grib:oedov

Bol. Khariton:evsky per.

Furmanny per.

Muzey-kvartira AM Vasnetsova (Apollari Vasnetsov Museum)

Kurskaya

PARK IM. 1 MAY

olshoy teatr

TsUM

Detsky Mir

Lubyanka

Menshikova bashnya (Menshikov's Tower)

Muzey istorii gorodskovo osveshcheniya

Armyansky per.

Chistye prudy (Clean Ponds)

Zemlyanov Val

Kurskaya

Kursky vokzal

Maly teatr

Metropol

Lubyanka

Novaya pl.

Ogni Moskvy (Fires of Moscow)

Figurny dom ("Figured House")

ulitsa Pokrovka

Podsosensky per.

oskva

Teatralnaya pl.

Ploshchad Revolyutsii

Politekhnichesky muzey (Polytechnic Museum)

Staraya pl.

Kitai-gorod

Pokrovsky bul.

Chkalovskaya

orichesky uzey

Kazansky sobor (Kazan Cathedral)

Khoralnaya sinagoga

Kolpachny per.

osobnyak Morozovich

Krasnaya ploshchad

GUM

Gostiny dvor

Kitai gorod

Kiril e Metody

Khram Troitsy Zhivonachalnoy v Khokhlakh

ul. Vorontsovo Pole

Muzey i obshchestvenny tsentr Andreya Sakharova (Sakharov Museum and Public Centre)

Syromyatnicheskaya naberezhnaya

Zolotorozhskaya nab.

Mavzoley Vl Lenina

ul. Varvarka

Solyanka

Yauzsky bulvar

em Kreml remlin

Sobor Vasiliya Blazhennovo (St Basil's)

Muzey Palaty v Zaryade

Tserkov Zachatiya Anny (Conception of St Anne)

Yauzsky

Yauza Nikoloyamskaya

Spaso-Andronikov monastyr (Andronikov Monastery)

emlyovskaya nab.

Moskvoretskaya nab.

Serebryanicheskaya nab.

Bernikovskaya nab.

Nikoloyamskaya ul.

Nikoloyamskaya ul.

ofiyskaya nab.

Raushskaya naberezhnaya

Balchug-Kempinski

Bol. Shkolnaya ul.

Bolotny ostrov

oitnaya loshchad

Sadovnicheskaya nab.

Dom na Kotelnicheskoy

Gon_charnaya

Dobrovolcheskaya ul.

Bibliotechnaya ul.

hevskaya nab.

Muzey russkovo pitiya (Museum of Drinking Traditions)

Kotelnicheskaya nab.

Moskva

Tsentr-muzey VM Vysotskovo (Museum to Vysotsky)

Bol. Kommunisticheskaya pereulok

Teatr na Taganke

Andronevskaya ul.

Bol. Rogozhsky Val

Tretyakovskaya galereya (Tretyakov Gallery)

Ordynka

Novokuznetskaya

Sadovnicheskaya naberezhnaya

Taganskaya

Taganskaya ploshchad

Towarishchesky pereulok

Muzey mebeli (Furniture Museum)

Taganskaya

Marksistskaya ulitsa

Tretyakovskaya

Khram sv. Nikolaya v Pyzhakh (St Nicholas in Pyzhakh)

Ozerkovskaya naberezhnaya

Marksistskaya

Taganskaya

ul. Mal. Kamenshchiki

Vorontsovskaya ulitsa

Marksistskaya ulitsa

Abelmanovskaya ulitsa

Strojkovskaya ul.

Terualikhina

Dimitrov

Tserkov Grigoriya Neokessariyskovo (St Gregory of Neocaesarea)

yanka

ZAMOSKVORECHE

ulitsa

Bolshaya

Tatarskaya ulitsa

Shlyuzovaya nab.

ul. Bol. Kamenshchiki

Rachalinskaya

Volgogradsky pr.

Polyanka

ul. Mal. Ordynka

Pyatnitskaya ulitsa

Tatarskaya ulitsa

Bakhrushina

Krasnokholmskaya nab.

Novospassky proezd

N

Novospassky monastyr (Novospassky monastery)

Krestyanskaya Zastava

Proletarskaya

itnaya ul.

Korovy Val

Lyusinovskaya ul.

ulitsa Zatsepa

Paveletskaya

Paveletskaya

Kozhevnicheskaya ul.

Dubininskaya ulitsa

Kozhevnicheskaya ul.

obryhinskaya

Serpukhovskaya

Stremyanny per.

Valovaya ul.

Paveletsky vokzal

0   800 m

0   800 yds

The Kremlin Palace, as seen from over the River Moskva.

THE KREMLIN

As the symbol of Russia's religious heritage and the seat of today's political regime, the Kremlin is Moscow in a nutshell. Flash, presidential limos drive past historic cathedrals full of sacred icons, leaving tourists to gasp at tales of bygone intrigue and to gawp at extravagant displays of wealth.

T he Russian poet Konstantin Batyushkov described Moscow as 'a gargantuan city built by giants; tower upon tower, wall upon wall, palace next to palace. A strange mixture of ancient and modern architecture, of poverty and wealth, the morals of Europeans and the morals and customs of Easterners. A divine, incomprehensible synthesis of vanity, conceit and true glory, of ignorance and enlightenment, of humanity and barbarism.' That was in 1811, but the sentiments still ring very true today. And at the core of this megalopolis, a city within a city, is the Kremlin, the original fortress around which everything grew. It's arguably Moscow's, and possibly Russia's, biggest mustsee – an intoxicating mixture of old Muscovy, imperial elegance and remnants of the Soviet era awaits within its imposing walls.

The Kremlin fortress

The original citadel, the **Kremlin ❶**, was built by Yuri Dolgoruky (see page 31) in the 12th century as a humble, wooden stockade fortress. The site was chosen for its well protected location on a thickly wooded hill surrounded by rivers. The waterways later proved conducive to transport and trade, which, together with

rich mineral deposits in the area, encouraged rapid growth. Originally, the fortress was a city unto itself, with dwellings, churches and monasteries, traders and craftsmen. It was repeatedly devastated by fires and Tatar raids until 1340, when Tsar Ivan Kalita ('Moneybags') built a new oak fortress reinforced with stucco, which lasted an unprecedented 26 years. When this, too, burned to the ground in 1366, Dmitry Donskoy (see page 32) decided to build walls made of white stone quarried from the nearby

Main Attractions
Ivan the Great Bell Tower
Dormition Cathedral
Cathedral of the Archangel Michael
Annunciation Cathedral
Armoury Palace Museum
Diamond Fund

Maps
Pages 88, 100

The Tsar Bell at the Kremlin.

Red star on top of the Saviour Gate Tower.

town of Myachkovo. Construction went on for 15 years, and the resulting fortress with eight towers became the symbol of Moscow (to this day, the city is still referred to in literature as 'white-stone Moscow'). By the end of the 15th century, the famous white stone walls were crumbling. Tsar Ivan III asked the Italian builders who were assisting Russian architects in constructing churches in the Kremlin to re-fortify the walls. Between 1485 and 1495, the white stone walls were bricked over, and sturdy replacements erected to extend the fortress to its present size. To improve security, the new walls were made taller and thicker, topped by entry and defence towers and lined with swallow-tailed crenellation.

Despite periodic repairs and modifications, the walls we see today are essentially those commissioned by Ivan III. Napoleon and his armies blew up certain sections and destroyed several towers, but these were rebuilt to the original design by the architect Osip Bove in 1817.

Protective towers

Overall, the Kremlin wall has 20 towers, which vary in shape, height and design. The tallest is the **Trinity Tower Ⓐ** (*Troitskaya*, 80 metres/260ft), originally connected by a drawbridge extending over the Neglinnaya River to the **Kutafya Tower**, but replaced by one of the city's first stone bridges in 1516. The Trinity Tower is now the main entrance for visiting tourists. Russian leaders and delegations (and some tour groups) usually enter through the Borovitsky Gates on the southwest corner.

The **Saviour Gate Ⓑ**, on the other side of the Kremlin opposite St Basil's Cathedral, takes its name from an icon of the Saviour that graced the archway. Once fortified by two bastions and reached by a drawbridge over a moat that ran along the wall, this was the grandest tower of

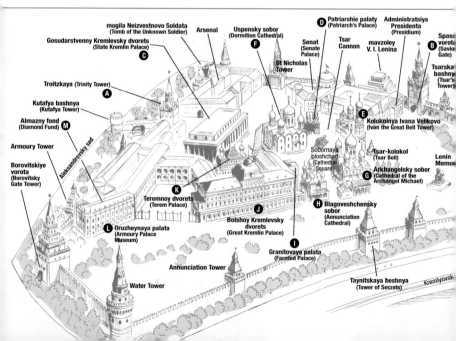

the fortress, through which tsars and foreign dignitaries entered. Today it is used by official visitors.

The Saviour Gates also house the famous clock that overlooks Red Square. The first clock was placed in the tower in the 16th century. In 1625 the tower was modified by English architect Christopher Halloway to its present Gothic appearance, and a new clock was installed. It was later replaced, but the Halloway clock was discovered in 1850, found to be functioning, and reinstated. It sustained damage in the Revolutionary fighting of 1917, and during repairs, the old melody that rang out on the hour (the *Preobrazhensky March*) was replaced with the opening tones of 'The Internationale', which the Kremlin Chimes play to this day.

Other towers along the walls have their own stories and secrets. The **Sobakina Tower** (at the corner of the Aleksandrovsky sad) and the **Taynitsky Tower** (Tower of Secrets; the third

tower from the left when facing the Kremlin from the Moscow River) reportedly have tunnels for escaping by boat. The Sobakina Tower's tunnel once led to the Neglinnaya River, now in the Aleksandrovsky sad (see page 119). The small **Tsar's Tower** (to the left of the Saviour Tower when viewed from Red Square) was added in 1680 in the place where Ivan the Terrible once watched ceremonies on Red Square.

The seat of power

When Ivan III moved the tradesmen outside the Kremlin walls and onto Red Square in the late 15th century, the Kremlin was no longer a small fortified town; it was now the seat of power for both state and Church, and was to become filled with palaces, administrative buildings, monasteries and churches. Over the centuries these buildings have been destroyed by fire, damaged by war or rebuilt to the taste of the rulers of the time.

FACT

The word *kreml* in Russian means 'fortress' and is often used to describe citadels in other historic Russian cities. The origins of the word are obscure, but it may have been derived from the Greek *kremn* or *krimnos*, meaning a hill over a ravine.

Tourists in front of Saviour Gate Tower.

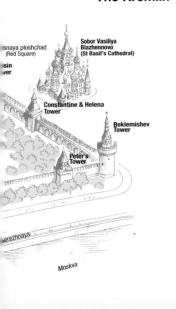

The Kremlin

Though visitors come to see the Kremlin's historic churches and museums, there is no escaping the fact that this is the centre of Russian power. After passing through the Trinity Tower, all buildings to the left belong to Putin's administration and are strictly off limits to tourists. The first building on the left is the **Arsenal**, built in 1736. In front are more than 800 cannons, some captured from Napoleon's army, others Russian-made.

Straight ahead and across a small garden is the former **Senate Palace**, commissioned by Catherine the Great to convene the Moscow senators. It was built by the Russian architect Matvey Kazakov between 1776 and 1787 in the classical style and shaped as a triangle to fit the space. Today it is the President's official residence, and guards will move dallying tourists on their way. The Senate and Great Kremlin Palace (see page 94)

The Tsar Cannon.

were refurbished and renovated at massive expense in the 1990s; a later investigation revealed the so-called Mabetex scandal – a case of suspected misappropriation of funds by officials. To the right of the Senate is the **Presidential Administration**, another administration building, erected on the site of the Miracles and Ascension monasteries, which were torn down in the 1930s.

To the right of the Trinity Gates is the **State Kremlin Palace ⓖ**, built in 1959–61 to house Communist Party Congresses. The large, deep stage has been used for opera and ballet, and the 6,000-seat auditorium is a venue for state festivities and pop concerts.

Patriarch's Palace

Just past the State Kremlin Palace on the right is the **Patriarch's Palace and Church of the Twelve Apostles ⓓ** (*Patriarshie palaty i Tserkov Dvenadtsati apolstolov*). The main entrance is

The Alexander Garden and Arsenal wall.

behind the Dormition Cathedral. Completed in 1656 at the behest of the then new Patriarch Nikon, it replaced the Metropolitan's modest apartments and the small private church used by the higher clergy, the Church of the Disposition of the Robe. It is now the **Museum of 17th-Century Life and Applied Art** and contains exhibitions of religious vestments and vessels, as well as rooms reconstructed to look as they would have been when used by a boyar. Of particular interest is the Cross Chamber, which was the largest room without supporting columns built at the time.

Ivan the Great Bell Tower

Still visible for miles around, though no longer Moscow's tallest building, the **Ivan the Great Bell Tower** **E** (*Kolokolnya Ivana Velikovo*) dominates the Kremlin's skyline. Named after the Church of St Ivan Climacus that once stood on this spot, it was built in two tiers: in 1505–8 Italian master architect Bon Fryazin constructed the main bell tower; in 1599 Tsar Boris Godunov commissioned its final tier

to make it, at 81 metres (265ft), the tallest building in Moscow. The adjacent Assumption Belfry was added in 1543, and the annexe was commissioned by Patriarch Filaret in 1642. The 21 bells, including the 64-ton Resurrection or Festival bell, are rung on special occasions.

The huge **Tsar Bell** was cast from the pieces of one that shattered during attempts to raise it into the belfry; the 200-ton bell was still in its casting pit when fire swept the Kremlin. To protect it, cold water was thrown into the pit, causing the surface to crack. It was then left in its pit for almost a century; when it was finally excavated, an 11-ton chunk broke off.

Cathedral Square

At the heart of the Kremlin lies Cathedral Square. This has been a ceremonial centre since the 14th century. Instead of a single state church, the tsars used several, and each of the four lining the square played a unique role in the life of the imperial family. The oldest, grandest and most important is the **Dormition Cathedral** **F** (*Uspensky sobor*), which

FACT

The main entrance for visitors to the Kremlin is Troitskaya Bashnya (Fri–Wed 10am–5pm). Ticket offices can be located in the Alexandrovsky Gardens – there are long queues in summer. Otherwise timed tickets can be bought in advance online. See www.kreml.ru for further details. You could also try calling the Kremlin Excursions Office (tel: 495-695 4146/697 0349; daily 9am–5pm). You are not allowed to take any luggage into the Kremlin – this must be left at the left luggage office beneath the Kutafya Tower. There are no restaurants or cafés in the Kremlin.

The Kremlin Regiment.

symbolises Moscow's claim to be the protector of Russian Orthodoxy. It is the only one of the four churches used for services just once a year, on the Feast of the Dormition (15 August). The current church was built between 1475 and 1479 by Aristotele Fioravanti. Its exterior is simple to the point of plainness, with only a decorative arcade band around the bays and helmet-like cupolas. Nevertheless, it has been the country's premier church since its inception, and has hosted coronations of the tsars and granted them intercession during times of trouble. Every grand prince and tsar was crowned here from 1498.

In contrast to its plain exterior, the interior of the church is richly decorated with a five-tiered iconostasis and frescoes on every surface of the walls, domes and pillars. The iconostasis dates from 1652, but some of its icons were made in the 14th century. Tombs of Church leaders, metropolitans and patriarchs line the walls. The Monomakh Throne, in the

The Annunciation Cathedral.

Cathedral's back right-hand corner, was installed for Ivan the Terrible in 1551; its carvings show scenes from the life of Vladimir Monomakh (see page 31). During the Napoleonic invasion of the Kremlin, the French army used this cathedral as a stable and gutted it of gold and silver. Later, Cossack soldiers recovered much of the looted metal and used it to create the 46-branch Harvest Chandelier that illuminates the interior.

Across from the main entrance of the Dormition Cathedral is the small **Church of the Deposition of the Robe** (*Tserkov Rizopolomeniya*), built by Pskov architects in 1486. Once the private chapel of patriarchs and metropolitans, it now houses a small collection of wooden religious sculpture.

The **Cathedral of the Archangel Michael** **G** (*Arkhangelsky sobor*), opposite the Cathedral of the Dormition, is the most unusual church on the square and the final resting place for the early tsars. Commissioned in 1505 by Ivan III to replace an older church, it was built by Aleviz Novyi

Choir performing in the Archangel Cathedral.

the 1360s. The iconostasis from the original church was preserved, and it is considered the finest in all Russia. Its icons and frescoes were painted by three of the finest icon-painters: Theophanes the Greek, Prokhor of Gorodets and Andrey Rublyov, who painted two icons in the upper, Feast Day or Festival Tier, the *Annunciation* and the *Nativity*. The church was constructed by builders from Pskov between 1484 and 1489, but rebuilt so many times that the sense of the original structure has been lost.

The Cathedral served as the private church of the tsars and grand princes. The extended porch, called the Ivan the Terrible Steps, was built after the Metropolitan banned him from entering the church, in punishment for his seven marriages and countless concubines. Here Tsar Ivan listened to the service from a space just outside the church walls.

The Kremlin palaces

Between Cathedral Square and the Borovitsky Gate are three palaces

The Dormition Cathedral.

and incorporates much Western ornamentation, such as the scalloping on the gables and Corinthian capitals, decoration unknown in Russia at the time. However, the structure of the church is the traditional Russian cross plan. The frescoes were painted by Simon Ushakov and his co-operative between 1652 and 1660. The original iconostasis was destroyed by the French in 1812, and the present one was installed the following year. The tsars were interred in this church from 1340 until 1712, when the capital was moved to St Petersburg. The first tsar in the Romanov dynasty, Mikhail Romanov and his family, are interred here, as is Ivan the Terrible, whose tomb is hidden behind the iconostasis.

The **Annunciation Cathedral**  (*Blagoveshchensky sobor*), opposite, was built on the basis of a church thought to have been constructed in

The Hall of Facets in the Kremlin building, completed in 1491, contains restored 16th century frescoes.

that combined the imperial family's living and reception quarters and are now connected under one roof.

The most striking of the three palaces is the **Faceted Palace** ❶ (*Granitovaya palata*), named after the unusual diamond-patterned facets decorating the facade and entered through Cathedral Square. It was built in 1487–91 by Marco Ruffo and Pietro Solario as one of the main administrative buildings for the tsar. The lower floor consists of chambers, and the upper floor is one enormous hall supported by a central pillar and lavishly painted with historical and Biblical scenes. Here the tsar held audiences, banquets and received foreign ambassadors. Later the Zemsky sobor (a proto-parliament) convened here. A small window allowed the tsarina and women family members to eavesdrop on the proceedings.

Leading down to Cathedral Square is the Red (or, more properly translated, 'Beautiful') Staircase by which the tsars entered Cathedral Square. It

a Peter the Great saw his relatives murdered in a rebellion, an experience so horrible it may have led him to found another capital – St Petersburg. The staircase was demolished by Stalin, but under Boris Yeltsin it was rebuilt according to the original plans.

Attached to the Faceted Palace and stretching westwards for 125 metres (410ft) along the Kremlin Wall overlooking the Moscow River is the **Great Kremlin Palace** ❶ (*Bolshoy Kremlevsky dvorets*). Built under Nicholas I by the Russian architect Konstantin Ton, it served as the residence of the imperial family. Two rows of windows on the second floor give the illusion of three storeys, but there are only two, the family occupying the ground floor, and the second floor given over to lavishly decorated reception and meeting halls named after Russia's most honoured saints. During the Soviet period two grand halls were turned into one room to house meetings of the Supreme Soviet. Boris Yeltsin made a point

Georgievsky hall in the Great Kremlin Palace.

the 'long box'; hence the Russian expression 'to put something in a long box' for future consideration.

Armoury Palace Museum

In the southwest corner of the Kremlin, between the Great Kremlin Palace and the Borovitsky Gates, is the highlight of any visit. The **Armoury Palace Museum** ❶ (*Oruzheynaya palata*) is believed to have been established as a workshop by Tsar Basil Ill in 1511. The current building, completed in 1851 by Konstantin Ton, houses an amazing collection of treasures that celebrate Russia's imperial heritage. Many items were created by master craftsmen of the Kremlin and Russian workshops; others were given as ambassadorial and state gifts.

The first, small room on the upper floor contains a collection of Russian gold and silver tableware from the 12th to 16th centuries, and includes a 12th-century chalice given by the founder of Moscow, Yuri Dolgoruky (see page 31), to a cathedral in the town of Pereslavl-Zalessky. There are

of restoring them both. Now the St Alexander and St Andrew halls serve vital functions in the ceremonies of the Russian Federation; the former as a backdrop to conclaves of the Federation Council, the latter for swearing in Russian presidents.

The third palace is the **Terem Palace** ❶ (*Teremnoy dvorets*), built in 1635 by a group of Russian architects. Much of the palace fell into disuse in the 18th century, but was restored in the original style in 1837. Under the low-vaulted and profusely decorated ceilings the early tsars had their residence and reception rooms – an antechamber, the Cross Chamber, where the tsar met with his boyars and noblemen, and the Throne Room. From the small petition window in the Throne Room, a box would be lowered to the square. Anyone – from peasant to prince – could put a written petition in the box for the tsar's consideration. Since these rarely brought a swift response, it was called

The Faceted Palace.

also a number of traditional drinking vessels encrusted with enamel and precious stones.

The dark-green hall beyond holds the famous Fabergé eggs, with their extraordinarily fine craftsmanship. Nicholas II, the last tsar, commissioned two eggs each Easter from the German jeweller Carl Fabergé from 1884 until 1917. Among the 14 eggs in the original Kremlin collection are the Clock Egg (nestled in a bouquet of diamond lilies) and the Trans-Siberian Railway Egg, which has a gold model train that could be wound up. Elsewhere in the green room are gold and silver items and a diamond-studded Bible.

The red room beyond is filled with European silver and gold items, mostly dinner sets, state gifts for imperial families. Weaponry and armour from Russia, Persia and Turkey fill the side rooms. The first room on the lower floor displays imperial clothing, from the enormous boots worn by Peter the Great while working in Amsterdam shipyards, to the ermine-lined cape worn by the last tsarina, Alexandra.

State regalia in the next room include Ivan the Terrible's ivory throne, the Diamond Throne of Tsar Aleksey (with over 800 diamonds) and the double throne made for young Peter the Great and his brother Ivan – with a small window through which their elder sister Sophia could whisper instructions. Among crowns on display is one believed to have been given to Grand Prince Vladimir of Kiev by Constantine XI of Constantinople. The octagonal room to the side houses a fine collection of equestrian regalia, while ahead is a room of grand carriages and coaches.

Diamond Fund

A short tour of the **Diamond Fund** (*Almalzny fond;* www.almazi.net; Fri–Wed 10am–1pm and 2–5pm), for those with the stamina after the Armoury Palace Museum, reveals an even more impressive collection of imperial jewels. Most noteworthy is Catherine the Great's coronation crown. There is a breathtaking array of imperial baubles, as well as diamond-encrusted victory orders awarded to Stalin's marshals.

The Kremlin Armoury.

Red Square and Lenin's Mausoleum.

RED SQUARE AND KITAI-GOROD

Red Square is the ceremonial heart of Moscow, the familiar scene of parades and proclamations. Steeped in history, it is home to the State Historical Museum, Lenin's Mausoleum and the magnificent St Basil's Cathedral. Close by are relics of tsarist-era trade – the Old English Court, Old Merchants' Quarters and the Stock Exchange.

The Old Russian word *krasny* translates as both 'beautiful' and 'red', and Russia's main public space was meant to be called 'Beautiful Square'. Whatever its name, for centuries **Red Square ❷** (*Krasnaya ploshchad*) has been the heart of Russia: a place of celebration and public execution, a stage for leaders' public appearances and the main hub for trade, news and gossip. The vast expanse (700 metres/yds long and 130 metres/yds wide) is enclosed by the Kremlin walls, the birthday-cake facades of GUM (State Department Store) and the State Historical Museum, with the riotous colours and forms of the Church of the Intercession on the Moat (St Basil's) rising on the fourth side.

Since Tsar Ivan III cleared the area of houses and moved the trading booths from inside the Kremlin in the 16th century, it had been filled with traders, shoppers and businessmen, or crowded with throngs of peasants and noblemen attending the nation's most important religious and state ceremonies.

The square was originally called Trinity Square, after the Church of the Trinity that stood where St Basil's is now. It was then called *Torg* (Market), until one of the fires that devastated

the timber-built city gave it the name of The Fire. 'What news did you hear at The Fire today?' traders would ask each other at one of the taverns in the side streets. Only in the 17th century did the square become 'Red'. Today however, Red Square is mostly empty but for tourists and the occasional limousine zipping through the Saviour Gates of the Kremlin.

Entering the square

Red Square is most impressive when entered through the **Resurrection**

Main Attractions
Red Square
GUM
Lenin's Mausoleum
St Basil's Cathedral
Old English Court
Chambers of the Romanov
 Boyars

Map
Page 100

Entrance to Red Square and St Basil's.

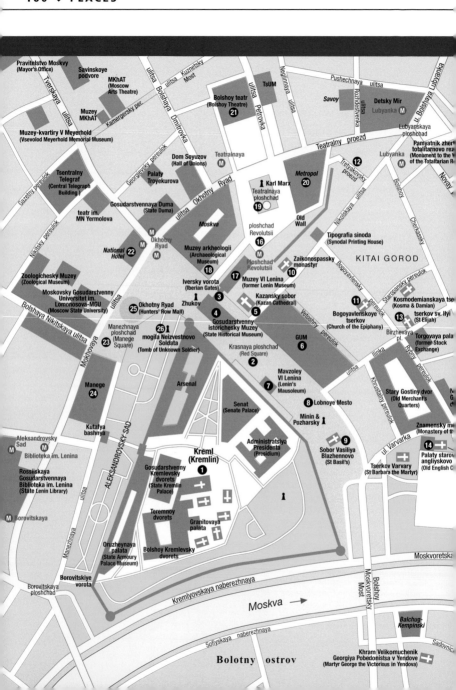

Pravitelstvo Moskvy (Mayor's Office)

Savinskoye podvore

MKhAT (Moscow Arts Theatre)

Muzey MKhAT

Muzey-kvartiry V Meyerhold (Vsevolod Meyerhold Memorial Museum)

Tsentralny Telegraf (Central Telegraph Building)

teatr im. MN Yermolova

Gosudarstvennaya Duma (State Duma)

Palaty Troyekurova

Dom Soyuzov (Hall of Unions)

Bolshoy teatr (Bolshoy Theatre) 21

TsUM

Savoy

Detsky Mir Lubyanka

Pushechnaya ulitsa

Lubyanskaya ploshchad

Pamyatnik zher totalitarnovo rez (Monument to the V of the Totalitarian R)

Lubyanka

Metropol 20

Teatralnaya

Karl Marx Teatralnaya ploshchad 19

ploshchad Revolutsii 16

Old Wall

Tretyakovsky proezd 12

Tipografia sinoda (Synodal Printing House)

KITAI GOROD

National Hotel 22

Zoologichesky Muzey (Zoological Museum)

Moskovsky Gosudarstvenny Universitet im. Lomonosova-MGU (Moscow State University)

Okhotny Ryad

Muzey arkheologii (Archaeological Museum) 18

Ploshchad Revolutsii 17

Zaikonospassky monastyr 10

Muzey VI Lenina (former Lenin Museum)

Iversky vorota (Iberian Gates) 3

Kazansky sobor (Kazan Cathedral) 5

Zhukov

Bogoyavlenskoye tserkov (Church of the Epiphany)

Kosmodemianskaya tse (Kosma & Damian) 11

tserkov sv. Ilyi (St Elijah) 13

Bolshaya Nikitinskaya ulitsa

Okhotny Ryad (Hunters' Row Mall) 25

Gosudarstvenny istorichesky Muzey (State Historical Museum) 4

Krasnaya ploshchad (Red Square)

GUM 6

Torgovaya pala (former Stock Exchange)

Manezhnaya ploshchad (Manege Square) 23

mogila Neizvestnovo Soldata (Tomb of Unknown Soldier) 26

Manege 24

Arsenal

Mavzoley VI Lenina (Lenin's Mausoleum) 7

Lobnoye Mesto 8

Stary Gostiny dvor (Old Merchant's Quarters)

Znamensky me (Monastery of th

Kutafya bashnya

Aleksandrovsky Sad

Biblioteka im. Lenina

Rossiiskaya Gosudarstvennaya Biblioteka im. Lenina (State Lenin Library)

Borovitskaya

Senat (Senate Palace)

Administratsiya Presidenta (Presidium)

Minin & Pozharsky

Sobor Vasiliya Blazhennovo (St Basil's) 9

Tserkov Varvary (St Barbara the Martyr)

Palaty starov angliyskovo (Old English C)

Kreml (Kremlin) 1

Gosudarstvenny Kremlevsky dvorets (State Kremlin Palace)

Teremnoy dvorets

Granitovaya palata

Oruzheynaya palata (State Armoury Palace Museum)

Bolshoy Kremlevsky dvorets

Borovitskiye vorota

Borovitskaya ploshchad

Moskvoretskaya

Moskva →

Kremlyovskaya naberezhnaya

Sofiyskaya naberezhnaya

Bolotny ostrov

Balchug-Kempinski

Khram Velikomuchenik Georgiya Pobedonositsa v Yendove (Martyr George the Victorious in Yendova)

Central Moscow

or Iberian Gates ❸ (*Iversky vorota*) from **Manege Square** (*Manezhnaya ploshchad*, see page 118). The gate was part of the wall (built 1535–8) that surrounded the area to the east of the Kremlin. In the 17th century an icon of the Iberian Mother of God (or the Iberian Virgin), from the Iberian Monastery on Mount Athos, was placed here, and in 1782 the gate was rebuilt outside the walls. Before entering the Kremlin, tsars and emperors would stop at the gate's tiny chapel to pay homage to this miracle-working icon.

Stalin had the gates torn down in 1931, but the structure was rebuilt according to the original plans and dedicated in 1996. Note the icon of St George and the dragon – the symbol of Moscow – above the left gate, and St Sergius – patron saint of Russia – above the right, as well as the marker on the pavement just outside the gate for 'kilometre zero', from which all distances in Russia are measured, a popular photo spot for tourists.

State Historical Museum ❹

Address: 1 Krasnaya ploshchad; www.shm.ru

Throwing a coin for good luck at the entrance to Red Square.

Tel: 495-692 3731
Opening Hrs: Mon, Wed, Fri–Sat
10am–6pm, Thu and Sun 11am–
8pm; closed first Mon of the month
Entrance Fee: charge
Transport: Ploschad Revolutsii,
Okhotny Ryad

Immediately on the right through the Resurrection Gates is the State Historical Museum (*Gosudarstvenny istorichesky muzey*). The museum was founded in 1872 as the Imperial Russian Historical Museum and is itself an important monument to Russian culture. Built by the architect Vladimir Shervud (of English descent; his surname was probably Sherwood) in 1874–83 in the Russian Revival style, its turrets, kokoshniki, gables and towers celebrate pre-Petrine architecture. Selections from the enormous collection narrate the country's history from the Stone Age to the 19th century, in halls decorated in old Russia styles and filled with paintings and murals of historical scenes.

Foreign-language audio tours are available in the excursion bureau off the first exhibition hall. The museum

also has an excellent shop selling a range of quality souvenirs, including museum jewellery reproductions.

Icons and idols

On the other side of the lane leading from the Resurrection Gates to Red Square is the diminutive, pink **Kazan Cathedral** ❺ (*Kazansky sobor*, daily 8am–8pm). The church was built in 1636 to celebrate Tsar Mikhail Romanov's victory over the Poles, and dedicated to the icon of the Virgin of Kazan, which was carried into battle by Prince Pozharsky (see page 34). It was torn down in 1936 but rebuilt in 1993 under the indefatigable erstwhile 'mayor-builder' of Moscow, Yuri Luzhkov. The interior has been fully restored, with remarkable frescoes and iconostasis.

GUM ❻

Address: 3 Krasnaya ploshchad;
www.gum.ru;
Tel: 495-788 4343
Opening Hrs: daily 10am–10pm
Entrance Fee: free
Transport: Ploschad Revolutsii,
Okhotny Ryad

Kazan Cathedral.

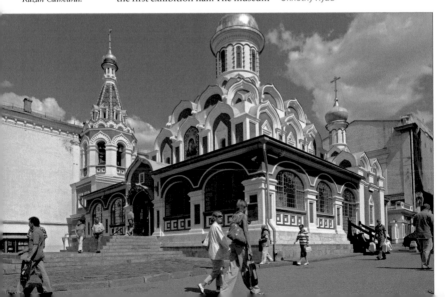

GUM Department Store.

Across Nikolskaya ulitsa is the entrance to GUM (pronounced 'goom'), the State Department Store. The marketplace was called the Upper Trading Rows when built in 1889–93, but the bland name GUM, given when it was nationalised in 1921, has remained. During the Soviet years, it was one of the few department stores with a constant and relatively high-quality selection of goods. It has been extensively renovated and is now filled largely with luxury foreign shops and snack bars, although the fountains, wrought-iron balconies and glass roof still give a sense of a swisher pre-Revolutionary shopping experience.

Lenin's Mausoleum ❼

Address: Mavzoley V.I. Lenina
Opening Hrs: Tue–Thu, Sat–Sun 10am–1pm
Entrance Fee: free
Transport: Ploschad Revolutsii, Okhotny Ryad

Opposite GUM, in front of the Kremlin wall, is the Mausoleum of V.I. Lenin (*Mavzoley V.I. Lenina*). Please note that the mausoleum is sometimes closed for long periods for the treatment of Lenin's body, and the entrance queue forms by the Kremlin wall in the Aleksandrovsky sad; as it begins to move, visitors are required to leave all bags and cameras in a room in the State Historical Museum.

When the leader of the October Revolution and Soviet state died on 21 January 1924, Party leaders overruled the objections of his wife, Nadezhda Krupskaya, and had a wooden mausoleum quickly built so the devoted could pay their last respects. Lenin's body was then embalmed according to a unique process that involves submerging the body in a special solution every 18 months or so. When the embalming process proved successful, the wooden mausoleum was replaced by the Constructivist pyramid of red granite and black labradorite, designed by Aleksey Shchusev, in 1930. From 1953 to 1961, Stalin was also preserved and placed on view. Up until 1991 the

Pro-Communist Muscovites queue up to enter Lenin's Mausoleum.

mausoleum and embalming were funded by the state but they are now financed from private contributions. Most Russians think the body should finally be buried.

Visitors file through the mausoleum in silence, hands at their sides (not in their pockets) and all hats removed. Steps and corridors lead down to the sombre viewing room, where Lenin lies in state under a glass dome. A few minutes later the queue emerges by the Kremlin wall, where over 400 luminaries of the Soviet state have their final resting place. Here are the graves of Stalin, cosmonaut Yuri Gagarin (see page 175) and American journalist John Reed, whose eyewitness account of the Revolution, *Ten Days That Shook the World*, was revered in the USSR.

Close to St Basil's is a round white stone platform called **Lobnoye Mesto** ❽ ('a high, protruding place') dating from 1534. It was made of brick, with pillars, a roof and a wooden fence surrounding it. The current podium, faced with white stone, was constructed in 1786. On this spot Ivan the Terrible confessed his sins after

St. Basil's Cathedral.

Statue of Minin and Pozharskiy.

the devastating fire of 1547; also from here state proclamations were read, religious ceremonies, held and, once a year, the tsar appeared before the people. It was also the custom to show the heir apparent when he reached the age of 16, so no usurper could later deceive the population.

St Basil's ❾

Address: 2 Krasnaya ploshchad; www.saintbasil.ru;
Tel: 495-698 3304
Opening Hrs: daily 11am–5pm; closed first Mon of the month
Entrance Fee: charge
Transport: Ploschad Revolutsii, Okhotny Ryad, Kitai-gorod

Red Square is dominated by the Cathedral of the Intercession on the Moat, known as St Basil's (*Khram Vasiliya Blazhennovo*). Ivan the Terrible commissioned the Cathedral to commemorate the Russian victory over the 'Tatar infidels' in Kazan on the

Volga River in 1552. When the Tsar succeeded in subduing the khanate in Astrakhan in 1556, the Cathedral became a symbol of the victory of the Russian state and Orthodoxy. Since the battle that led to victory in Kazan took place on the day of the Feast of Intercession of the Virgin, the full name of the church is the Cathedral of the Intercession by the Moat, referring to the moat that once flowed along the wall of the Kremlin by Red Square. Later it became known as St Basil's in honour of St Basil the Blessed (1468–1552), a popular and prophetic 'holy fool in Christ' who on occasion went around naked and in chains. His remains were later interred in a separate chapel added to the Cathedral.

Historians attribute the Cathedral to two architects from Pskov, Barma and Postnik Yakovlev; however, research carried out in the early 2000s indicated that this might have been one architect, who had the nickname of Barma ('the Mumbler'). The story that Ivan the Terrible had the builders blinded so they could never build anything more beautiful is apocryphal. Napoleon ordered it blown up in 1812 (it was saved from destruction, but pillaged by his army) and in 1936 Stalin planned to blow it up 'because it hindered automobile movement across the square'.

The present Cathedral is built on the site of the Church of the Trinity, which has been retained as an interior chapel. Until the final tier of the Ivan the Great Bell Tower in the Kremlin was erected in 1600, the Cathedral's spire was the highest in Moscow.

At first glance St Basil's seems exotically asymmetrical, but this is an optical illusion caused by additions that conceal the original design. It is in fact utterly symmetrical, an octagon with a central tent spire surrounded by eight cupolas. The cupolas at the four compass points are taller than the four at the diagonal points. The Cathedral is structured architecturally by the Trinity: there are three towers on each compass axis, diagonal and side; each tower has three sections: the main octagon or cube, the tiers of *kokoshniki* and then a culminating octagon topped by a cupola. In 1588 Tsar Fyodor added a small chapel for the remains

The Red Square and St. Basil's at night.

of St Basil. Some later additions, such as the covered terrace and bell tower (1630), have remained; others (such as 13 small chapels built around the structure) were dismantled in a large-scale reconstruction in the 1780s.

Inside, the Cathedral is not one large space, but nine small chapels linked by passageways painted dark red with white lines to look like brick, or decorated in profuse and brightly coloured geometric and floral designs. Entry is through the **Church of St Basil the Blessed**, where the saint's relics are kept in an elaborate gold-and-silver shrine, then up a very steep winding staircase into the **Church of the Intercession** under the tent steeple. This is surrounded by eight motley chapels. Some are gift shops, some are empty, but some are well preserved.

The exit is through the **Church of the Entrance of Christ into Jerusalem**. On Palm Sunday (called Pussy Willow Sunday in Russia), the tsar would ride on a horse from the Kremlin to this church. St Basil's is maintained by the State Historical Museum but it has been reconsecrated, and services are held occasionally.

A typical facade at Kitai-gorod.

Kitai-gorod

The area to the east of Red Square that stretches from GUM to New and Old squares (Novaya and Staraya ploshchad respectively) was called **Kitai-gorod**. The name is either derived from the Russian word *kila* (wattle) used in its original fences, or a Mongol word that meant 'central fortress'. In 1535–8, the area was enclosed by a thick (6-metre/ 20ft) wall with 14 towers. To prevent attacks through tunnels, the wall extended 12 metres (40ft) underground and contained listening chambers with hanging copper sheets that jangled at the slightest disturbance.

This was the main trading district of old Moscow: streets were full of shops, outdoor markets, tenements, taverns and trading houses – as well as four monasteries and 18 churches. Armenians, Persians, Jews and countless other nationalities mingled and haggled over prices at rowdy outdoor markets on Red, Old and New

A CITY OF CHURCHES

Moscow was once called the city of '40 times 40' churches. Spires filled the skies with gold, and bells rang out across the city. In the Soviet period and during the campaign against religion in the 1930s, most churches were emptied of their religious treasures, destroyed or turned into offices, warehouses or apartments. A few remained functioning; others were stripped of religious meaning and called 'monuments of Russian architecture'. Today, nearly all of Moscow's churches and cathedrals have been returned to the patriarchy. However, some churches are still closed for refurbishment, while others are only open for services (usually at 8am and 5pm). While many churches have had their exteriors repaired, the interiors can often be disappointing: bare walls and a few modern icons where once there were frescoes, a gleaming multi-tiered iconostasis and shelves of golden vessels. Women should cover their heads with scarves when visiting a church. Photography, talking, touching the icons and turning one's back to the altar are considered disrespectful. It is acceptable for anyone to buy a candle and place it in front of an icon, and there is usually a box by the door for donations.

squares. In the late 19th and early 20th centuries, elegant shopping centres, banks, insurance companies and the Stock Exchange appeared on the narrow streets.

During Soviet times much of the area was taken over by government buildings; Old Square was occupied by the Central Committee of the Communist Party, the USSR's ruling body. Today, the area's lanes are taken up by various ministries and higher courts, the ground-floor windows often discreetly curtained. Only the streets closest to Red Square have emerged as up-market shopping areas. Three main streets cross the district from Red Square to Old and New squares: Nikolskaya ulitsa (closest to the Resurrection Gates), ulitsa Ilinka and ulitsa Varvarka (leading from St Basil's), the latter is the main street of the old Zaryade neighbourhood.

Nikolskaya ulitsa

Taking its name from the Nikolskaya (St Nicholas) Tower of the Kremlin, **Nikolskaya ulitsa** runs from the Historical Museum in Red Square to New Square. It is lined with low- to medium-end stores, cafés and dense crowds of shoppers. On the left when walking from Red Square are tightly packed buildings with archways leading to courtyards. The arch at No. 9 leads to the **Zaikonospassky Monastery** ❿ *(Zaikonospassky monastyr)*. The name translates as 'The Saviour Monastery behind the Icon', which identified it as 'the monastery behind the icon-seller's stand'. In 1687 the monastery was converted into Russia's first institution of higher learning, called the Russian-Greek-Latin Academy. Mikhail Lomonosov, founder of the Moscow State University (see page 138), studied here. The monastery was returned to the patriarchy in the 1990s. Only the church, which is renowned for its choir, is open for services.

Further down Nikolskaya at No. 15, and rather out of kilter with the downbeat shops and cafés, is the former Synodal Printing House, a magnificent pale-blue Gothic edifice with white floral carvings and a whimsical lion and unicorn

Woman sweeping up at Russurection Gate.

Synod Printing House, Nikolskaya Street.

The Church of Epiphany.

dating from 1815. Tradition has it that Russia's first printed book, The Apostles, was produced on this site in 1563. Later it housed the Russian newspaper Vedomosti.

Next to it, and now part of the Humanities University, is the former **Slavyansky Bazar Hotel and Restaurant**. Here the theatre directors Stanislavsky and Nemerovich Danchenko spent an evening enjoying food, drink and conversation that culminated in their decision to found the Moscow Art Theatre (see page 158). It is now home to the Pokrovsky Theatre.

Still in Kitai-gorod, it's worth walking down **Bogoyavlensky** (Epiphany) **pereulok** from Nikolskaya towards Stock Exchange Square. On the right is the renovated Baroque **Church of the Epiphany ⑪** (*Bogoyavlenskaya tserkov*, 2 Bogoyavlensky pereulok), with rows of mosaic saints on the drum of the cupola and an impressive gold dome. The church is in the grounds of a monastery founded in 1296; it now houses a liturgical music school, and is worth a visit for the chance of catching the talented students rehearsing inside the church.

Building on Ilinka Street.

On the left just before Stock Exchange Square is a narrow street, **Staropansky pereulok**, originally settled by traders from Lithuania. Halfway down the street on the right is the tiny **Church of Kosma and Damian**, a bright patch of pink and gold nearly hidden by the tall buildings around it. Across the street at No. 5 is the former **Arshinov Trading House**, built in 1899 in the Russian *style moderne* by Fyodor Shekhtel.

Back on Nikolskaya ulitsa and heading west, you'll come to one of Moscow's most exclusive shopping streets. **Tretyakov Passage ⑫** (Tretyakovsky proezd), painted gleaming white, was built by the Tretyakov brothers in 1872. It is now packed with luxury cars, stylish women and super-rich oligarchs buying baubles at Gucci, Tiffany & Co. and other exclusive boutiques.

Ulitsa Ilinka

Bisecting Kitai-gorod from the centre of Red Square, **ulitsa Ilinka** (from Ilya, the Russian translation of Elijah), was once the centre of the Russian business world. The street takes its name from the Monastery of Elijah that once stood here. The small 16th-century **Church of St Elijah ⑬** has been restored at No. 3.

The biggest attraction on ulitsa Ilinka is the architecture on **Stock Exchange Square**, where it meets Rybny pereulok. It is dominated by the orange **Chamber of Commerce** (formerly the Stock Exchange). Built in classical style between 1873 and 1875, it stands in contrast to the more highly decorated pale-green structures surrounding it. Across the square is the former Ryabushinsky Bank, another *style moderne* building by Shekhtel. Ryabushinksy, the head of the Stock Exchange and an ardent art collector, later commissioned Shekhtel to build his private home. On the left side of the street as you walk towards Red Square is the

northern end of the **Old Merchants' Quarters** *(Stary Gostiny dvor)* that covers the large square stretching to ulitsa Varvarka. It once housed trading booths of visiting merchants, but has been rebuilt many times. The current structure was built by Catherine the Great's favourite architect, Giacomo Quarenghi, in the late 18th century, and restored in the early 2000s. The vast central hall is used for trade fairs and temporary exhibitions. It's still worth stopping in the shops along ulitsa Ilinka selling *Vologda* linen and traditional Russian crystal. The rest of ulitsa Ilinka is mostly filled with drab ministries, courts and state offices.

Zaryade and ulitsa Varvarka

The area from St Basil's to the river (called *Vasilevsky spusk*) and to the east where the Rossiya Hotel once stood, bounded by **ulitsa Varvarka**, was originally called **Zaryade**, which meant 'beyond the rows' of traders' booths on Red Square. It was settled in the 14th century by builders brought in to put up the Kremlin walls, then occupied by foreign traders, boyars and princes. By the 17th

century it was a teeming slum of crooked streets and emitted a stench so bad that, as one writer noted, 'Once you broke out of there, you joyfully gulped the fresh air.'

Virtually nothing but the churches and buildings on ulitsa Varvarka remain, but they are still lovely. Nearby once stood the Rossiya Hotel, built in 1964–7 and touted as the world's largest (with 6,000 rooms). It was bemoaned as the world's greatest eyesore before being demolished in 2006. A new complex of office and shopping buildings has been planned for years.

At the corner closest to Red Square is the **Church of St Barbara the Martyr** *(Tserkov Varvary)*, built in 1796–84 to replace an earlier structure.

Old English Court ⓮

Address: 4 ulitsa Varvarka
Tel: 495-298 3952
Opening Hrs: Tue–Sun 11am–6pm; closed last Fri of the month
Entrance Fee: admission and photo charges
Transport: Kitai-gorod

Tretyakov Passage.

Next to the Church of St Barbara the Martyr is the white, wooden-eaved Old English Court (*Palaty starovo angliysk-ovo dvora*). Built as a merchant's palace and one of the oldest secular buildings in the city, it was given to the Muscovy Company by Ivan the Terrible after the visit of Richard Chancellor, and became the house of visiting merchants and dignitaries from England. After the expulsion of the British Trade Company in 1649 following the execution of King Charles I, the building was bought for 500 roubles by a local boyar; it later passed through many hands before being so completely hidden by an apartment house that 19th-century guidebooks listed the Court as 'not preserved.' It was restored for the 1994 state visit of Queen Elizabeth II, and is a fine concert venue. An exhibition (with explanations in Russian and English) narrates the history of relations between England and Russia. Of note is the **Official Hall** upstairs, with its Russian-style ceramic corner stove decorated with fantastical animal figures.

Three other churches line ulitsa Varvarka: the **Church of Maxim** *The Old English Court.* the Blessed (*Tserkov Maksima Blaz-henovo;* 4 ulitsa Varvarka), built in 1698–9 by Novgorod merchants; the Cathedral of the Monastery of the Sign (*Znamensky monastyr,* 8a ulitsa Varvarka), founded in 1634; and the **Church of St George** (*Tserkov Georgiya na Pskovskoy Gorke;* 12 ulitsa Varvarka). All have been returned to the patriarchy and are open for services. There is a small store selling books, icons and other religious items at the monastery.

Chambers of the Romanov Boyars ⓰

Address: 10 ulitsa Varvarka; www.shm.ru
Tel: 495-698 1256
Opening Hrs: Thu–Mon 10am–5pm, Wed 11am–7pm; last ticket one hour from closing; closed first Mon of the month
Transport: Kitai-gorod

Just before you reach the Church of St George is a small museum called the Chambers of the Romanov Boyars (*Palaty boyar Romanovykh*), where the first of the Romanov tsars, Mikhail, was born. Entered from a

The Old English Court.

Exhibition at the Old English Court.

Nikolsky pereulok is the tiny **Church of St Nicholas of the 'Beautiful Sound'** *(Khram Svyatitelya Nikolaya 'Krasny Zvon')*, built in 1561 and named for the sweet tones of its bells. Further down ulitsa Varvarka towards Old Square, turn left on Ipatyevksy pereulok to see the **Church of the Trinity in Nikitniki** (see page 72). Built in 1634 and modified over the centuries, it is a spectacularly ornamented small gem. The bell tower was the first to be built into the structure of a church in Moscow. Frescoes from 1652–8 by the school of Simon Ushakov fill the walls.

At the end of ulitsa Varvarka, on the street to the right leading down to the river, are remains of the Kitai-gorod wall. Several sections of the wall are preserved behind glass in the pedestrian underpass.

On the Moscow River in front of the old Rossiya Hotel site is the small white **Church of the Conception of St Anne** *(Tserkov Zachatiya Anny)*, built in the 1530s. It was once a wealthy church, at an important intersection in Zaryade, where tsars and their families attended services.

courtyard adjacent to the old Rossiya car park, it is a beautifully reconstructed medieval Russian dwelling, with low-vaulted ceilings, deep-set mica windows, chased leather 'wallpaper' and a *terem* – a section at the top floor of the house where women were secluded. The practice of secluding women in a *terem* (not a corruption of the word *harem*, but derived from the Greek *teremnon*, meaning 'special quarters') was instituted in Russia in the 15th century. One of the rooms, the 'Bright Room', was well lit by natural light and used for embroidery and other handicrafts.

On the other side of the street, opposite the Church of Maxim the Blessed, is the southern facade of the Old Merchants' Quarters *(Stary Gostiny dvor)*.

Historic churches

Three old churches worth noting are tucked away on nearby side streets. On

Dining room at the Palace of the Romanov Boyars.

The Bolshoi Theatre.

THEATRE AND MANEGE SQUARES

Remnants of the Revolution are fading, world-famous theatres are being refurbished, and a multi-million-dollar development has brought even more shopping to the heart of old Moscow. Theatre and Manege squares are in the vanguard of Moscow's evolution from cloak-and-dagger capital to modern metropolis.

The centre of Moscow's street life has shifted. No longer is it set amid the traditional architecture of Red Square. It now focuses on the three redeveloped open spaces to the north that separate the Kremlin from Tverskaya ulitsa: Revolution, Theatre and Manege squares. This vast expanse of construction sites and building refurbishments reveals the vision of city planners since the end of the Soviet Union. Soviet relics such as the Moskva Hotel have been destroyed. Elite shopping centres have become a priority, while reminders of Russia's great, tsarist past – such as the Bolshoi Theatre – are being comprehensively spruced up. Even the long-forgotten Neglinnaya River, which once ran beside the walls of the Kremlin, has been allowed to return to the surface, if only to water a parade of traditional Russian fairy tale characters.

In a country where history is constantly being rewritten, this is where the full story of 'New Russia' is emerging, from the pageantry of its history to some of the most expensive shopping centres in Europe.

The three squares covered in this chapter are well served by the metro and can be visited in any order. We start in the middle, at ploshchad

Revolutsii, head north to Teatralnaya ploshchad and then on to Manezhnaya ploshchad to the southwest.

Revolution Square

Despite its name, the most revolutionary sight today on **Revolution Square** ⑯ (*ploshchad Revolutsii*) is of old people hawking Communist papers and (now probably fake) memorabilia by the steps of the former **Lenin Museum** ⑰ (*Muzey V.I. Lenina*; 112 Krasnaya ploshchad). The largest collection of Lenin

Main Attractions
Metropol Hotel
Bolshoi Theatre
Moscow State University
Okhotny Ryad
Aleksandrovsky sad
Tomb of the Unknown
  Soldier

Map
Page 100

A Lenin lookalike in Revolution Square.

A rather incongruous inscription around the facade of the five-star Metropol Hotel – a favourite place for business travellers – reads: 'Only the dictatorship of the proletariat can free the world of the oppression of capitalism.'

General Vhukousk statue at Revoltution Square.

memorabilia in the world was once housed in this red-brick building, just west of ploshchad Revolutsii metro station. But it has been transferred to the State Historical Museum (see page 101), and the space is now used as a gallery.

Lenin's museum may be history, but much Soviet heritage remains underground. Crammed with bronze statues celebrating ordinary citizens of the Communist workers utopia, Ploshchad Revolutsii is one of the finest metro stations in Moscow. Amid the kiosks to the east of the station are steps up to a passage lined with tiny clothing and electronics stores that leads onto Nikolskaya ulitsa (see page 107). There is also a bit of reconstructed Kitai-gorod wall here, with a kitschy restaurant in a faux tower. During the summer, outdoor café-bars and snack stands fill the square. For an original section of the Kitai-gorod wall, look a little further to the east behind the Metropol Hotel.

At the rear of the State Historical Museum rises an equestrian statue of

Marshal Zhukov, erected in 1995 to commemorate the 50th anniversary of the end of World War II.

Archaeological Museum ⑱

Address: 1a Manezhnaya ploshchad; www.mosmuseum.ru
Tel: 495-692 0020
Opening Hrs: Tue, Wed and Fri–Sun 10am–8pm, Thu 11am–9pm; closed Mon and last Fri of the month
Entrance Fee: charge
Transport: Ploschad Revolutsii, Okhotny Ryad, Teatralnaya

Just before the statue of Marshal Zhukov, on the northern side of the square, a marble pavilion covers the entrance to the underground Archaeological Museum (*Muzey arkheologii*). The museum includes a large collection of artefacts found during excavations of Manege Square, with some captioning in English. Some of the items date from the 12th century and include a pile of Spanish doubloons. The highlight is a portion of the Voskresensky Bridge (16th–17th century) that once

Metropol Hotel dining room.

spanned the Neglinnaya River and connected the White City (*Bely Gorod*, see page 141) to Red Square.

Theatre Square

On the other side of Revolution Square is a monument to Karl Marx in the centre of the southern section of **Theatre Square** ❶⑨ (*Teatralnaya ploshchad*), incongruous among its elegant neighbours, the Metropol Hotel and the Bolshoi and Maly theatres across the street.

Theatre Square has certainly seen better days. During the 19th century, when it wasn't coarsely bisected by the eight lanes of ulitsa Okhotny Ryad, it made a grand impression. In the evenings it was filled with carriages awaiting elegant theatre-goers, and in December an enormous Christmas-tree market made it look like a Siberian spruce and pine forest in the snow, with bonfires to warm the patrons and vendors of hot drinks and rolls touting their wares among the shoppers.

Now much of this once lively square is taken up by car parks. On the square's eastern side is the elegantly renovated **Metropol Hotel** ❷⓪ (1/4 Teatralny proezd; tel: 499-501 7800). An Englishman named William Walcot, who was born in Odessa and educated in Russia, finished this *style moderne* masterpiece in 1901. Its north wall is decorated with *The Princess of Dreams*, a mosaic panel designed by Mikhail Vrubel. It's worth a pause to examine it; it's also worth a short stop in the hotel to see the fountain with its statue *Cupids at Play* in the glass-domed main dining room. On the eastern side of the Metropol Hotel is one of the original Kitai-gorod towers.

Home of the arts

Until the 19th century Theatre Square was called St Peter's Square, then it briefly became Flower Square as it was the main outdoor market for flowers. It was renamed Theatre Square in the 1820s, when the main venues for the performing arts, the Bolshoi (Great) and Maly (Small) theatres, were built.

The **Bolshoi Theatre** ❷① company started life in 1776 when Prince

The Princess of Dreams, Metropol Hotel.

Karl Marx statue.

The interior of the Bolshoi Theatre.

Urusov, backed by the English entrepreneur Michael Maddox, received imperial permission to found a permanent performing-arts troupe. Performers were drawn from serf troupes, private and university theatres. After the first building burned down, the theatre was given the status of Great Imperial Theatre in 1805, and its original architect, Osip Bove, was entrusted with redesigning the square and its two theatres. The Bolshoi was again destroyed by fire in 1853, after which the architect Albert Kavos rebuilt the theatre as it is today. Its clean, classical lines, eight enormous columns and figure of Apollo riding his chariot along the top (by Pyotr Klodt) are emblems of Russian excellence in opera and ballet. Inside, the gold-and-red velvet decor, elegant cafés, shimmering chandeliers and sconces have delighted ballet- and opera-lovers for generations.

Between 2005 and 2011 the entire building was renovated at huge cost – it is estimated that US$1.1 billion was spent shoring up the theatre, which had developed serious structural flaws, and giving it a new lease of life. Once again it is Moscow's main theatre, employing over 900 actors, dancers, singers and musicians. A performance here is a highlight of any visit to Moscow and tickets are not as expensive as you might imagine, especially for matinees.

The Bolshoi's near neighbours are the **Maly Teatr** (Maly, 'little', Theatre), the oldest drama hall in the city, and to its left, the **Detsky Teatr** (Central Children's Theatre). The Detsky opened in 1921 and was Moscow's first professional theatre for children.

Across from the Bolshoi Theatre in the centre of the square is a stolid statue of Karl Marx, who seems to be emerging from an angular piece of rock. The inscription reads 'Proletariat of all countries, unite!'.

West of the Bolshoi along ulitsa Okhotny Ryad is an unimposing, but graceful pale-green classical building with white columns. Built for the Club of the Russian Nobility by Matvey Kazakov in the 1770s, it was nationalised in 1919 and renamed the Hall of Unions (dom Soyuzov; 1 ulitsa Bolshaya Dmitrovka). Both Lenin and Stalin were laid in state here before

being moved to the mausoleum on Red Square (see page 103). Several thousand mourners are said to have been trampled to death trying to see Stalin's body. Many other Bolsheviks met their fate here when it was used for the show trials of the late 1930s. Today it is used for state functions, concerts and special events.

Towards Manege Square

The stretch of ulitsa Okhotny Ryad between ulitsa Bolshaya Dmitrovka and Tverskaya ulitsa was once a boggy warren of small lanes, shacks and booths where trappers sold their catches. Cleared in the 1930s, they were replaced by the Hotel Moskva – now destroyed – and the grey and imposing edifice on the corner of Tverskaya ulitsa, which is now the **State Duma** (*Gosudarstvennaya Duma*), the lower house of parliament (see page 47).

On the other side of Tverskaya is the elegant **National Hotel** ❷ (*Hotel National;* Mokhovaya ulitsa, str. 1; tel: 495-258 7000; www.national.ru), built in 1903. From 1918 until the late 1920s it housed state officials moved from St Petersburg (then Petrograd) and was called the 'First House of Soviets'. Since its renovation in the 1990s, it has competed with the Metropol and Balchug-Kampinski for the reputation of Moscow's finest hotel. Its rooms and restaurants have good views of the Kremlin. Next to the National is a building erected in 1934 in mock 16th-century Italian style. It once housed the **American Embassy**, and on 9 May 1945, when word came that World War II in Europe was over, crowds gathered and cheered. George Kennan, then chargé d'affaires, described in his memoirs the thousands of people who stood in front of the Embassy all day and into the evening. When anyone ventured into the street, he was, in Russian fashion, kissed soundly, tossed in the air and carried off for more merriment, presumably involving jubilant toasts to victory.

Further down Mokhovaya ulitsa is Moscow **State University**, considered one of Russia's finest neoclassical buildings. It was built by Matvey Kazakov in 1793 and rebuilt after the fire of 1812. On the other side

The Hotel National.

FACT

Mokhovaya ulitsa gets its name from the many stalls that once stood here and sold moss (*mokh* in Russian), which was used as insulation in log houses.

of Bolshaya Nikitskaya ulitsa is the 'new building' of the university, built in 1836 with a statue to its founder, Mikhail Lomonosov, in the courtyard. Both buildings are still part of the university, though the main campus is now in Sparrow Hills (see page 138). A church dedicated to St Tatyana, patron saint of students, is in the corner of the new building – a refuge during the rigorous exam season.

Manege Square

The broad square on the other side of Mokhovaya ulitsa is **Manege Square** ㉓ (*Manezhnaya ploshchad*). Once the site of rag and food markets, it was completely redeveloped in the post-Soviet years. In USSR days the area would often be filled with crowds or tanks waiting to enter Red Square for parades, celebrations or protests. Crowds of almost a million demonstrated here against the Soviet authorities and, in 2002, it was the scene of

Mikhail Lomonosov statue outside Moscow State University.

Guards at the Tomb of the Unknown Soldier.

a riot of soccer fans watching large outdoor screens.

At the southern end of the square is the **Manege** ㉔, a neoclassical yellow structure with white columns. Built as a riding school under Alexander I in 1817, it had an uninterrupted roof-span of 45 metres (148ft). After serving as a garage in the early Soviet years, it was turned into the Central Exhibition Hall. In 1962 Nikita Khrushchev attended an exhibition of modern art here and started a shouting match with the artists by sensitively calling one work 'dogshit'. In March 2004, on the eve of the presidential elections, it burned almost to the ground. It was quickly restored, reopened the following summer and now holds exhibitions.

Okhotny Ryad ㉕

Address: Manezhnaya ploshchad
Tel: 495-737 8449
Opening Hrs: daily 10am–10pm

Entrance Fee: free
Transport: Okhotny Ryad

The centrepiece of the Manege Square redevelopment is the deluxe underground mall known as Okhotny Ryad or Hunters' Row. This was the name once given to the former meat market nearby that was famous in the 19th century for its taverns and nightlife. The mall today has a much more contrived nature. It was funded under Mayor Luzhkov, who gave free reign to his favourite artist, Zurab Tsereteli, to decorate the building to mixed effect. From above ground all that is visible is the mall's glass cupola – a dome map of the northern hemisphere. Tsereteli also designed a modern garden to lead to **Aleksandrovsky sad** (gardens), which was laid in 1819–22 when the Neglinnaya River was forced into underground pipes.

Today these gardens are enlivened by a trickle of the Neglinnaya River that has been released above ground to flow amid sculptures of fairy-tale characters. Across from the fountain is a **Grotto**, or 'Ruins', designed by Bove as a romantic nook for poetic thoughts. The nearby obelisk was dedicated in 1913 to the 300th anniversary of the Romanov dynasty, but was soon converted into a Monument to Revolutionary Thinkers.

At the gardens' north end is the **Tomb of the Unknown Soldier** 26 (*Mogila Neizvestnovo Soldata*), which was dedicated in 1967, on the 25th anniversary of the battle of Moscow. Under an eternal flame is a tomb decorated with a helmet and banner inscribed: 'Your name is unknown, your deed is immortal.' Wreaths are laid here for the war dead on Victory Day (9 May), and newlyweds come to pay their respects (and take photos) in between the registry office ceremony and their wedding reception. The guard changes every hour with great ceremony. In winter they change every 30 minutes. The nearby gates open onto the rear of the Historical Museum.

The Manege.

PALACES BENEATH THE STREETS

Muscovites are extremely proud of their metro system, and rightfully so – it is clean, fast, efficient, cheap and spectacular to look at, if occasionally a bit crowded.

Public transport in Moscow seems more like entertainment than a daily grind to visitors. You leave street reality, step on a fast-moving escalator that plunges you deep under the earth, and step off into a palace of marble and coloured stone lit by chandeliers and decorated with sculpture and mosaics. The Moscow metro is one of the world's most beautiful modes of public transport, and also one of the most efficient. It handles around 9.7 million passengers every day, ferrying them to 200 stations over 333km (207 miles). And the stations – particularly the older ones on the Circle Line and in the city centre – are shockingly elegant and majestic, even if the mosaics of farm workers or bas-reliefs of hearty athletes seem anachronistic in today's materialistic post-Soviet Moscow. But the sleek, stainless-steel-arched Mayakovskaya station that won the Grand Prix at the New York World's Fair in 1938 fits right into postmodernist Moscow. In the completely restored station, be sure to glance up at the ceiling mosaic designed by the artist Alexander Deneyka. This station served as a bomb shelter during World War II and was the venue of Moscow City Council's celebration of the 24th anniversary of the October Revolution in 1941.

Mayakovskaya, with its elegant arches, is true Art Deco chic.

Many metro stations were built in the war years and used as shelters. Park Pobedy, opened in 2003, is the deepest station in the world and features two enamelled panels depicting the Great Patriotic War.

The grand mosaics at Kievskaya tell the 'happy story' of Russian-Ukrainian relations: two peoples working to the same communist goal.

A chandelier-lit subway at Komsomolskaya metro station.

DIGGING TUNNELS FOR SOCIALISM

Although the Moscow City Council had discussed building a metro system as early as 1902, the first tunnels were not dug until 1931. Designed to be the showcase of the Soviet Union's first Five-Year Plan to modernise industry, the metro combined technical innovation with artistic celebration of the proletariat. It was also a symbolic project, intended to show that Socialism could achieve anything capitalism could.

The first line (the Red Line) was opened with much pomp in 1935. Kropotkinskaya is one of the most beautiful and restrained stations. It is lined with marble taken from the facade of the demolished Cathedral of Christ the Saviour, now reconstructed nearby (see page 129).

Newer stations in the outer districts are not as elegant or as deep as those in the centre. The exception to the rule is the station at Park Pobedy, completed in 2003. It is the deepest station in the city with the world's longest escalator: an ear-popping 126 metres/yds.

The names of stations are not always obvious, so visitors should listen for the recorded announcements: 'Doors closing, next stop…'

The escalator at Kurskaya–Koltsevaya station.

Now that Socialist Realist statuary is out of fashion, Ploshchad Revolutsii (Revolution Square) is one of the few places you can see monumental Soviet art.

Crowds on Arbat Street.

CLASSIC ART AND OLD ARBAT

Celebrated in song and verse, the Arbat was once the Bohemian centre of the capital, and it is still vibrant today, even if it has lost some of its edge. Along with a visit to Moscow's most celebrated street, there's also the chance to see two world-class museums, Russia's largest church and a host of homes that once belonged to Russia's literary heroes.

The part of the city southwest of the Kremlin is filled with museums and good shopping. Further afield, two visual feasts await: the surreal beauty of Novodevichy Convent and the view over the city from the Sparrow Hills.

Opposite the Kremlin's southwest tip stands the magnificent **Pashkov House** (*Dom Pashkova*; metro Boroyitskaya), designed by Bazhenov for Pytor Pashkov, a captain in the Semyonovsky regiment, who was granted the land by Peter the Great. Today, obscured by an enormous billboard, it is difficult to appreciate its graceful proportions and grandeur, which earned it the name of 'the enchanted castle'. In 1861, the Rumyantsev Library and art collection was brought here from St Petersburg. In 1924 it was turned into the Lenin Library, and the non-book collections were distributed among other Moscow museums. It is still part of the State Library. The street that begins at Borovitskaya ploshchad, a massive roadway in front of the Kremlin's Borovitsky Gates, is ulitsa Znamenka, named after a church that once stood here: the Mother of God of the Sign (*znamenie*).

Shilov Art Gallery ❶

Address: 5 ulitsa Znamenka
Tel: 495-203 4450
Opening Hrs: Tue–Wed and Fri–Sun 11am–7pm, Thu noon–9pm
Transport: Borovitskaya

At No. 5 ulitsa Znamenka is the Shilov Art Gallery (*Kartinnaya galereya A. Shilava*). Alexander Shilov's portraits of famous Russians, still lifes and landscapes are hugely popular. In 1997 Shilov (b.1943) donated more than 300 canvases to the State, which provided this

Main Attractions
Pushkin Museum of Fine Arts
Cathedral of Christ the Saviour
Old Arbat
Skriabin House-Museum
Pushkin Apartment-Museum
Tolstoy House Museum
Novodevichy Convent
Novodevichy Cemetery
The Sparrow Hills
The Mosfilm Studios

Map
Pages 124, 133

Shilov Gallery.

19th-century manor house to house them.

Street of the arts

Ulitsa Volkhonka starts at Borovitskaya ploshchad and goes to the southwest. This area leading down to the Moscow River was called Chertole ('The Devil's Land') from Chertomaya, a tributary of the Moscow River. Another tributary, the Volkhonka, gave the street its name. The area was once settled by Ivan the Terrible's *oprichniki* (see page 33), but by the 19th century it was lined with noble mansions. Today this short street boasts four major museums and the country's main church, the Cathedral of Christ the Saviour.

Pushkin Museum of Fine Arts ❷

Address: 12 ulitsa Volkhonka; www.arts-museum.ru
Tel: 495-697 7415
Opening Hrs: Tue–Sun 11am–8pm, Thu–Fri until 9pm
Entrance Fee: charge
Transport: Kropotkinskaya, Borovitskaya, Biblioteka im. Lenina

The Pushkin Museum of Fine Arts (*Muzey izobrazitelnykh iskusstv imeni*

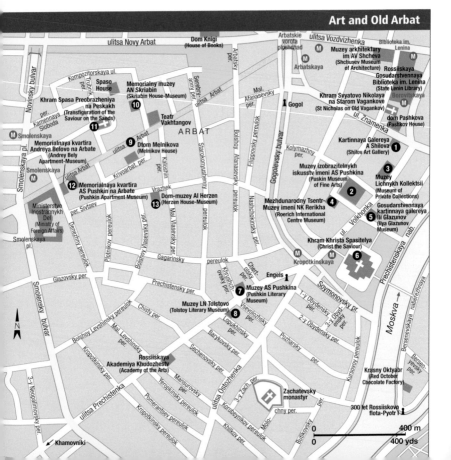

Art and Old Arbat

A.S. Pushkina) is a handsome classical building set back among tall pines. It was the 'child' of Ivan Tsvetaev (1847–1913), a professor of art history and father of the poet Marina Tsvetaeva, who was possessed with the idea of creating a museum that would present the finest examples of Western art to the public. The museum was finally opened by Tsar Nicholas II and his family. Under Soviet power the collection grew to include expropriated private collections from Sergey Shchukin, Ivan Morozov, Sergey Tretyakov, the Yusupov and Shuvalov families and other Soviet museums. The bulk of the collection was fortuitously evacuated to the east during World War II. In 1953 the museum resumed displays of its main collection and began to exhibit art 'saved' from Nazi Germany.

Today the museum has more than half a million works of art, with many copies of antique and European statuary, and retains its founder's concept of an educational institution. English audioguides are available; maps of the museum and Moscow are available in the basement.

Highlights of the Pushkin

Our tour begins at the top of the stairwell accessed from the cloakroom. Please be aware that not all the works listed below may be in the location indicated as collections are changed, lent out and moved about regularly.

Stop in Hall 7, straight ahead at the top of the stairs, where the **Schliemann Gold** is usually on display, while the debate as to which country the collection truly belongs continues. Heinrich Schliemann discovered the huge cache of gold jewellery and objects, dated to 2500 BC, in Turkey in 1873. The hall also showcases antiquities and special exhibits.

To see the Pushkin's collection chronologically, turn left at the top of the stairs and go through Halls 3

and 4, where you turn left again into Hall 2 and then into Hall 1, which holds the museum's small, but truly excellent collection of **Egyptian art**.

Hall 2 showcases the art of Ancient civilisations: bas-reliefs from Persepolis and Babylon, pottery and statues from India and pre-Columbian America. Before visiting 13th- and 14th-century Italy (Hall 4), look at the eerily lifelike Fayum funeral masks (1st century AD) in Hall 3, as well as the still bright and festive Coptic textiles.

The museum's collection of early Italian art in Hall 4 (13th–15th centuries) is not extensive, but the *Virgin and Child Enthroned*, by an anonymous Florentine artist, and the icon *The Twelve Apostles* (Hall 3), both from the 1330s, are exquisite. Halls 5 and 6 highlight the museum's collection of art from the medieval to Renaissance periods in Italy, Germany and the Netherlands. In Hall 5 the masterpiece is the *Annunciation*, part of an altarpiece painted by Sandro Botticelli in the 1490s. It overpowers the delicate *Madonna and Child* by Lucas Cranach the Elder (1525) and

Annunciation, c.1489, by Sandro Botticelli, at the Puskin Museum.

Pushkin Museum stairs.

Room 15, the Italian Courtyard, at the Pushkin Museum.

Room 25, the Art of Ancient Italy and Ancient Rome, at the Pushkin Museum.

several lovely landscapes, including Pieter Brueghel the Younger's *Winter Landscape with a Bird Trap*.

EI Greco's *St John the Baptist*, thought to have been lost in World War II, graces Hall 6, which is otherwise devoted to the **Renaissance art of Venice**. Note Tintoretto's *Portrait of a Man* and Paolo Veronese's *Minerva*. Hall 6 is a dead end, so backtrack to the central lobby. Off the lobby on either side in Halls 14 and 15 are the Greek and Italian courtyards, brightly lit from skylights, beautifully appointed and filled with plaster casts and copies of statuary.

Directly opposite Hall 3 is Hall 11, which contains Flemish art of the 17th century, with some Spanish art from the same period. The museum's collection of Spanish art is not representative, but Bartolomé Murillo's *The Fruit Seller* and *Archangel Raphael and Bishop Domonte* are excellent. The Flemish school is well represented by Peter Paul Rubens's *Bacchanalia*, several canvases by Van Dyke and Snyders, and the lush Jacob Jordeans paintings of *Ulysses in the Cave of Polyphemus* and *The Flight into Egypt*.

To the left in Hall 10 is one of the museum's finest collections: 17th-century Dutch art. The highlight is **Rembrandt**. Canvases include the luminous *Ahasuerus, Haman and Esther* and three portraits of Rembrandt's family: *An Old Woman, An Old Man* and *An Elderly Woman*. From the dead-end Hall 10 backtrack through Hall 11 to Hall 12, Italian art of the 17th and 18th centuries. This collection is also excellent, containing works from all the main centres: Rome, Florence, Bologna, Naples, Genoa and Venice. The museum's collection of **French art** begins in Hall 13. The Pushkin Museum is second only to the Louvre in the scope and size of its French collection, mostly expropriated from Moscow's great arts patrons, Shchukin, Morozov and Tretyakov. Hall 13 displays the 17th and 18th centuries, with splendid works by Greuze, Fragonard, Wateau, Boucher and Poussin.

From Hall 13 you can enter the Italian Courtyard (through a copy of the Golden Arch of the Cathedral in Freiburg) and take the stairs to the second floor. The halls in the back

half of the museum (24–9) and the first halls at the top of the stairs (16 and 16a) are taken up by plaster casts and copies. The central halls (19, 20 and 30) are used for temporary exhibits, but the five halls on this floor devoted to painting are the museum's Holy Grail: the magnificent collection of **Pre-Impressionist**, **Impressionist** and **European art** of the late 19th and early 20th centuries.

To continue chronologically, walk past the main staircase and through Hall 24 (Greek art) to Hall 23 and 22 on the left. These exhibit European art of the first half of the 19th century. Wonderful canvases of the Barbizon school include fine works by Courbet, Corot and Millet. The museum has several landscapes by John Constable and an excellent landscape by the German Romantic painter Caspar David Friedrich. Delacroix's *After the Shipwreck* is one of the collection's treasures, as is the study for Rodin's *The Kiss*.

Hall 21 has a changing exhibition of **French Impressionists**. Renoir's *Portrait of Jeanne Samary* and his luscious *Nude* are usually on display, as are Monet's *Luncheon on the Grass* and one of his series of the Cathedral in Rouen. Across the staircase landing and past the halls for temporary exhibits, the collection continues in Hall 18 with the **Post-Impressionists**: primarily Van Gogh, Cezanne and Gauguin, whose *Red Vineyard in Arles* and *The Prisoner's Walk* are breathtaking. The last large hall, No. 17, displays works of the late 19th and early 20th century.

Collectors Shchukin and Morozov each bought nearly 50 paintings by **Picasso** and **Matisse**; three or four are on display. Picasso's *Girl on a Ball* and the *Portrait of Ambroise Vollard* are usually exhibited, as are Matisse's bright *Goldfish* and one of the smaller versions of *The Dance*. The hall only displays two canvases by Marc Chagall, but there are excellent works by Kandinsky, Léger and Miró, and the Maillol sculpture *Pomona*.

Museum of Private Collections ❸

Address: 8/10 ulitsa Volkhonka
Tel: 495-697 1610
Opening Hrs: Wed–Sun noon–8pm
Entrance Fee: charge

The Renaissance collection at the Pushkin Museum.

Transport: Kropotkinskaya

Across Kolymazhny pereulok, just opposite the exit of the Pushkin Museum, is another branch of the institution – the Museum of Private Collections (*Muzey lichnykh kollektsii*). The museum makes no pretence of being comprehensive, but there is a bit of everything. The focus is on Russian art, including icons, 18th- and 19th-century folk art, paintings by such masters as Polenov and Repin, as well as the world's largest collection of art by **Alexander Rodchenko** and **Varvara Stepanova**.

This is Russia's first truly international-standard museum, and it is a delight to view the art in the airy, well-lit and comfortable building.

Nikolay Roerich International Centre Museum ❹

Address: 3/5 Maly Znamensky pereulok; http://en.icr.su/museum

Moscow State Art Gallery of the People's Artist of the USSR Ilya Glazunov.

Tel: 499-271 3404
Opening Hrs: Tue–Sun 11am–7pm
Entrance Fee: charge
Transport: Kropotkinskaya

To the left of the Pushkin Museum, at the end of a small side street, is the Nikolay Roerich International Centre Museum (*Mezhdunardny tsentr-muzey imeni N.K. Rerikha*). The museum displays every aspect and period of Roerich's life: from his work as a set designer for Diaghilev and his ethnographic and artistic travels through Asia, to his paintings and his philosophical and political activities to promote the Banner of Peace. The museum is well annotated in Russian and English.

Ilya Glazunov Gallery ❺

Address: 13 ulitsa Volkhonka; www.glazunov.ru
Tel: 495-691 8454
Opening Hrs: Tue–Sun 11am–6pm, Thu until 9pm

Song of Shambhala, 1943, by Nikolay Roerich.

Entrance Fee: charge
Transport: Kropotkinskaya

On the other side of ulitsa Volkhonka is a turquoise neoclassical mansion that houses paintings by Roerich's artistic and philosophical opposite: the Ilya Glazunov Gallery (*Kartinnaya galereya Ili Glazunov*). Glazunov (b.1930) is one of Russia's most controversial figures, whose nationalistic views and kitschy canvases have earned the scorn of the intelligentsia and the love of the masses. If you want to see what the fuss is about, stop in to see his wall-sized canvases filled with stale leaders, historical figures, sad-eyed old women, poor people holding signs 'selling Russian children', nuclear explosions, vulgar Bolsheviks, Bill Clinton and Monica Lewinsky.

Christ the Saviour

Opposite the gallery is the **Cathedral of Christ the Saviour** ❻ (Khram Khrista Spasitelya; ulitsa Volkhonka 15), famously rebuilt in the 1990s and opened in time to mark Moscow's 850th anniversary. The church is a copy of the original, which was erected between 1818 and 1858. It soon became the outstanding symbol of the city – it was not just a church, it was also a monument to the Russian victory over Napoleon, a symbol of the idea that, with God's help, Russia could overcome any catastrophe. However, to the new Soviet regime the cathedral was little more than an ugly reminder of the autocratic regime.

In 1931, to the horror of Muscovites, Stalin had the cathedral dynamited. In its place he planned to erect a gigantic skyscraper, which would be the largest in the world. It was called the Palace of Soviets, and it was in effect a temple of Communism. It was to be crowned with a statue of Lenin so colossal that its upper half would have been permanently lost in the clouds – it's claimed Lenin's forefinger would have been big enough

to hold a cinema! But the megalomaniac plan was never realised – the skyscraper could not be made to stand up, and the gaping hole of the foundations was turned into the Moscow open-air swimming pool.

The demolished cathedral became a forbidden topic in the USSR, a non-building. But when Communism collapsed, the resurrection of the church became a cause célèbre. The then mayor of Moscow, Yuri Luzhkov, took up the baton. It was built in the astonishingly short space of three years and stands as much as a monument to Luzhkov's tenure of office as a place of divine worship. In 2007 Boris Yeltsin's funeral was held here, the first religious service since 1917. In 2012 it hit the news again when the Russian female punk band, Pussy Riot, famously staged an anti-Putin protest there. The members' trial and imprisonment caused international outrage until they were released by President Putin in time for the Sochi Winter Olympics in 2014.

FACT

Nikolay Roerich (1874–1947), painter, set designer, teacher and philosopher, spent many years in Asia. To protect the world's cultural treasures, he developed the Banner of Peace to be flown by cultural monuments to protect them during times of hostilities. The Roerich Pact to protect cultural treasures in war and peace was signed in 1935 by members of the Pan-American Union, including the US. It is still in force today.

Cathedral of Christ the Saviour.

Pushkin Literary Museum.

Literary heritage

Ulitsa Volkhonka splits into two formerly aristocratic streets as it heads southwest: Ostozhenka (closer to the Moscow River) and Prechistenka, with a statue to **Friedrich Engels** standing between them. Most buildings on Prechistenka are graceful 19th-century classical and Empire-style mansions.

Pushkin Literary Museum ❼

Address: 12/2 ulitsa Prechistenka; entrance in Khrushchovsky pereulok; www.pushkinmuseum.ru
Tel: 495-637 5674
Opening Hrs: Tue–Wed and Fri–Sun 10am–6pm, Thu noon–9pm; closed last Fri of the month
Entrance Fee: charge
Transport: Kropotkinskaya

The former Khrushchev mansion at No. 12/2 houses the Pushkin Literary Museum (*Muzey A.S. Pushkina*). The biggest museum devoted to Alexander Pushkin outside St Petersburg is filled with manuscripts, possessions and extensive collections of applied and fine arts that recreate the life and times of Russia's premier poet.

Tolstoy Literary Museum ❽

Address: 11 ulitsa Prechistenka; www.tolstoymuseum.ru
Tel: 495-637 7518
Opening Hrs: Tue and Thu noon–8pm, Wed and Fri–Sun 10am–6pm; closed last Fri of the month
Entrance Fee: charge
Transport: Kropotkinskaya

The Tolstoy Literary Museum (*Muzey L.N. Tolstovo*) is in the former Lopukhin mansion. The focus is on Leo Tolstoy's legacy, with books, manuscripts and memorabilia. Further down is the **Academy of the Arts** (at No. 21) and the gallery dedicated to its president, Zurab Tsereteli (at No. 19). The Academy's building is considered one of Moscow's finest examples of classicism. Before the Revolution it belonged to the Morazovs and housed the family's art collection.

Friedrich Engels statue.

Boulevard Ring to Old Arbat

The first long leg of the Boulevard Ring is called Gogolevsky, in honour of the writer Nikolay Gogol, who lived near here. It stretches up a gentle slope to the north past a few urban mansions on the east side (note the pink-and-white mansion at No. 10 – now the Russian Cultural Foundation) and apartment houses-turned-offices on the west side, to Arbatskie vorota ploshchad. In 1951 Stalin drove past the original 1909 statue of Gogol at the top of the boulevard and is reported to have said that it 'did not fit in with post-war optimism'. Gloomy Gogol was removed – he's tucked in the court-yard of 7 Nikitsky bulvar – and a newly commissioned 'Happy Gogol' (by Nikolay Tomsky) put in its place.

Old Arbat

The labyrinth of lanes between Prechistenka and Povarskaya ulitsas on the far side of ulitsa Novy Arbat (see page 147) are still celebrated in songs and poetry as the charming 'Arbat lanes', even though much of the neighbourhood's charms have been destroyed by successive build-ing booms. Ulitsa Prechistenka was originally called Chertolskaya, after the small river here, and known as the road that led to the Novodevichy Convent. But in 1658 Tsar Aleksey renamed it in honour of the church of the 'Most Pure *(prechistaya)* Mother of God of Smolensk' in the convent.

The heart of the neighbourhood is **ulitsa Arbat ❾**, which stretches from the southwest from Arbatskie vorota ploshchad. The street's name is believed to come from the Turkic word *rabat*, meaning 'caravan', and was settled by traders from the south.

Over the centuries it remained a trading street, the lanes around it slowly filling with the middle and upper-middle classes, and, by the

Arbat Street.

Melnikov House.

Ministry of Foreign Affairs.

turn of the 20th century, Moscow's poets, writers and artists. In the early 1980s the Arbat was pedestrianised and immediately overtaken by artists, street vendors and bearded singers doing their best imitations of the Russian bard Vladimir Vysotsky (see page 182).

The Arbat is graced at one end by the elegant Praga restaurant at Arbatskie vorota ploshchad and overshadowed at the other by the Stalinist giant of the **Ministry of Foreign Affairs** at Smolenskaya ploshchad on the Garden Ring Road. As you walk from Arbatskie vorota ploshchad, just past Arbatsky pereulok you'll see a confused mass of colour on a wall. This is the **Wall of Peace** – tiles decorated by Soviet schoolchildren in the 1980s, now covered with post-Soviet graffiti. Among the dozens of souvenir shops, the one at No. 27 has a large selection of high-quality crafts of every kind, from glassware to *Palekh* boxes. Past it is the **Vakhtangov Theatre**, a grey Stalinist structure on the right, enlivened by a delicate statue of Turandot (now a teenage hang-out).

Skriabin House-Museum ⑩

Address: 11 Bolshoy Nikolopeskovsky pereulok
Tel: 499-241 1901
Opening Hrs: Wed and Fri–Sun 11am–7pm, Thu 1–9pm; closed last Fri of the month; tours in English by appointment
Entrance Fee: charge
Transport: Smolenskaya

After the Vakhtangov Theatre, make a short detour to the Skriabin House-Museum (*Memorialny muzey A.N. Skriabina*). The composer and pianist Alexander Skriabin lived in this second-floor apartment for the last three years of his life, from 1912 to 1915. You can see the simple but elegant *style moderne* furniture and personal possessions in several modest rooms, but the highlight of the museum is the 'light keyboard'. Here, as he played the *Prometheus* symphonic poem on the piano, his wife would 'play' the colours that Skriabin 'saw' as the notes. The museum staff play the light keyboard to a recording of *Prometheus* and there is a programme of concerts and other events.

Exploring the Arbat

On the other side of the Arbat is the small Krivoarbatsky pereulok ('Bent Arbat'), notable for the wall near the Arbat plastered with graffiti in honour of the rock musician Viktor Tsoy, who died in a car accident in 1990. Tsoy is still one of the biggest names in Russian popular music and spend any time in Russia and sooner or later you will hear his gravelly voice on a radio somewhere.

As you follow the crooked lane, you come across one of Moscow's most famous architectural landmarks, tucked behind a wall amid renovated apartment buildings. The Constructivist masterpiece of the **Melnikov House** (*Dom Melnikova*) at No. 10 is easy to miss behind the ramshackle fence; if you peer between the posts, you can see the

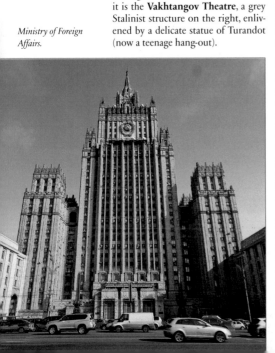

two cylinders decorated by rhomboid windows of the only private residence Konstantin Melnikov built in the Soviet period (1927–9). He fell out of favour at the end of the 1930s, but continued to live in the house until his death in 1974.

You can continue on Krivoarbatsky pereulok and then turn right on Plotnikov pereulok to return to the Arbat – passing on the way the statue of the Arbat's most famous poet, Bulat Okudzhava (see page 57). Across the street and a few paces back to the north, you can take another detour along Spasopeskovsky pereulok to see the charming white stone **Church of the Transfiguration of the Saviour on the Sands** ⓫ (*Khram Spasa Preobrazheniya na Peskakh*), named because the land here under the high-rises is sandy. The five-domed church was first built in stone in 1689, with a lovely tent spire over the belfry. The church has been immortalised in the Polenov canvas *Moscow Courtyard*

(1878) now in the Tretyakov Gallery: it is strange to see the delicate church, now dwarfed by modern buildings and blocked by cars, standing amid farmland and small wooden houses just a little over 135 years ago.

On the far side of the square is **Spaso House**, the residence of the US Ambassador, a beautiful neoclassical mansion built in 1913 by the Vtrorov family. The US was granted the house in 1933; two years later the Ambassador held a Spring Ball, with hundreds of animals and birds on loan from the Moscow zoo, roses and tulips filling the mansion, mountains of food and rivers of champagne. One of the guests was the writer Mikhail Bulgakov, and the lavish evening reappears as Satan's Ball in *The Master and Margarita* (see page 55).

Pushkin Apartment-Museum ⓬

Address: 53 ulitsa Arbat; www.pushkinmuseum.ru

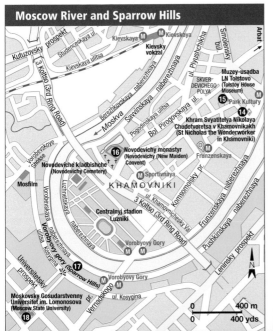

Moscow River and Sparrow Hills

Tsoi Wall.

Tel: 495-637 5674
Opening Hrs: Tue–Wed and Fri–Sun 10am–6pm, Thu noon–9pm; closed last Fri of the month; tours in English by appointment
Entrance Fee: charge
Transport: Smolenskaya

Back on the Arbat, the Pushkin Apartment-Museum (*Memorialnaya kvartira A.S. Pushkina na Arbate*) was home to Pushkin and his bride for five months immediately after their marriage. Although they only rented the second floor, the first floor has an exhibition on Moscow and Pushkin's life and friends. Much of the museum requires a guide, but on the first floor you can soak up the atmosphere of literary and aristocratic 19th-century Moscow. The second floor, where Pushkin lived, consists of a drawing room and several rooms with a few pieces of furniture and manuscript copies that serve as foils for the tour guide's discourses.

Next door is the **Andrey Bely Apartment-Museum** (*Memorialnaya kvartira Andreya Belovo na Arbate*; 55 ulitsa Arbat; tel: 499-241 9293; Wed noon–9pm, Thu–Sun 10am–6pm;

closed last Fri of the month), where Boris Bugayev (the writer's real name) was born and lived for the first 26 years of his life. Bugayev, novelist, poet and literary critic, led the group of Symbolists that appeared on the Russian literary scene at the end of the 19th century.

Herzen House-Museum ⑬

Address: 27 pereulok Sivtsev Vrazhek
Tel: 499-241 5859
Opening Hrs: Tue, Thu and Sat 11am–5pm, Wed and Fri 1–5.30pm; closed last day of the month
Entrance Fee: charge
Transport: Smolenskaya

At the Smolenskaya ploshchad end of the Arbat, you may choose to turn left on Denezhny pereulok, just before the massive Ministry of Foreign Affairs, and then left again on pereulok Sivtsev Vrazhek. The name means 'Sivtsev Gully' and refers to a creek no longer here. Literature buffs may want to visit the Herzen House-Museum (*Dommuzey A.I. Herzen*). Alexander Herzen (1812–70) lived in this cosy home, now filled with his personal effects, manuscripts,

Pushkin Apartment-Museum.

Church of St. Nicholas the Wonderworker.

portraits and memorabilia, with his family from 1843 to 1846, where he was visited by leading liberal thinkers and writers. In 1847 he wrote his most famous novel, *Who is to Blame?*

Khamovniki

Just beyond the Garden Ring Road at the Park Kultury metro station are two lovely sights that are well worth a visit. On the corner of Komsomolsky prospekt and ulitsa Lva Tolstovo is the **Church of St Nicholas the Wonderworker in Khamovniki** ⓮ *Khram Svyatitelya Nikolaya Chudotvoretsa v Khamovnikakh*). Built in the late 17th century by weavers, its bright-green and orange-red domes and layers of *kokoshniki* make it one of Moscow's most striking churches. Inside the lavishly decorated church is a gold canopy over a small icon of the Mother of God, *The Helper of Sinners*, a miracle-working icon brought to the church in 1848.

Tolstoy House Museum ⓯

Address: 21 ulitsa Lva Tolstovo
Tel: 495-246 9444
Opening Hrs: Tue and Thu noon–8pm, Wed and Fri–Sun 10am–6pm; closed last Fri of the month
Entrance Fee: charge
Transport: Park Kultury

Midway down ulitsa Lva Tolstovo on the left is the wonderful **Tolstoy House Museum** (*muzey-usadba L.N. Tolstovo*). In 1881, when Leo Tolstoy's children needed to go to school, the family decided to find a house in Moscow to spend the winters. They settled on a 16-room wooden house with no running water, sewage system or electricity. The family spent 19 winters here and Tolstoy wrote some of his most famous late works here including *What Do I Believe In? What is to Be Done?* and *The Kingdom of Heaven within Us.* The interior of the house is simple and comfortable. In the upstairs hall guides can play the waltz Tolstoy composed, and a recording of his voice. Down the narrow, dark hall that the family called the Catacombs is Tolstoy's modest study. Near-sighted and vain,

Tolstoy House Museum.

he refused to wear reading glasses; instead he sawed down the legs of his chair to sit lower and closer to his work.

Novodevichy Convent

Address: 1 Novodevichy proezd
Tel: 499-246 8526
Opening Hrs: daily 7am–7pm; tours in English by appointment
Entrance Fee: admission and photo/video charges
Transport: Sportivnaya

Not far from Khamovniki stands the Novodevichy Convent (*Novodevichy monastyr*). The convent was founded in 1524 in honour of the taking of Smolensk from the Poles and Lithuanians by Grand Prince Vasily III, and is one of the best-preserved and most peaceful of Moscow's fortress cloisters.

For most of its history it was a kind of prison for unwanted princely and royal wives and relatives, including Irina Godunova, Tsar Fyodor's widow and the sister of Boris Godunov. Boris Godunov was at the convent when the people of Moscow came three times to ask him to take the crown.

Novodevichy Convent.

Peter the Great sent his first wife, Yevdokia, and his sister, Sophia, here. Because the convent had such distinguished nuns, it received lavish gifts from the tsars, and by 1700 it was one of the richest cloisters in Russia, with over 15,000 serfs working in 36 villages. Although it was plundered by the French army in 1812, the nuns managed to disarm the fuses that were set to blow the entire convent to the heavens. It was also saved from destruction when the Bolsheviks decided to turn it into a museum in 1922. It was partially returned to the Church in 1944, when an agreement was signed for the Church and State museum to share the premises.

This peaceful and beautiful place is best seen first from the far side of the small duck-filled pond near the river. Inside the gate, with the **Transfiguration of the Saviour Church** (*Preobrazhenskaya nadvratnaya tserkov;* 1687–8) beyond it, there is a pleasing combination of medieval and baroque architecture, best expressed in the magnificent bell tower that rises 72 metres (236ft) above the walls. Tombs of nuns,

CLASSIC ART AND OLD ARBAT

military leaders and wealthy families are scattered about the grounds; note the beautiful family crypt of the Prokhorov textile magnates in front of Smolensk Cathedral. It was built in 1911 in the *style moderne.*

The central church in the convent is the **Smolensk Cathedral** (*Smolensky sobor*), built in 1524–5 and similar to the Dormition Cathedral in the Kremlin. Here the five domes (one gold and four lead) are shifted slightly to the east, with stone galleries running around three sides. The interior is magnificently preserved, with unusual floral fresco ornamentation in the galleries and late 16th-century frescoes in the body of the church, their deep blues and reds both grand and solemn. The five-tiered gilded wooden iconostasis was installed in 1683–5.

Behind the Smolensk Cathedral is the **Refectory** and **Church of the Dormition** (*Uspenskaya tserkov*), built in 1685 and considered an architectural wonder for the lack of supporting pillars in the vast hall (4,300 sq ft/400 sq metres). The museum in the **Lopukhin Chambers** (to the

right through the entrance gates) displays a variety of temporary exhibitions. A permanent exhibition of ecclesiastical vestments and vessels, icons and frescoes is displayed in the Irina Godunova Chambers (behind the Smolensk Cathedral to the left). Look out for the model of the convent inside the entrance gates by the ticket kiosk.

Novodevichy Cemetery

Address: 2 Luzhnetsky proezd
Opening Hrs: daily 9am–5pm
Entrance Fee: free
Transport: Sportivnaya

In 1898 church and city authorities decided to expand the convent cemetery to the south. The new area opened in 1904 and became a prestigious cemetery. The Novodevichy Cemetery (*Novodeviche kladbishche*) is now open to visitors. The cemetery is a *Who's Who* of Russia. You can see Chekhov's modest *style moderne* gravestone; the monument to Vladimir Mayakovsky; the clown Yuri Nikulin and the ballet dancer Ulanova; the monuments to the aircraft designers Tupolev and Ilyushin. By the south

Grave of Leonid Brezhnev, Novodevichy Cemetery.

Grave of famous clown Yuri Nikulin and his dog, Novodevichy Cemetery.

wall is the grave of Raisa Gorbachev: a simple gravestone with a delicate and graceful muse standing watch. Be sure to find Nikita Khrushchev's grave: the family asked Ernst Neizvestny, with whom the Soviet leader publicly argued at the Manege in 1962 (see page 118), to design the gravestone. A bust of Khrushchev rests between white and black blocks, symbolising the two sides of this complex leader. He is the only Soviet leader not to have had a state funeral or to be buried by the walls of the Kremlin.

The Sparrow Hills

On the top of a high bluff across the Moscow River from Novodevichy Convent are the **Sparrow Hills ⑰**, once a favourite spot for Muscovites to rent dachas in the hot summer months and enjoy the view of the city. Anton Chekhov once said, 'If you want to understand Russia, you

People walking in the Sparrow Hills.

must come here and look out over Moscow.' Today the view is slightly different than in those days but still pretty breathtaking. You can easily get here from the Vorobyovye Gory metro stop (exit from the front of the train and follow the path to the right, up the hill). Next to the viewing platform is the classical **Church of the Life-Giving Trinity on Sparrow Hills** (*Khram Troitsy Zhivonachalnoy na Vorobyovykh gorakh*), built in 1811–13. Behind the church are some former government dachas, still hidden behind tall fences.

Towering over the scene is the main building of **Moscow State University ⑱** (*Moskovsky gosudarstvenny universitet imena Lomonosova*), the greatest of the Stalinist skyscrapers. The university complex consists of over 50 buildings (the number-loving Soviet authorities liked to tell you there were 160km/110 miles of corridors), with 6,000 rooms for students and over 200 apartments for staff, all located in a beautiful park and botanical gardens.

The Mosfilm Studios

Address: 1 Mosfilmovskaya ulitsa; www.mosfilm.ru
Tel: 499-143 9599
Opening Hrs: tours 3pm daily
Entrance Fee: charge
Transport: trolley 34 from Kiev Station

Film buffs may want to arrange a tour of the Mosfilm Studios. Universal Studios it ain't, but the two-hour tour does give a glimpse of one of the world's greatest film companies. Visitors see a small part of the enormous collection of costumes and props (the largest in Europe), an outdoor set of Moscow at the end of the 19th century, old film equipment and a wonderful display of models used in special effects. The tour ends with Mosfilm's celebrated collection of transport: over 80 antique cars, trucks, motorcycles, carriages and carts, including a 1913 Rolls Royce.

View towards the Sparrow Hills and Moscow State University.

NEW ARBAT AND THE WEST

Moving westwards from the Kremlin, the city develops in distinct areas, from the old White City, dating from tsarist times, with its concert halls and the Patriarch's Ponds, to the former working-class districts where revolution was fomented. On the far side of the river, the Napoleonic and Second World wars are commemorated in Victory Park.

Divided into four distinct areas, Moscow's western sector has a medley of sights. Within the inner Boulevard Ring, a charming assembly of tsarist-era buildings awaits exploration. This atmosphere continues out as far as the Garden Ring (*Sadovoye Koltso*) – with the exception of Novy Arbat, a street Soviet planners took enormous pride in, which is now lined with super-casinos and looks more like a mini Las Vegas. Beyond the Garden Ring lies Krasnya Presnya, a former working-class district and home to the Russian White House and World Trade Centre. War monuments attract people across the river and down Kutuzovsky prospekt, the fourth area, where there is a hidden gem of a church in Fili.

White City treasures

From Manege Square west to the Boulevard Ring lies the western section of Moscow's old **White City** (*Bely gorod*) – a preserve of buildings and houses from tsarist times. The performing arts are well represented along these cosy streets, with first-rate productions at the Tchaikovsky Conservatory and the Mayakovsky and Gelikon Opera theatres. Museums are dedicated to zoology and the influential actor Konstantin Stanislavsky.

Conductor at the Tchaikovsky Conservatory.

Once known as a 'museum of classicism' because of its fine buildings, **Bolshaya Nikitskaya ulitsa** starts at Manege Square between the two buildings of Moscow University (see page 117). It was named after a monastery that existed here from 1582 until the 1930s.

Zoological Museum ❶

Address: 6 Bolshaya Nikitskaya ulitsa; www.zmmu.msu.ru
Tel: 495-629 4435
Opening Hrs: Tue, Wed and Fri–Sun

Main Attractions
Moscow Tchaikovsky
  Conservatory
Patriarch's Ponds
Vagankovskoe Cemetery
Hotel Ukraina
Battle of Borodino
  Panorama Museum
Church of the Intercession
  at Fili

Maps
Pages 142, 150

Pyotr Ilyich Tchaikovsky statue outside the Conservatory.

10am–6pm, Thu 1–9pm; closed last Tue of the month

Entrance Fee: charge

Transport: Okhotny Ryad, Aleksandrovsky Sad

From the Manege, on the right-hand side, is the pale-blue Zoological Museum (*Zoologichesky muzey Moskovskovo universiteta*). Nostalgically old-fashioned and smelling of formaldehyde and camphor, the ground floor has squiggly things in glass jars; on the upper floor you can see indigenous Russian creatures, such as the polar fox and the European bison, and several animals that have become endangered.

Arts venues

Further up the street, past sushi bars and boutiques, are a couple of hidden gems. At No. 18 is the lovely Church of the Little Ascension (*Tserkov Malovo Vosneseniya*), tucked behind white stucco walls decorated with carvings. Across the street is a statue of Tchaikovsky conducting an imaginary orchestra in front of the columned portico of the **Moscow Tchaikovsky Conservatory ❷** (*Moskovskaya gosudarstvennaya konservatoriya im. P.I. Chaikovskovo*; 13 Bolshaya Nikitskaya ulitsa; tel: 495-629 8183). The city's premier concert hall was founded in 1866 by Nikolay Rubenstein and is the venue for the prestigious Tchaikovsky competition. The Grand Hall where concerts take place is decorated with medallions of composers and has an old-world elegance and impeccable acoustics.

Two more worthy performing-arts venues, the red-brick **Mayakovsky Drama Theatre** and the green-and-white **Gelikon Opera Theatre**, sit further up the left-hand side of the street. If you'd rather take your art home with you, visit the friendly, cluttered **Murtuz Gallery** at No. 22. It has an eclectic assortment of contemporary art by more than 300 artists, and will arrange export (www.murtuz.ru; tel: 495-290 3139; Mon–Sat 10am–7pm).

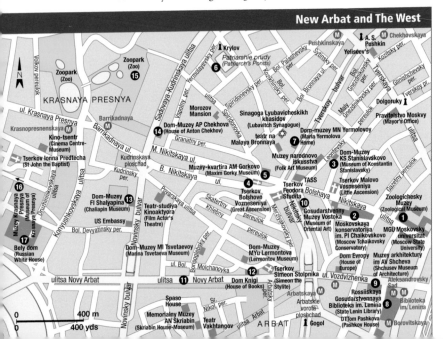

New Arbat and The West

Museum of Konstantin Stanislavsky ❸

Address: 6 Leontevsky pereulok
Tel: 495-629 2855
Opening Hrs: Thu and Sat–Sun
11am–6pm, Wed and Fri 2–7pm;
closed last Thu of the month
Entrance Fee: charge
Transport: Pushkinskaya

At the top of Bolshaya Nikitskaya ulitsa, just before Nikitsky vorota, Leontevsky pereulok heads off to the right, and on its right-hand side is the Museum of Konstantin Stanislavsky (*dom-muzey K.S. Stanislavskovo*). The actor, director and founder of the 'method school' of acting lived in this ground-floor apartment with his wife, the actress Maria Lilina, from the late 1920s to his death in 1948. The apartment, with several rooms decorated in Stanislavsky's favourite European medieval style, is filled with memorabilia from the Moscow Art Theatre (MKhAT), including stage-set models and manuscripts.

On the left side of Bolshaya Nikitskaya is Kalashny pereulok, where an antique shop, Antikvar, is filled with silver, icons, paintings and other small treasures.

Towards the Gorky Museum

The Boulevard Ring meets Bolshaya Nikitskaya ulitsa at **Nikitsky Gates** (Nikitskie vorota), the former entry gate in the walls of the White City. The square here is dominated by the ITAR-TASS building, but turn your back to the monolith of the regime's propaganda machine to see the majestic **Church of the Great Ascension** ❹ (*Tserkov Boishovo Vozneseniya*). Built in the first half of the 19th century, it suffered severely during the Soviet period. Many icons were burned, and more than 23kg (50lbs) of gold and 12kg (27lbs) of silver in icons and vessels were confiscated before the church was turned into offices. Now the interior is restored

and once again filled with frescoes, and a dazzling gold sun-ray cross crowns the sanctuary gates. In 1831 the writer Alexander Pushkin married Natalya Goncharova here, an event commemorated by bronze statues on the fountain in front of the church.

The more diminutive **Church of Theodore Studites** (*Tserkov Feodora Studita*), built in 1626, stands on the other side of Nikitskaya Bolshaya. The famous 18th-century general Alexander Suvorov was baptised here and even sang in the choir.

Maxim Gorky Museum ❺

Address: 6/2 Malaya Nikitskaya
ulitsa, entrance in ulitsa Spiridonovka
Tel: 495-690 0535
Opening Hrs: Wed–Sun 11am–
5.30pm; closed last Thu of the month
Entrance Fee: free
Transport: Pushkinskaya

On the corner of ulitsa Spiridonovka and Malaya Nikitskaya ulitsa is the Ryabunshinsky mansion, built by Fyodor Shekhtel in 1900 for the banker Ryabunshinsky and recognisable by the swirling wrought-iron fence and the frieze under the roof.

ITAR-TASS news agency building.

Most visitors are interested only in the building, which is officially the Maxim Gorky Museum (*Muzey-kvartiry A.M. Gorkovo*), since the writer lived here from 1931 to 1936.

This is one of Moscow's finest examples of *style moderne* architecture and decor, as Shekhtel also turned his attention to the furniture, fixtures, wrought-iron fence, floors and nine stained-glass windows. The architectural centrepiece of the house is the curved limestone staircase called 'The Wave', which is decorated with lamps that look like jellyfish – *medusa* in Russian. It was nearly ruined by the built-in bookshelves Gorky installed. His bedroom and sparsely decorated study, with a collection of oriental figurines, strikes a discordant note with Shekhtel's lush ornamentation. On the third floor is the restored chapel and a small bookshop.

Next to the Gorky Museum is an elegant, L-shaped house that follows the bend in Spiridonovka. It has an excellent art gallery, the **New Hermitage** (*Novy Ermitazh;* tel: 495-290 4515; Mon–Fri noon–6pm), on the main floor. Further down

Spiridonovka, at No. 17, is another Shekhtel mansion, this one executed in High Gothic style for the magnate Savva Morozov; it is now used for diplomatic receptions.

Patriarch's Ponds

Turn down ulitsa Malaya Bronnaya, named after the armour-makers (*bronniki*) who lived and worked here, and head north to reach one of Moscow's most picturesque, elite and expensive neighbourhoods – **Patriarch's Ponds** ❻ (*Patriarshy prudy*). Named after the Patriarch's court that was once here, the heart of Patriarch's Ponds is a quiet stretch of water enjoyed by swans in summer and ice-skaters in winter, and surrounded by apartments, cafés, boutiques and embassies. Much of Bulgakov's *The Master and Margarita* takes place here, and there is no escaping the black cat and devil theme to the cafés. At the end of the pond are statues of the fabulist Ivan Krylov and of his fairy-tale characters. In 2001 the Patriarch's Ponds community found the pond surrounded by fences and bulldozers; the city council had decided to face the pond in granite

Patriarch Ponds.

Marble Staircase in the Gorky Museum.

On the Tverskoy bulvar is the museum of the famous Russian actress Maria Yermolova (*Dommuzey M.N. Yermolovoy*). The premier actress at the Maly Theatre lived in this house from 1853 until her death in 1928.

Classic books and buildings

Running roughly parallel to Bolshaya Nikitskaya ulitsa to the south is **ulitsa Vozdvizhenka**, the street of 'the Exaltation of the Cross', named after a monastery that was here. The lushly ornamented building at the start of the street is the reception offices of the State Duma. On the other side is the stark-white marble **State Lenin Library ❽**. Built in 1940, and known as 'Leninka', it is the main library of record and houses more than 40 million volumes. There is a small **Museum of Books** (3/5 ulitsa Vozdvizhenka, through entrance 3, fourth floor; tel: 495-695 5790; Mon–Sat 10am–5pm; closed last Mon of the month; free), which displays examples of printing, from ancient Egyptian papyrus to the

and erect several statues to Bulgakov and his literary characters, including a statue of Christ walking on the water. The community rebelled and won – virtually the only successful challenge to Mayor Luzhkov's projects of 'urban improvement'. Returning to Nikitsky vorota from here, you pass the Theatre of Malaya Bronnaya (4 Malaya Bronnaya ulitsa), once the State Yiddish Theatre. Around the comer at No. 6 (building 3, Bolshaya Bronnaya ulitsa) is the Lubavitch Synagogue. Built in 1883, it was turned into the Moscow House for Amateur Performers in Soviet times and returned to the Jewish community in 1991. Its small museum can be viewed by appointment (tel: 495-202 4530).

Maria Yermolova Home ❼

Address: 11 Tverskoy bulvar
Tel: 495-290 5416
Opening Hrs: Mon and Wed–Sun 11–7pm; closed last Mon of the month

State Lenin Library and Fyodor Dostoyevsky statue.

present, and has a rich collection of early Russian liturgical texts. On the right side of Vozdvizhenka, at No. 16, is the House of Friendship (dom Evropy), an odd, neo-Moorish palace built in 1894–9 by Arseny Morozov. It is rumoured that when his mother saw the house she exclaimed, 'Before, only I knew that you were a fool; now, all Moscow will know'. Arseny didn't live long enough to enjoy the house; to prove his strength of will, he shot himself in the leg – and died of sepsis.

Shchusev Museum of Architecture ⑨

Address: ulitsa Vozdvizhenka 5/25; www.muar.ru
Tel: 495-691 2109
Opening Hrs: Tue–Sun 11–8pm, Thu 1–9pm
Entrance Fee: charge
Transport: Arbatskaya

Nearby is the Shchusev Museum of Architecture (muzey arkhitektury im A. V. Shchuseva), which inhabits a late 18th-century building with spacious halls, trompe l'oeil ceilings, crystal chandeliers and temporary

The State Museum of Oriental Art.

exhibitions. The Chambers of the Tsar's Apothecary in the delightful courtyard is a small exhibition space, built in 1670 to dry herbs for the tsar's private pharmacy. Any of the streets off ulitsa Vozdvizhenka to the north lead back to Bolshaya Nikitskaya ulitsa. Their modest classical mansions include the State Institute for the Dramatic Arts at No. 6 Maly Kislovsky, and the blue-and-white skyscraper at No. 10/2 Nizhny Kislovsky designed by avant-garde artists Alexander Rodchenko and Varvara Stepanova. It now houses the studio of the artist Ilya Glazunov (see page 128).

Museum of Oriental Art ⑩

Address: 12a Nikitsky bulvar; www.orientmuseum.ru
Tel: 495-695 4846
Opening Hrs: Tue and Fri–Sun 11am–8pm, Wed–Thu noon–9pm
Entrance Fee: charge
Transport: Arbatskaya

An exhibition at the Schusev State Museum of Architecture.

Heading north from Arbat Square, it's a pleasant stroll along **Nikitsky bulvar**. On the right are numerous cafés and bars, and the Museum of Oriental Art (*Gosudarstvenny* muzey Vostoka). This has a small but representative collection of Eastern art, with a rare collection of rugs from the Middle East and Caucasus. On the first floor are stores selling gifts, crafts and antiques. **Bookberry** (*Bukberi;* 17 Nikitsky bulvar), on the opposite side of the street, has a small café and a good selection of art books written in English.

Novy Arbat

Ulitsa Novy Arbat ⓫ (New Arbat), a baleful mix of grey Soviet architecture and gaudy shopping centres, restaurants and casinos, runs from Arbatskie vorota ploshchad to the Moscow River. Only the lovely 17th-century **Church of Simeon the Stylite** (*Tserkov Simeon Stolpnika*) adds a note of beauty. The large **House of Books** ⓬ (*Dom Knigi;* 8 Novy Arbat) by the church has a good assortment of English books, maps and posters.

Two small, but charming, literary museums nestle to the north of New Arbat. Go through the alleyway to the left of the House of Books to reach the wooden **House-Museum of Mikhail Lermontov** (*Dom-muzey M.Yu. Lermontova;* 2 ulitsa Malaya Molchanovka; www.goslitmuz.ru; tel: 495-691 5298; Tue and Fri–Sun 11am–6pm, Wed–Thu 2–8pm; closed last day of the month; charge), which has a modest exhibition of memorabilia and personal possessions. The **House-Museum of Marina Tsvetaeva** is also a cultural centre (*Dom-muzey M.I. Tsvetaevoy;* 6 Borisoglebsky pereulok; tel: 495-516 5693; Wed–Sun 10am–6pm; charge). Tsvetaeva lived in this odd, two-storey apartment she called a 'surprise box' from 1914 until she emigrated in 1922. Her small study has 11 corners, the walls of which she covered with drafts of her poems.

Arts and chocolate

Near Borisoglebsky pereulok are a number of streets where purveyors to the royal court lived and worked. The street names identify their wares: Skaterny (*Tablecloth*), Khlebny

FACT

Mikhail Lermontov (1814–41) was one of Russia's finest Romantic poets and prose writers. His most well-known prose work is *A Hero of Our Times*. Exiled for his poem about the death of Pushkin, he was killed, like Pushkin, in a duel in the Caucasus a few years later.

Garden Ring Road, New Arbat.

(*Bread*) and Povarskaya (*Cook*). *Style moderne* architecture abounds in the neighbourhood. At No. 44 Povarskaya is a masterpiece built by the architect Kukushev in 1903–4. Across the street, the **Red October Sweet Shop** is worth stopping in, if only for a sample. Another culinary treat is the elegant restaurant at the nearby **Central Writers' House** (No. 50). The International Association of Writers' Unions next door at No. 52 is a classical Russian mansion said to be the model Leo Tolstoy used for Natasha Rostova's house in *War and Peace*. In the tranquil courtyard pleasant cafés cater to the local creatives. Across the street, at No. 33, is the **Film Actors' Theatre**, built in 1934 by the avant-garde Vesnin brothers.

On Garden Ring Road

Povarskaya ulitsa ends at Kudrinskaya ploshchad on the Garden Ring Road, which has two interesting museums nearby – the former homes of opera star Fyodor Chaliapin and writer Anton Chekhov. The 'birthday cake' building towering over the square, completed in 1954, was one of the seven Stalinist skyscrapers built in Moscow.

To the left, across the 10 lanes of the Garden Ring Road (here called Novinsky bulvar), is the older part of the **US Embassy**. The new part is behind it.

Fyodor Chaliapin Museum ⑬

Address: 25 Novinsky bulvar
Tel: 495-605 6236
Opening Hrs: Tue 10am–6pm, Wed and Thu 11.30am–7pm, Sat and Sun 10am–4pm; closed last day of the month
Entrance Fee: charge
Transport: Krasnopresnenskaya, Barrikadnaya

At No. 25 is a two-storey yellow classical mansion housing the Fyodor Chaliapin Museum (*Dom-muzey F.I. Shalyapina*), which also hosts concerts and events. The house is as extravagant as one would wish of an opera star.

House of Anton Chekhov ⑭

Address: 6 Sadovaya-Kudrinskaya ulitsa

Entrance to the House of Anton Chekhov.

Feodor Chaliapin.

Tel: 495-691 6154
Opening Hrs: Tue, Wed and Sat–Sun 11am–6pm, Thu–Fri 2–8pm; closed last day of the month
Entrance Fee: admission and photo charges
Transport: Krasnopresnenskaya, Barrikadnaya

On the right side of Kudrinsky ploshchad, on what Muscovites call the 'inner' side of the Garden Ring Road, is a narrow, pink two-storey house that looks, in the words of its owner, 'like dresser drawers'. This is the House of Anton Chekhov (*Dommuzey A.P. Chekhova*), where he lived with his family from 1886 to 1890. It is filled with photographs, posters, theatre, literary and medical memorabilia. It also hosts concerts and events.

Spirit of revolution

If there is a dark spirit of revolution in Moscow, for the last century it has been focused in the area of the city below Kudrinsky Square. It is here that Russian governments seem to meet their demise. Once called simply Presnya (probably meaning 'fresh water', from the small rivers and ponds), the area consisted of villages and monasteries beyond old Moscow. In 1729 Peter the Great gave one of the villages to the Georgian king in gratitude for help in fighting the Persians, and several streets called 'Georgian' (*Gruzinskaya*) testify to this, as does the statue on Bolshaya Gruzinskaya by Zurab Tsereteli dedicated to 'Friendship For Ever' between Russia and Georgia, an ironic statue indeed these days as relations between the two countries hover just above freezing.

This industrial and working-class neighbourhood became the site of fierce revolutionary battles in 1905 and again in 1917. To commemorate these conflicts, in 1918 the neighbourhood was renamed Red (Krasnaya) Presnya, and a number of streets were given appropriately revolutionary names. The cobblestones on Barrikadnaya ulitsa leading down past the Stalinist tower

Kudrinskaya Square Building.

Entrance to Moscow Zoo.

from Kudrinsky Square – the bane of drivers in winter – were left by Soviet authorities to honour the fighting spirit of the proletariat.

Still enslaved are the residents of the **Zoopark** ⑮ (1 Bolshaya Gruzinskaya; www.zoo.ru; tel: 495-255 6034; daily 10am–8pm in summer, until 5pm in winter; charge). The main entrance is at the corner of Bolshaya Gruzinskaya and Barrikadnaya streets. Founded in 1864, it's an excellent place to watch Moscow families enjoying themselves, and the polar bears always look as if they are having fun. At No. 2 Malaya Predtechenskaya ulitsa is the **Church of St John the Baptist** (*Tserkov Ionna Predtecha*), which has remained open since it was completed in 1730.

Museum of Krasnaya Presnya ⑯

Address: 4 Bolshoy Predtechensky pereulok
Tel: 499-252 3035
Opening Hrs: Tue–Fri 10am–6pm, Sat–Sun 10am–5pm; closed last Fri of the month
Entrance Fee: charge
Transport: Krasnopresnenskaya

For a sense of the various Russian revolutions, visit the much-praised Museum of Krasnaya Presnya (*Muzey Krasnaya Presnya*). The highlight of the museum is an enormous, room-sized diorama of the 1905 battles, with sound effects, that shows the city in historical detail. Other exhibits portray life in the district at the turn of the 20th century, and the history of the various revolutionary movements up to 1990.

The White House

From the zoo, Konyushkovskaya ulitsa leads to the new US Embassy compound on the left and the building commonly called the **Russian White House** ⑰ (*Bely dom*) on the right. Just before the White House

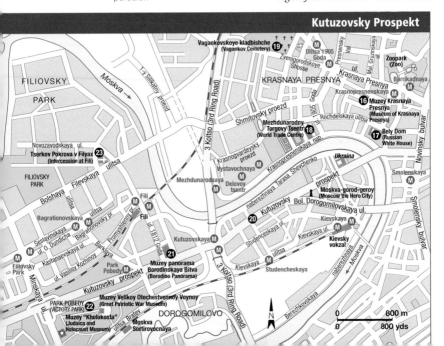

Cheetah at the Zoo.

misery. Further down the embankment to the right is a complex of grey buildings called the **World Trade Centre** ⓲ (*Tsentr mezhdunarodnoy torgovli*). They were built by the American industrialist and friend of the USSR, Armand Hammer, and opened in 1980 in time for the Olympics. During Soviet years, the Mezh, as it was called by expats (an abbreviation of the Russian for 'international'), was a haven for foreigners, with decent restaurants and shops selling such unheard-of delicacies as cucumbers in winter.

Vagankovskoe Cemetery ⓳

Address: 15 ulitsa Sergeya Makeyeva
Tel: 499-252 2541
Opening Hrs: daily 9am–5pm in winter, until 7pm in summer
Entrance Fee: free
Transport: Ulitsa 1905 Goda

A short walk from the 1905 metro station is Vagankovskoe Cemetery (*Vagankovskoye kladbishche*). This traditional, rambling Russian cemetery is less official than the Novodevichy Cemetery (see page 137), though it is the final resting place for the poet Sergey Yesenin (in section 17), the singer-songwriter Vladimir Vysotsky

there is a monument to those who died in the events of 1990 and the **Hunchbacked Bridge**, which once crossed the narrow Presnya River, now underground, when it was built in 1683. It figured prominently in the 1905 fighting and was restored as a monument to the revolution.

The White House held the Council of Ministers of the Russian Federation when Russia was just one of 16 Soviet republics. During the coup attempt in 1991, it was the rallying point for Yeltsin's supporters; in 1993, the building switched sides when it was occupied by the parliament opposed to Yeltsin. It was besieged by tanks and snipers until the occupiers surrendered. Repaired immediately afterwards, the building was enclosed by an iron fence.

Across the street is the **Mayoralty**, a building shaped like an open book, that once housed the Council on Mutual Economic Achievement that successfully united the Eastern Bloc countries in common economic

The White House and Hunchbacked Bridge.

(see page 182), the TV personality Vlad Ustev (immediately to the right through the gates) and many other stars of sports, literature, science, the military and the performing arts. Here, too, are buried those who died on the Khodynka field during the coronation celebrations for the last tsar, Nicholas II, when 1,389 were trampled to death racing for the free food and drink. Don't be surprised to see families enjoying vodka and a bite to eat at a graveside; it is a tradition on holidays and anniversaries.

Kutuzovsky prospekt

As traffic-filled Novy Arbat crosses the Moscow River, it becomes **Kutuzovsky prospekt** , one of the city's smartest neighbourhoods, built in the 1950s. It is still one of the most expensive districts, filled with top-end bars, restaurants and boutiques, but it's not good for strolling, as 10 lanes of non-stop traffic rush by immediately over the bridge from the city centre. On the right is the five-star luxury **Hotel Ukraina**,

Radisson Royal Hotel.

another of the seven Stalinist high-rises that carve out the city's skyline. Completed in 1957, it featured in the 1990 film *The Russia House.*

Where Dorogomilovskaya ulitsa meets Kutuzovsky prospekt, there is an **obelisk** dedicated to those who fought and died in World War II. On the right side of the road, the ornamented house at No. 26 was the city apartment of Leonid Brezhnev during his term as Secretary General of the Communist Party.

Battle of Borodino Panorama Museum ㉑

Address: 38 Kutuzovsky prospekt; www.1812panorama.ru
Tel: 499-148 1927
Opening Hrs: Tue–Sun 10am–6pm, Thu until 9pm; closed last Thu of the month
Entrance Fee: charge
Transport: Kutuzovskaya

The war monuments continue as you drive away from the city centre. On the right is the Battle of Borodino

Cyclists at Kutuzovsky Prospekt.

Panorama Museum (*Muzey-panorama Borodinskaya Bitva*). This contains a 115-metre (377ft) circular painting depicting, in obsessive historical detail, one of the key battles of 1812. It was painted by Franz Rubo in 1912 and installed in this specially constructed, round building in 1962. Spectators stand on a raised podium in the centre to spot characters from Tolstoy's *War and Peace*. Not far from here, Kutuzovsky prospekt narrows, and the traffic snarls around the Triumphal Arch. Designed by Osip Bove, it is decorated with the coats of arms of the 48 Russian provinces (*guberniya*) and bas-reliefs of 'The Expulsion of the French'.

Central Museum of the Great Patriotic War ㉒

Address: 11 ulitsa Bratyev Fonchenko; www.poklonnayagora.ru
Tel: 499-449 8179
Opening Hrs: Tue, Wed and Sat–Sun 10am–8pm, Thu–Fri 10am–8.30pm
Entrance Fee: charge; tTours: in English by appointment
Transport: Kutuzovskaya

Just beyond the arch on the left-hand side of the road on Poklonnaya Gora is the vast **Victory Park** and the Central Museum of the Great Patriotic War (*Tsentralny muzey Velikoy Otechestvennoy Voyny*). The park is situated in the Poklonnaya Hills and has strong historical associations. In centuries past tsars would ride out to this hilltop to greet foreign delegations. Knowing this tradition, Napoleon waited in vain here for Russian noblemen to bring him the keys to the Kremlin. In 1983 the area was established as a park and museum dedicated to World War II. It is dominated by a 140-metre (460ft) obelisk decorated by an angel of Victory and a sculpture of emaciated bronze figures called *The Tragedy of Nations*, all by Tsereteli. A church, mosque and synagogue were built to encourage religious observances.

The synagogue also has a small **Museum of Moscow Judaica and the Holocaust** (*Muzey Kholokosta*; tel: 499-148 1907; Sun–Tue and Thu 10am–5.45pm, Wed 10am–8pm, Fri

FACT

The name of Poklonnaya Gora comes from the Russian 'to pay obeisance', and visitors entering or leaving Moscow stopped here to 'bow down' to the city before them. It could also refer to *poklon*, a kind of duty paid in feudal times for temporary residence in a principality. Most Russians now understand Poklonnaya Gora as 'the Hill of Homage' to those who fought for victory in the Great Patriotic War.

Tragedy of Nations, Victory Park.

10am–5pm), but the main attraction of the park is the **Central Museum of the Great Patriotic War**. Its main room, the Hall of Glory, depicts the course of the war; on the lower level, dioramas show the fiercest battles. Despite its solemn memories the site has become one of the city's most popular meeting places, filled on weekends with children climbing on the World War II weaponry and tanks, grandmothers with strollers, and teens rollerblading and flirting.

Church of the Intercession at Fili

Address: 6 ulitsa Novozavodskaya
Tel: 915-278 9493
Opening Hrs: daily 8am–5pm
Entrance Fee: charge
Transport: Fili

Near by is a Baroque masterpiece: the Church of the Intercession at Fili (*Tserkov Pokrova v Filyax*). In the late 17th century the noble Naryshkin family commissioned estate and monastery churches that have become synonymous with Moscow Baroque. This one is like a pale, frothy wedding cake crowned by six golden domes: four

Central Museum of the Great Patriotic War.

semicircular apses form the main church on the upper floor, and the tiered style is reminiscent of both the early Russian 'tent' churches and Western architectural forms.

The building has two churches: the church at ground level was stripped of ornamentation when it was closed in 1941 but its iconostasis has been re-created and it is open for weekend services.

Yet even during the waves of anti-religious campaigns in Soviet times, no one could destroy the interior of the church on the upper floor. One entire wall, from the plank wooden floor to the very top of the tent spire, is a nine-tiered iconostasis with myriad icons framed in heavily ornamented and gilded carved wood. At the very top, under the tip of the spire, is a wooden statue of the Crucifixion – a very unusual Western innovation in an Orthodox church. The icons, also more naturalistic in the Western style, are lit by shafts of sun streaming through the windows in the tent roof. The Naryshkin family and their royal guests sat in the gilded Tsar's Box suspended across from the iconostasis.

TVERSKAYA AND THE NORTHWEST

Shopping and family fun are the essence of this slice of the city. Following the 'Tsar's Road' that leads towards St Petersburg, you pass through lively Pushkin Square and see the famous Moscow Art Theatre. Nearby attractions include a puppet theatre, doll museum and the Moscow Circus, plus the chance to take a plunge in the famous Sandunovsky Bathhouse.

This chapter begins with a trip along Tverskaya ulitsa, from the shadow of the Kremlin to the sprawl of warehouse-sized shopping centres along the Outer Ring Road. We then follow the Boulevard Ring to the northeast with short excursions on Malaya and Bolshaya Dmitrovka ulitsas before a longer exploration of ulitsa Petrovka and Karetny Ryad, where shopping and the Upper Peter Monastery are the main attractions. Then it's on to Trubnaya ploshchad, the intersection of four picturesque boulevards where you can be pampered at the Sandunovsky Bathhouse, before heading north to three classic Moscow attractions: the Moscow Circus, Durov's Circle and the Obrazstov Puppet Theatre.

The 'Tsar's Road'

Moscow's main shopping street, its Fifth Avenue or Oxford Street, is **Tverskaya ulitsa** ❶. Built as a road to Tver – the nearest principality to Moscow at the time – it later grew in importance when Peter the Great established St Petersburg as his capital, becoming the main road connecting Russia's two principal cities. Tsars coming from St Petersburg arrived for coronations, holidays and

official visits along Tverskaya, hence the name 'Tsar's Road'.

Tverskaya's appearance changed dramatically in the 1930s when the General Plan for Moscow's reconstruction called for the road to be widened from 18 metres (60ft) to 60 metres (200ft). Buildings were demolished or moved back, and the Stalinist neoclassical apartment houses and buildings that define the street were built around them. It is now a busy shopping district and civic centre.

Main Attractions

Yeliseev's emporium
Museum of Contemporary
  History of Russia
Museum of Unique Dolls
Sandunovsky Bathhouse
Moscow Circus
Obrazstov Puppet Theatre

Map

Page 158

Designer clothing store on Tverskaya ulitsa.

Central Telegraph Building.

Exploring on foot

Starting at Okhotny Ryad metro, the most interesting stretch to walk is from the start of the street by the Historical Museum up to Pushkin Square. Here the main street and courtyards are lined with ethnic restaurants, foreign clothes shops and easy-going coffee houses.

The elegant green-and-white **Yermolova Theatre** can be found at No. 5, while further up the imposing 1927 **Central Telegraph Building** (*Tsentralny Telegraf*) is marked by a distinctive, bulging globe. On Tverskaya's eastern side, step through

the arched gateway onto Georgievsky pereulok to glimpse the **Troyekurov Palace**, a lovely 17th-century boyar house behind the heavily guarded Duma building.

Moscow Arts Theatre

Further up Tverskaya, Kamergersky pereulok to the right is a pedestrianised street of restaurants and cafés. On its northern side at No. 3 is the elegant *style moderne* **Moscow Arts Theatre** (MKhAT), one of Fyodor Shekhtel's masterpieces (1902). The sea theme in the 1903 sculpture over the right door, by A. Golubkin,

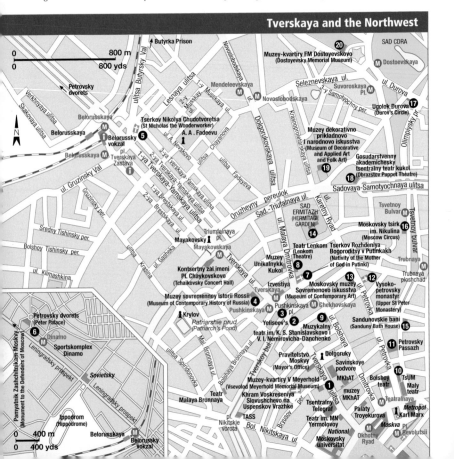

Tverskaya and the Northwest

reflects the seagull that became the theatre's emblem in honour of Chekhov's famous play.

The **MKhAT Museum** (*Muzey MKhATa im. A.P. Chekhova*; 3a Kamergersky pereulok; www.mxatmuseum. com; tel: 495-692 3866; Wed–Sun 11am–6pm; charge) has several halls filled with stage sets, old photos, dioramas and sketches of set decorations by celebrated Russian artists.

Before going back out onto Tverskaya, step through the wrought-iron gates closest to the main street on the north side of Kamergersky pereulok; in the courtyard is the turreted and tiled **Savinskoye podvore**, a magnificent apartment block built in 1907 by the patriarchy. The huge apartments inside are worth millions of dollars when they come up for sale.

Further up Tverskaya on the eastern side is a 1954 equestrian statue of Moscow's founder, **Prince Yuri Dolgoruky**, looking suitably heroic, opposite the red, classical-style Mayor's Office, built in 1782 by Kazakov for the Governor Generals of Moscow. In October 1993, when Yeltsin's government seemed about to be overthrown, it was a rallying point for the democratic forces. Just past the Dolgoruky statue is the enormous **Moskva bookstore**, which has a reasonable stock of English-language paperbacks and art books.

Yeliseev's emporium

In the middle of the next block is **Yeliseev's ❷** (No. 14), a magnificent *style moderne* food emporium with panelled shelves, chandeliers and elegant marble counters, once the mansion of Princess Volkonskaya, famous for her literary soirées. It was bought by the Yeliseev family in 1898 and turned into Moscow's most fashionable food store. Even as Gastronom No. 1 during the Soviet period, it was always stocked with goods unavailable elsewhere.

Turn left just before Pushkin

Square through the arches to Bolshoy Gnezdnikovsky pereulok to see Moscow's first skyscraper at No. 10. The 10-storey *style moderne* **Nirnzee House** was built in 1913 with fine detailing both on the facade and in the lobby.

Pushkin Square

If Tverskaya is Moscow's Fifth Avenue or Oxford Street, then **Pushkin Square ❸** (*Pushkinskaya ploshchad*) is its Times or Leicester Square – lively, but a bit seedy. Located at the intersection of the Boulevard Ring with Tverskaya ulitsa, it's a place that makes nostalgic Muscovites weep. Once an elegant open space surrounded by graceful buildings, churches and monastery walls, its garishly lit buildings now include what was once the world's largest McDonald's and a remarkably lurid casino.

All the same, the monument to Pushkin – installed in 1880 and moved to its present site in 1950 – is still a favourite meeting spot; at every hour of day and night you can see earnest men holding bouquets of flowers as they wait for their dates.

Yeliseev's.

The square is decorated when film festivals or premieres are held in the **Pushkin Movie Theatre**.

It's now incredible to think that the square was once the site of pro-democratic rallies, as it was the centre of Moscow's post-Soviet liberal press, with *Izvestiya* on one side and *The Moscow News* on the other. The original **Izvestiya Building** is a fine example of Constructivism. Built in 1927 by Grigory Barkhin, it is a study in geometric forms with nothing to soften its angularity.

Museum of Contemporary History of Russia ❹

Address: 21 Tverskaya ulitsa; www.sovrhistory.ru
Tel: 495-699 6724
Opening Hrs: Tue, Wed and Fri–Sun 11am–7pm, Thu noon–9pm; closed last Fri of the month
Transport: Pushkinskaya

Northwest of Tverskoy bulvar at 21 Tverskaya ulitsa are the white lions immortalised by Alexander Pushkin in his poem *Evgeny Onegin*. They guard the entrances to the large red mansion which is the Museum of Contemporary History of Russia (*Muzey Sovremennoy istorii Rossii*).

Museum of Contemporary History of Russia.

In 1831 it became the English Club (see box), famously frequented by Russia's intelligentsia and celebrated in fiction. From 1924 until 1991 it was the Museum of the Revolution.

The museum's exhibitions include a recreation of the English Club's famous library, an extensive collection of fascinating Soviet propaganda posters and bizarre home-made gifts presented to Stalin.

Pushkin Square to Belorussian station

North of Pushkin Square, Tverskaya is lined with up-market European clothes shops, hotels and restaurants. The next square's name has reverted to the pre-Revolutionary Triumfalnaya ploshchad, but many Muscovites still call it **Mayakovka**, because of both the 1958 statue of the poet Vladimir Mayakovsky (1893–1930), frozen mid-stride, and the avant-garde steel arches of the metro station bearing his name. Next to the monument is the famous **Tchaikovsky Concert Hall** (*Kontsertny zal imeni P.L. Chaykovskovo*) – seating 1,600, it is the largest in Moscow, and home of the State Symphony Orchestra – and the **Satirical Theatre**. Behind them the

---

THE ENGLISH CLUB

In the 19th century, it was said that there were four milestones in a gentleman's life: birth, receiving a government rank, marriage and membership of the English Club. This was a true gentlemen's club: no women allowed (even the floors were washed by men) and hence no dances or costume balls. Poets, writers, politicians, merchants, publishers and noblemen enjoyed evenings in the comfortable library, reading European newspapers and discussing politics without fear of police informers. In fact, it was said that Tsar Nicholas I regarded the club as a kind of barometer for the mood in the country and would regularly ask his advisers: 'What do they say about it in Moscow at the English Club?' There were halls for card games, and in 1862 Leo Tolstoy lost 1,000 roubles to an army officer and was nearly blacklisted when he found himself short of cash; luckily, a kind-hearted publisher lent him the money. The Club's kitchen was renowned for its sumptuous meals. During the Soviet period, Russian readers salivated over a scene in War and Peace in which Count Rostov discusses a menu at the English Club, much of which no one had ever tasted.

ornamented Stalinist towers of the **Peking Hotel** rise over the square.

The last square before the Garden Ring overpass is **ploshchad Tverskaya Zastava**, the main ceremonial gate to the city, through which tsars entered from St Petersburg. A Triumphal Arch celebrating the routing of the French in 1812 stood here until 1936.

East of Tverskaya on **ulitsa Butyrsky Val** is an imposing Old Believers' church with an icon of *The Image of the Saviour Not Made by Human Hands* above the main portal. The church, dedicated to **St Nicholas the Wonderworker** ❺ *(Tserkov Nikolaya Chudotvoretsa)*, was not completed until 1921, and remained open for 14 years. It later became the studio of Sergey Orlov, one of the sculptors of the statue to Yuri Dolgoruky (see page 159), and in 1993 it was returned to the Old Believers.

Yar restaurant

On the other side of the overpass at Belorussian train station, Tverskaya becomes the main road out of the city, changing its name to **Leningradsky prospekt**. The grand Stalinist apartment buildings here include the last grande dame of Soviet hotels – the **Sovietsky**. In the 19th century the **Yar restaurant**, one of the most famous in Moscow, was on this site. Poets, writers and men about town would spend the night carousing and listening to gypsy music. By the mid-20th century it had become dilapidated, and in 1951 it was reconstituted into the present hotel. The Yar restaurant is still here, and the tradition of gypsy songs and dance continues at the Romen Gypsy Theatre in the hotel's concert hall.

Peter Palace and Beyond

Ten minutes' walk up the road, just past the **Dynamo soccer stadium**, is a miniature Kremlin in the round. This is **Peter Palace** ❻ *(Petrovsky dvorets)*, built in 1775–82 under Catherine the Great by the architect Kazakov

as a place for the imperial retinue on their way from St Petersburg to Moscow to rest and dress for their ceremonial entrance into the city. When Napoleon left the burning city in 1812, he stayed here.

In the 19th century the park behind the palace was famous. Full of dachas and country houses, it was a place for feckless young men to go riding, followed by an evening of gypsy music in the park restaurant or the Yar, or perhaps an evening at Voksal, the park theatre named after the Vauxhall Pleasure Gardens in London. Ambitious merchant families would bring their daughters for promenades in the square nicknamed 'the bride fair'. Only a small piece of the park remains.

Near Sokol metro, the **Triumph-Palace apartment building** towers 264 metres (866ft) over the area – the tallest apartment house in Europe and what the developers call the 'eighth Stalinist skyscraper'.

The city of Moscow ends and Moscow *oblast* (province) begins 10km (6 miles) from Peter Palace at the Outer Ring Road along and beyond which

Performance at Yar restaurant.

Spring festival on Bolshaya Dmitrovka.

stretch department stores and malls. Near the turn-off to the Sheremetevo airport is the **Monument to the Defenders of Moscow** (*Pamyatnik zashchitnikam Moskvy*). Three enormous tank traps mark the spot where the German Army was stopped in its advance on the capital.

Malaya Dmitrovka

We now return to Pushkin Square. The boulevard that intersects Tverskaya here is **Strastnoy bulvar**, named after the Strastnoy monastery that once stood on Pushkin Square. A block to the east along Strastnoy bulvar, just past the Izvestiya Building, is **ulitsa Malaya Dmitrovka** and the lovely and ornately decorated **Church of the Nativity of the Mother of God in Putinki** ❼ (*Tserkov Rozhdeniya Bogoroditsy v Putinkakh*). This was the last tent church built in Moscow, in 1653. Patriarch Nikon banned the architectural style as inappropriate, because the thick walls that were needed to support the spires made the interiors small and cramped.

A few doors north of the church at No. 6 is the **Lenkom Theatre** ❽

on the site of the elegant 1907 *style moderne* Merchants' Club. According to contemporary accounts this was a rowdy place with musical entertainment, theatrical performances, dances and costume balls. It was briefly occupied after the Revolution by left-wing squatters and called the House of Anarchy. It later served as the first Communist University and is where Lenin addressed budding Communist leaders. The theatre established here in 1938.

Near Lenkom, next to the chic Hotel Golden Apple, is the **Museum of Unique Dolls** (*Muzey unikalnykh kukol*; 9 ulitsa Malaya Dmitrovka; tel: 495-625 6405; Fri–Sun 10am–6pm; guided tours only Wed–Thu noon, 2pm and 4pm; charge), opened in 1996 to house a private collection of over 6,000 dolls from all over the world, with an emphasis on rare Russian dolls.

Bolshaya Dmitrovka

In the 19th century **ulitsa Bolshaya Dmitrovka**, which begins at Okhotny Ryad at the House of Unions and ends at the Boulevard Ring,

was known as Club Street for the Noblemen's Assembly, Doctors' Club and first site of the Merchants' Club. Contemporaries complained about the stream of carriages dropping off well-to-do patrons and making the narrow street impassable. Today, lined with shops and cafés, it is clogged with weekday traffic heading for the **Prosecutor General's Offices** (No. 15, with impressive reliefs of Marx, Engels and Lenin) or the upper chamber of the Russian Parliament, the **Federation Council**, at No. 26.

About halfway down the street, the small pedestrian **Stoleshnikov pereulok** (Tablecloth Lane) leads east to ulitsa Petrovka. The lane is lined with up-market boutiques and cafés. Further up Bolshaya Dmitrovka at No. 17 is the **Stanislavsky and Nemirovich Musical Theatre** ❾, founded in 1941 when Konstantin Stanislavsky's Bolshoi Theatre Opera Studio joined Nemirovich-Danchenko's Musical Studio of the Moscow Art Theatre. Rejecting opera as 'concerts in costumes', they introduced method acting into the opera repertoire. The building was an enormous 18th-century mansion belonging to the Saltykov family; part of the original is preserved in the foyers and the grand staircase.

Russia's first department store

Ulitsa Petrovka, which leads off between the Bolshoi and Maly theatres, takes its name from the monastery at the top of the street. Built up after the Neglinnaya River was funnelled underground, Petrovka was inhabited by well-to-do traders, craftsmen and carriage-makers. Start exploring the street from behind the Bolshoi Theatre. On the right is **TsUM** ❿ (2 ulitsa Petrovka; www.tsum.ru), the Russian acronym for Central Department Store. It was the country's first department store, opened by the Scottish firm of Muir and Mirrielees.

The neo-Gothic pile was built in 1908 by Roman Klein, using revolutionary steel-and-concrete techniques. Chekhov and his family bought everything here, and the writer named his two farm dogs Muir and Mirrielees.

While middle-class shoppers are well served by TsUM, the more well-to-do head for the elegant **Petrovsky Passage** ⓫ at No. 10. This style *moderne* structure, built in 1903 as an elite arcade, has resumed its reputation for high prices despite the Revolutionary statues added in 1920.

Upper Peter Monastery ⓬

Address: corner of ulitsa Petrovka and Petrovsky bulvar
Opening Hrs: daily 9am–8pm
Entrance Fee: free
Transport: Chekhovskaya

According to legend, Tsar Ivan I was passing a snow-covered hill, when suddenly the snow melted. Seeing it as a sign, he had a church built on the site, and by 1330 it was part of the Upper Peter Monastery (*Vysokopetrovsky monastyr*). The complex was rebuilt several times, notably by the Naryshkin family, who are buried here.

Upper Peter Monastery.

TsUM at dusk.

A fine Baroque bell tower leads to four churches, including the impressive **Church of the Icon of the Mother of God of Bogolyubovo** (*Bogolyubsky sobor*) at the entrance, and the **Church of the Metropolitan Peter** (*Tserkov Petra-Metropolita*), built in 1517 by the Italian architect Aleviz Novyi.

Moscow Museum of Contemporary Art

Address: 25 ulitsa Petrovka;
www.mmoma.ru
Tel: 495-231 4406
Opening Hrs: Fri–Wed noon–8pm,
Thu 1–9pm
Entrance Fee: charge
Transport: Chekhovskaya

Across the street in a lovely 18th-century manor house is the Moscow Museum of Contemporary Art (*Moskovsky muzey Sovremennovo iskusstva*). Based on the private collection of Zurab Tsereteli and featuring rather more of his works than one might like, the museum is attempting to fill in the lost years of Soviet non-conformist art. There are only a few canvases of note by such artists as Oscar Ryabin and Anatoly Zverev. Early 20th-century art on the second floor includes works by

New Opera, Hermitage Gardens.

Chagal, Kandinsky, Rodchenko and some truly excellent Malevich canvases. A kiosk by the entrance sells art books and contemporary artworks.

The Hermitage Gardens

Ulitsa Petrovka continues across Tsverskoy Boulevard, with its plethora of cafés and restaurants, and becomes **ulitsa Karetny Ryad** (Carriage Row), named after carriage-makers who lived and worked here. The **Hermitage Gardens** (*sad Ermitazh*) on the left is a well-kept pleasure garden with an illustrious history. It opened in 1894 with pavilions and theatres, including one in which the Lumiére brothers showed the first film in Russia and where the Moscow Art Theatre performed Chekhov's plays until their own theatre was completed. Filled with cafés, the garden is the venue of music festivals. The **New Opera** next door (3 ulitsa Karetny Ryad) stages traditional and unconventional musical theatre.

Four boulevards

At the intersection of ulitsa Petrovka and the Boulevard Ring, Petrovsky

THE FATE OF 20TH-CENTURY ART

After the great avant-garde innovations of art during the Revolutionary period, officially sanctioned art in the USSR was Socialist Realism: glorified workers and peasants portrayed bringing peace and prosperity to the Soviet people and little else was tolerated. 'Non-conformist' art (anything that was non-representational and did not conform to official canons) was banned from public exhibition, and non-conformist artists were persecuted, jailed, incarcerated in psychiatric hospitals or packed off to Siberia. Between the 1960s and 1980s, many of the Soviet Union's greatest works of this underground art were sold to a handful of insightful private Western collectors; a few curators at the Tretyakov and other Russian museums used state funds to buy some works. The turning point came with the Sotheby auction of Russian contemporary art in 1988: a painting by an unknown artist, Grisha Bruskin, sold for more than $400,000. Suddenly 'non-conformist' art was hot. But back in the USSR, when the Gorbachev reforms threw open the country's doors, many artists left with their works or signed exclusive contracts with foreign galleries. Several generations of contemporary art had disappeared from Russia.

bulvar slides gracefully downhill to the east amid lush greenery and pastel buildings. At the bottom of the hill four boulevards intersect: Petrovsky, Rozhdestvensky, Neglinnaya and Tsvetnoy. This is **Trubnaya ploshchad**, once a noisy, swampy square with The Crimea, Hell and other infamous taverns of cardsharps, crooks, swindlers, merchants and provincials looking for diversion. In the 19th century the green-and-white building on the corner of Petrovsky and Neglinnaya (No. 14), now a theatre, housed the Hermitage restaurant whose French chef, Olivier, invented the now ubiquitous Russian salad 'Olivier'.

Neglinnaya ulitsa stretches south from Trubnaya ploshchad to just above Theatre Square. One of the most important landmarks on the street owes its existence to the former Neglinnaya River. In 1806 an actor named Sandunov built a stone bathhouse by the river bank, at No. 14. In 1896 a complex of elegant buildings opened here, known as the **Sandunovsky Bathhouse** ❶ (entrance is on Zvonarsky pereulok, on the right one block up; tel: 495-625 4631; www.sanduny.ru; daily 10am–11pm; see page 166). The men's side is lavishly decorated with columns and statues. The women's is smaller and less ornate, but elegant nevertheless.

Moscow Circus ❶

Address: 13 Tsvetnoy bulvar
Tel: 495-780 3133
Entrance Fee: charge
Transport: Tsvetnoy Bulvar

To the north of Trubnaya ploshchad is one of the city's most famous entertainments, Moscow Circus (*Moskovsky tsirk im. Nikulina*). Founded in 1880, the circus became popular in the last century when Yuri Nikulin, a brilliant clown, singer and actor, made it a national institution. As with many Russian circuses, acts include performing lions, bears and tigers, along with tight-rope walkers, trapeze artists and clowns. Audience members can also pay to have their photo taken in the lobby taken with a chimpanzee, a bear or even one of the big cats, which animal-lovers may find unsettling.

A kilometre and a half (a mile) to the north, across the Garden Ring

Moscow Circus.

The Bathhouse

Whether a simple village log house or an elegant city building, the bathhouse – *banya* – is a beloved tradition across the Russian Federation.

Russians firmly believe that steaming cures a variety of ailments, rids the body of toxins, relieves stress and revives both body and soul. Many have a regular bath day with friends, chatting and drinking tea between the steam rooms. For women there are pampering massages, manicures and pedicures, for men beer and conversation.

Bring plastic slippers, shampoo, soap, hand cream, comb and brush. Bathhouses provide hairdryers and usually sell flip-flops, shampoo and bath gel or soap. Men and women have separate facilities. At the door, buy your ticket and ask for a sheet (*prostyn*), towels (*polotensta*) and cloakroom (*khranenie*). You might also buy a felt hat and a bunch of birch branches, which are soaked in hot water to soften them so you can beat yourself, or have yourself beaten, to improve circulation.

Bathhouses have three sections: a changing room, often with separate cabins,

Steam room in a banya.

a washing room with marble benches and lined with shower stalls, and a steam room. City bathhouses usually have saunas (dry heat) and cold-water pools, as well as additional massage rooms, barber shops and hair salons.

After disrobing and checking in your valuables, wrap yourself in a sheet (or not, as you wish) and head for the steam room, a wood-lined room with a huge stove and tiered benches. Some announce 'steam time', others let patrons handle the steam themselves. First rule for novices: sit on the bottom bench and cover your head with a towel or bathhouse hat, and your shoulders with a sheet. Only experienced bathers should sit on the top benches, where the temperature is highest. Second rule: no talking. Steaming is serious business.

The attendant will close the door, open the stove hatch and begin to ladle hot water on the red-hot rocks. Usually there is a pause at some point, when the attendant will spray water mixed with aromatic oils on the ceiling or wave a towel to force the steam to descend. After more water is tossed on the rocks and everyone agrees the temperature is just right (which can be over 66°C/150°F), the stove door is closed, and everyone waits. After a minute the steam will descend like a blanket of fire (which is why your shoulders should be covered), and for several minutes you sit and sweat.

From the steam room, head straight for the cold water pool and plunge in. After 10 seconds of feeling you are about to die, you receive a jolt of energy: your skin tingles and you think you could run a marathon. If the pool is too daunting, try taking a cool shower or pouring water over your head from one of the plastic tubs available. Once you're refreshed, you can go back into the steam room where, for a fee, you can lie on a bench and have an attendant whip you with birch branches. When you feel like jelly, it's time for water, tea or beer. The ritual is several steams interspersed with massages and, for women, other pampering.

When your skin is marbled and soft, it's time for a final shower. As you leave, the attendants will say *S loykhim parom*, a hope that the steam was light and refreshing.

Road, is another Moscow institution, **Durov's Circle** ⓱ (*ugolok Durova*; 4 ulitsa Durova; www.ugolokdurova.ru; tel: 495-631 3047). The Durov family has been training animals since 1894, and performances are a delight.

Obrazstov Puppet Theatre ⓲

Address: 3 Sadovaya-Sarnotyochnaya; www.puppet.ru
Tel: 495-699 5373
Entrance Fee: charge
Transport: Tsvetnoy Bulvar

For the full experience of the city's light-hearted entertainments, see an innovative and sophisticated show at the Obrazstov Puppet Theatre (*Gosudarstvenny akademichesky tsentralny teatr kukol*). Every hour the little doors on the facade open and a puppet pops out.

Museum of Decorative and Applied Art and Folk Art ⓳

Address: 3 Delegatskaya ulitsa; www.vmdpni.ru
Tel: 495-609 0146
Opening Hrs: Mon, Wed, Fri and Sun

10am–6pm, Thu 10am–9pm, Sat noon–8pm; closed last Mon of the month
Transport: Tsvetnoy Bulvar

In a sprawling mansion off the Garden Ring Road where ulitsa Karetny Ryad ends is the Museum of Decorative and Applied Art and Folk Art (*Muzey dekorativno-prikadnovo i narodnovo iskusstva*). It has an extensive collection of crafts, folk costumes and applied arts.

Dostoyevsky Memorial Museum ⓴

Address: 2 ulitsa Dostoyevskovo; www.goslitmuz.ru
Tel: 495-681 1085
Opening Hrs: Tue and Fri–Sun 11am–6pm, Wed–Thu 2–9pm; closed last day of the month
Transport: Novoslobodskaya

In a wing of what was the Mariinsky Hospital for the Indigent is the **Dostoyevsky Memorial Museum** (*Muzey-kvartiry F.M. Dostoyevskovo*). This 19th-century furnished apartment is where Fyodor, the son of a struggling doctor, grew up.

Bear statue on the V. L. Durov Animal Theatre.

Art at the Museum of Decorative and Applied Art and Folk Art.

Monument to the Conquerors of Space,
and statue of Konstantin Tsiolkovsky.

ЦИОЛКОВСКИЙ

ОСНОВОПОЛОЖНИК
КОСМОНАВТИКИ

LUBYANKA AND THE NORTH

Sense the sinister power of the Soviet state in Lubyanka Square, erstwhile headquarters of the infamous KGB. Not far away is the fantastic Futurist museum of Vladimir Mayakovsky. Further from the centre is a museum to Russia's cosmonauts and the delightful private theatre of the Ostankino Estate.

This chapter begins at Lubyanka, the notorious former headquarters of the KGB, and ends in Moscow's northern suburbs at the VDNKh (see page 176), a collage of golden fountains and buildings recalling Soviet ambitions. There is also a monastery, a convent and smart shopping on Kuznetsky Most. The highlights, however, are two intriguing museums: the experimental museum to Futurist poet Vladimir Mayakovsky, and the fascinating Museum of Cosmonautics.

Lubyanka and the KGB

The word 'Lubyanka' is indelibly associated with the square's main tenant: the KGB, who had their headquarters here until they were disbanded in the early 1990s. Before December 1917, **Lubyanskaya ploshchad** ❶ was a bustling trading area filled with carters and carriage drivers who plied their services with nothing more sinister than cheap taverns for the drivers. But the new Soviet power expropriated the 1898 Russia Insurance Company building, which dominates the square, for the secret police. They stripped its facade and built around and under the square to occupy most of the expanse. In the early post-Soviet days the building

housed the KGB Museum, but this closed a long time ago as the political weather in Russia changed. The grey building on the northeastern side of Lubyanskaya ploshchad is the former **Lubyanka Prison**, now the headquarters of the FSB (Federal Security Service), today's KGB. It goes without saying that no part of the building is open to the public. The square is also a popular meeting place for Moscow's die-hard Communists.

Opposite the KGB building is the enormous **Detsky Mir** ❷ (Children's

Main Attractions

Lubyanka
Detsky Mir
Polytechnic Museum
Mayakovsky Museum
Perlov Tea Shop
Chistye Prudy
VDNKh
Ostankino Estate Museum
Ostankino Television
  Complex

Map

Page 171

Looking out over Lubyanskaya Square.

World; daily 9am–9pm), opened here because one of the KGB's founders, 'Iron' Felix Dzerzhinsky, had an interest in child welfare. This huge department store is unmissable if you're travelling with children; adults will enjoy the panoramic city centre views from the top floor.

The **Polytechnic Museum** ❸ (*Politekhnichesky muz*ey; ¾ Novaya ploshchad) is in the frothy building that fills an entire block on the southeast side of Lubyanskaya ploshchad. It was established as early as 1872 by the Imperial Society of Amateur Naturalists, Anthropologists and Ethnographers and located in a Russian Revival building completed five years later. Today its extensive collection of every kind of technological gadget is under renovation and the museum is set to reopen with a modern, Western, rebranded feel. Sadly no one seems to know when that might be.

In front of the museum is the **Monument to the Victims of the Totalitarian Regime**, a simple stone brought from the island monastery that became the Solovky prison camp in Russia's far north. Remembrance

ceremonies are held at the monument on 30 October each year.

The pale-blue mansion just north of the Lubyanka Building on ulitsa Bolshaya Lubyanka is the Rostopchin House, where the eponymous Governor General of Moscow lived. It was Rostopchin who ordered Moscow to be set ablaze when Napoleon and his army entered the city in 1812 (see page 36).

Churches and monasteries

On the western side, just before ulitsa Bolshaya Lubyanka meets the Boulevard Ring, is the **Sretensky Monastery** ❹. Founded in 1397 and restored to the Church in 1994, it includes the **Church of the Icon of the Vladimir Mother of God** (*Tserkov Ikony Vladimirskoy Bogomal*eri), nestled in a peaceful garden behind the monastery's white stone fence decorated with tiles and icons. The icon is supposed to have invoked a vision of the Virgin Mary which convinced the Turco-Mongol conqueror Tamerlane not to attack the city in 1395, and it has been one of Russia's most revered icons ever since.

At the top of Rozhdestvensky bulvar, where ulitsa Bolshaya Lubyanka

Sretensky Monastery.

Nadezhda Krupskaya statue.

crosses the Boulevard Ring to become ulitsa Sretenka, sits the cosy white **Church of the Dormition of the Mother of God ❺** (*Tserkov Uspeniya Bogoroditsy*), built in 1695 and rebuilt in 1902, with elaborate *kokoshniki* gables and a gold dome. An art gallery in the Soviet period, it is once again a church, its bare interior relieved by a fresco above the portal. The religious-looking statue across the street in the park is in fact **Nadezhda Krupskaya**, Lenin's wife.

The Boulevard Ring drops from Sretenskie vorota down a hill so steep that extra horses were once required to pull the trams up it. This stretch is Rozhdestvensky bulvar (Nativity Boulevard), which is named after the **Nativity of the Mother of God Convent ❻** (*Bogorodilse-Rozhdeslveny monastyr;* daily 8am–8pm) whose fortified walls line its south side. The convent was founded in 1386 and was a place for unwanted wives, most famously the wife of Grand Prince Vasily III, Solomonia, who was sent to the nunnery for her inability to bear children, but gave birth soon after her arrival. She pretended the child had died and had him spirited away

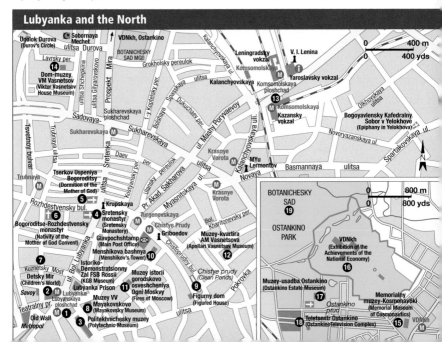

to the south, where he became a war-lord. A grave containing a doll was found in the monastery in 1930. The convent is under reconstruction, but still tidy and peaceful. Most impressive is the 16th- to 18th-century **Cathedral of the Nativity** (*sabar Razhestva Bogoroditsy*), a white stone church with clusters of gables.

'Smithy's Bridge'

Ulitsa Rozhestvenka leads south to Kuznetsky Most and past the pretty **Church of St Nicholas of the Bellringers** at No. 15 and the pale-green and tiled **Architectural Institute** at No. 9. The section of **Kuznetsky Most ❼** between Rozh-destvensky and Neglinnaya ulitsas is worth further exploration. This was once the 'Smithy's Bridge', which crossed the Neglinnaya River until the water was shuttled underground in the early 19th century. Its paving blocks were used to lay out Moscow's most aristocratic shopping street, filled with dozens of French fashion and jewellery shops that were so small that one writer said he felt like Gulliver among the Lilliputians. Kuznetsky Most has not reclaimed its

Menshikov's Tower.

former glory, but it's trying: Versace and Valentino have shops here, as does Fabergé (at No. 20).

Mayakovsky Museum ❽

Address: 3/6 Lubyansky proezd
Tel: 495-621 9075
Opening Hrs: Fri–Tue 10am–5pm, Thu 1–8pm; closed last Fri of the month
Entrance Fee: admission and photo charges
Transport: Lubyanka

Myasnitskaya ulitsa, 'Butcher's Street', is named after the meat stores that predominated here. It begins at the eastern corner of Lubyanskaya ploshchad. A monumental bust of Futurist poet Vladimir Mayakovsky peers from a portal in the Mayakovsky Museum (*Muzey v.v. Mayakovskovo*). Walk up to the fourth floor to the small room where Mayakovsky lived the last 11 years of his life, and where he shot himself in the heart on 14 April 1930. Then enter a maelstrom of

Constructivist and Futurist madness, which spirals down a ramp through twists of girders, displays of photographs piled willy-nilly around old furniture, Mayakovsky's hand-drawn posters, Constructivist drawings and models, manuscripts, letters, posters and photographs of his plays. The exhibitions are designed to plunge you into the dizzying days when Mayakovsky wrote the essay 'A Slap in the Face of Public Taste', and the artistic and literary avant-garde thought they had overthrown Russia's moribund culture along with the tsar.

The bright-blue Baroque mansion behind the FSB building was once the town house of the Saltykov-Chertikov family and is now a cultural centre. You can't miss the **Perlov Tea Shop**, decorated in lavish fake Chinese style – supposedly to impress the Chinese ambassador on his state visit in 1893. The envoy never turned up, but the pagoda still graces the roof. Next to it on the right is the Moscow School of Painting, Sculpture and Architecture, founded in 1844. Mayakovsky was one of its students.

Myasnitskaya ulitsa meets the Boulevard Ring at Turgenevskaya ploshchad, with the modern **Lukoil Building** on one side, the **Main Post Office** (*Glavpochshtamp*) on the other, and a statue of the playwright Alexander Griboyedov in the centre.

Clean ponds

The broad park in the boulevard is called **Chistye Prudy** ❾ (Clean Ponds). Once called 'Foul Ponds', because butchers on Myasnitskaya ulitsa dumped their waste here, in 1739 the ponds were cleaned and renamed, but only one remains. It is graced by swans in summer and ice-skaters in winter. This expensive area is filled with cafés and restaurants serving wealthy residents and businesses.

It is a pleasant stroll along the park, but you may wish to take a detour into what was once the Armenian neighbourhood. Turn south on Archangelsky pereulok and you'll soon see the gold spire of the Church of the Archangel Gabriel (*Tserkov Arkhangela Gavriila*), commonly called **Menshikov's Tower** ❿ (*Menshikova bashnya*). It was completed in 1707 by Prince Menshikov, Peter the Great's close friend, in imitation of Western religious architecture. The archangel that once topped its salmon-pink tower was destroyed when the tower was struck by lightning. It was replaced with a more modest finial in 1780. In the courtyard is the Antioch Patriarch's Court.

The Fires of Moscow ⓫

Address: 3/5 Armyansky pereulok, str.l, code 1
Tel: 495-924 7374
Opening Hrs: daily 11am–5pm
Entrance Fee: charge
Transport: Lubyanka

In nearby Armyansky pereulok is an offbeat museum called The Fires of Moscow (*Muzey istorii gorodskovo osveshcheniya Ogni Moskvy*). The museum has lights and lamps from

Shoppers on Kuznetsky Most.

1730 to the present, and the friendly staff run unusual city light tours.

Apollinary Vasnetsov Memorial Flat ⑫

Address: Furmanny pereulok, apt 22
Tel: 495-208 9045
Opening Hrs: Wed–Sun 10am–5pm
Entrance Fee: charge
Transport: Chistye Prudy, Krasnye Vorota

The area beyond the Boulevard Ring holds some unique attractions, which are best reached via metro. East of Lermontovskaya ploshchad, two long blocks from Krasnye Vorota metro station, turn right on Furmanny pereulok and enter the quiet neighbourhood where the painter Apollinary Vasnetsov lived for the last 30 years of his life, until 1933. The Apollinary Vasnetsov Memorial Flat (*Muzey-kvartira A.M. Vasnetsova*) displays his study and living room, with furniture he designed, and wonderful paintings and drawings of old Moscow.

Moscow's stations

*People outside
Leningrad Station.*

'Three Station Square' is the popular name for **Komsomolskaya ploshchad**

Yaroslavl Station.

⑬, a hopeless confusion of car parks, dreary cafés and myriad kiosks. The three magnificent train stations here deserve a far better backdrop but are rather lost in the melee. Each reflects the city or country it serves: the Leningrad station (opened in 1851 by Tsar Nicholas I and his family) duplicates, in smaller form, the classical masterpiece of the Nicholas station in St Petersburg – there are countless television and film skits about drunken travellers unable to understand what city they are in. **Yaroslavl station**, a masterpiece of neo-Russian fantasy built in 1902 by Fyodor Shekhtel, mimics the walls and fortresses of Moscow and Yaroslavl. It is the western terminus of the world's longest railway route, the Trans Siberian. The **Kazan Station**, built in 1926 by Alexander Shchusev, is reminiscent of Kazan's fortress walls. Between 1925 and 1927 Shchusev also designed and built the ornamented brick-and-stone

Central House of Culture for Railway Workers across from Kazan station. It is one of Moscow's finest 'worker's cultural centres'.

Vasnetsov Museum and Prospekt Mira

The once important road leading to the Holy Trinity Monastery of St Sergius (see page 205) was built over by **Prospekt Mira** (Peace Avenue), the least pleasing of the Stalinist highways. However, not far north from Prospekt Mira metro station is a gem, the **House-Museum** of the artist **Viktor Vasnetsov** ⓮ (*dom-muzey V.M. Vasnetsova;* 13 pereulok Vasnetsova; tel: 495-681 1329; Wed–Sun 10am–5pm; closed last Thu of the month; charge).

Tucked amid a depressing conglomeration of rough tower blocks and tin garages is this small fairy-tale house designed by the prolific artist, architect and set designer Viktor Vasnetsov in 1894. It was his home and studio until his death in 1926. The interior is decorated in an utterly charming late 19th-century Russian combination of *style moderne* and folk art.

South of the Olympic Stadium, Moscow's **main mosque** (*Sobornaya Mechet*) rises incongruously on pereulok Vypolzov. The original 1904 building was controversially demolished in 2011 and what you see today is a new incarnation designed to hold over 10,000 worshippers. The president of Turkey, Recep Tayyip Erdoğan, today one of the Kremlin's biggest adversaries, was present at the opening of the new mosque in 2015.

Museum of Cosmonautics ⓯

Address: 111 Prospekt Mira; www.kosmo-museum.ru
Tel: 495-683 7914
Opening Hrs: Tue, Wed and Fri–Sun 10am–7pm; closed last Fri of the month
Entrance Fee: admission, photo and video charges
Transport: VDNKh

In 1964 a huge space-rocket obelisk was erected at the intersection of Prospekt Mira and Ostankinsky pereulok in honour of Yuri Gagarin's first manned space mission on 12 April 1961. The rocket towers nearly

Museum of Cosmonautics.

100 metres (330ft) over the Alley of Cosmonauts, with busts of the USSR's first men and women in space and a statue to Konstantin Tsyolkovsky (1857–1913), the father of Russian cosmonautics. It also houses the Museum of Cosmonautics (*Muzey Kosmonavtiki*). The largest part of the exhibition is devoted to Gagarin's flight. Be sure to note the first dogs in space, Belka and Strelka, who have been stuffed for posterity. Khrushchev gave Jacqueline Kennedy one of Strelka's puppies, so space-dog progeny may still be roaming the US.

The majestic arches behind are the entrance to the grandly named **VDNKh** ⑯ (*Vystavka Dostizheniy Narodnogo Khozyaystva*; Exhibition of the Achievements of the National Economy; www.vdnh.ru; daily 9am–7pm), which you walk to via a bustling market of CDs, DVDs and other items, which attract gaggles of teenagers. This Stalinist exhibition centre opened in 1959 and today the buildings, mosaics, statues and glorious fountain still comprise the country's finest collection of Socialist Realism statuary. In 2014, the centre was spruced up after a couple of decades in the doldrums, the various pavilions now housing myriad exhibitions on topics ranging from Russian history to Moscow's fashion industry. There are also sports facilities and events to enjoy, from ice hockey to horse riding.

Ostankino Estate Museum ⑰

Address: 5 1-ya ulitsa Ostankinskaya; www.ostankino-museum.ru
Tel: 495-602 1852
Opening Hrs: Currently closed for rennovation – please see website for further details.
Entrance Fee: admission, photo and video charges
Transport: VDNKh

From the VDNKh turn right on Ostankinsky pereulok and left on ulitsa Akademika Korolyova, following the small elevated monorail, and after a 20-minute walk among faceless estates, you'll come to one of Moscow's most delightful palaces, the Ostankino Estate Museum (*Muzey-usadba Ostankino*). When Count Nikolay Sheremetev became bored with the old family manse at Kuskovo

Ostankino Palace.

Ostankino TV tower.

(see page 195), he decided to remodel a neglected family estate in Ostankino. Passionate about theatre, he envisioned a Theatre Palace where guests would be both actors and spectators. The Theatre Palace, built from 1793 to 1797 and used for just four years, was meant for summer pleasures. In the luxurious Italian Pavilion the count's guests would gather before the evening's opera or concert. This 'theatre within a theatre' has a stage 22 metres (72ft) deep and 17 metres (56ft) wide that opens to a circular seating area, ringed by a balcony. The enormous columns could be moved to change scenes; wooden machines made the sounds of wind, thunder and rain (the last by tossing dried peas down a chute lined with curved metal blades).

Another part of the museum displays an exhibition of the dazzling and ingenious lighting fixtures that were essential to the theatricality of the count's entertainments.

Just past the palace stands the **Ostankino Television Complex ⑱** (www.tvtower.ru; Tue–Sun 10am–8pm)

– the production-and-broadcasting studios that were stormed in the second coup attempt of 1993 – and the 540-metre (1,770ft) television tower. In August 2000 fire swept through the tower, but it has since been renovated. There are panoramic, 360-degree views from the top. Tours leave hourly but you must book in advance and bring photo ID (passport).

Botanical Gardens ⑲

Address: 4 ulitsa Botanicheskaya
Tel: 499-977 9145 (to arrange orangery tours)
Opening Hrs: gardens open all year during daylight
Entrance Fee: charge
Transport: Vladykino

If you walk past the TV centre to the end of ulitsa Akademika Korolyova and turn right on Botanicheskaya ulitsa, you will come to the main entrance to the Botanical Gardens (*Botanichesky sad*). The gardens have an astounding 16,000 types of flora, ranging from the tropics to the tundra, all laid out in an beautifully landscaped park.

Moscow Botanical Gardens.

IVANOVSKAYA HILL TO TAGANKA

Explore the quiet lanes and grand mansions of this area rich in places of worship and old monasteries. This was where the city's first Stalinist skyscraper was erected and, by way of contrast, the location of the Theatre on Taganka.

Moscow's southeast section once had a reputation for debauchery and imprisonment. Now it is made up of quiet little lanes lined with old mansions, the city's oldest Stalinist skyscraper and one of its most experimental theatres.

The 'Little Russia' quarter

This tour begins just south of the Polytechnic Museum (see page 170), where a large boulevard (called Lubyansky proezd on the eastern side and Staraya ploshchad on the western side) slopes down past ulitsa Varvarka to the Moscow River.

The tree-shaded park in the centre of this boulevard is called the **Ilinsky Gardens ❶** (*Ilinskie sady*, named after the Ilinsky Gates that once stood at the end of the street Ilinka) and has monuments at each end. The bell-like monument across from the Polytechnic Museum is dedicated to the Russian soldiers who died in 1878 while defending the Bulgarian city of Plevna from the Turks.

At the bottom of the hill, on Slavyanskaya ploshchad, is the monument to Cyril and Methodius (*Kirill i Metodiy*), Greek monk-scholars and patron saints of all the Slavs who developed the Cyrillic alphabet to translate the Bible in the 9th

century. Across from the statue is the bright little **Church of All Saints in Kulishkakh**, originally built to honour the dead of the battle of Kulikovo Fields in 1380.

Ulitsa Maroseyka runs to the east of the Polytechnic Museum and becomes ulitsa Pokrovka before it crosses the Boulevard Ring. The word Maroseyka is a corruption of the Russian word for 'Little Russia', which – in the big Russian Empire – meant Ukraine. In the 17th century the Ukrainian representative had his

Main Attractions
Choral Synagogue
Foreign Literature Library
Theatre on Taganka
Museum of Vysotsky
Andrey Rublyov Museum

Map
Page 180

Morozov's mansion.

headquarters here in a bright-blue mansion at No. 17, now the **Belarus Embassy**, and the area was inhabited by a mix of foreigners and local families. Maroseyka and Pokrovka ulitsas are now lined by a rather garish assortment of shops and restaurants, but the streets to the right that twist and curve down towards the river on Ivanovskaya Hill are filled with little churches and mansions.

Ivanovskaya Hill

The highlight of the area is a walk down **Kolpachny pereulok** ❷ past four unique mansions on the left side: one Gothic (No. 5), the next bright blue-green Baroque, the next a little pink classical jewel box and the last (No. 11) in *style moderne*. They were all built by wealthy traders in the 19th century as dwellings. *Kolpachny* means the street of hatmakers. *Khokhlovsky* means the street of Ukrainians, from the word *khokhol*, the characteristically Ukrainian long

tuft of hair at the brow (beware, this is now a derogative term for Russia's southern neighbour).

At the bottom of the hill, turn left up Khokhlovsky pereulok past the walled gardens and pistachio-coloured **Morozov Mansion** that was once owned by the Old Believer Morozova, and follow along two sharp bends, between which stands the **Trinity Church** (*Troitskaya tserkov*), a magnificent example of Naryshkin Baroque – and, just before it, an odd white warehouse building decorated with dark-red paint. This 17th-century dwelling was the archives of the Russian Foreign Service and, oddly enough, one of the favourite spots for Russia's golden artistic youth in the 19th century. Writers like Pushkin and Turgenev (and composers including Tchaikovsky) whiled away the hours here, plumbing the empire's ancient documents for raw material.

Ivanovskaya Hill has several landmarks to Moscow's non-Russian

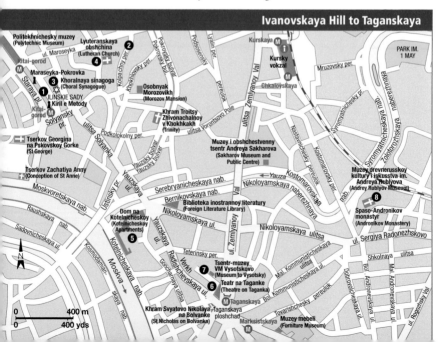

Kotelnicheskoy apartments.

River. From 1826 to 1923 this area was the labour market Khitrovka – a foul, swampy mass of tenement houses and taverns with names like 'Transit Camp', 'Siberia' and 'Hard Labour', filled with prostitutes of every age and both genders, thieves, escaped convicts and murderers. The area on the south side of the Yauza River was first inhabited by craftsmen who settled here so that the river would protect the city from any blaze that might be ignited as they worked. Today the community's little churches and lanes are dwarfed by the Stalinist skyscraper on the embankment, the first of the city's seven to be completed (1948–52). This skyscraper is the **Kotelnicheskoy apartments** ❺ (*Dom na Kotelnicheskoy*), once given to the Party's faithful but now sold for prices as high as its Stalinist spire.

Across the street on the same side of the Yauza is the four-storeyed brick-and-glass office block of the

The interior of the Choral Synagogue.

population. The yellow-and-white classical-style **Choral Synagogue** ❸ (*Moskovskaya khoralnaya sinagoga*) has been standing at 10 Bolshoy Spasoglinishchevsky pereulok for well over 100 turbulent years. Synagogue construction was banned in Kitai-gorod, so this ornate building stands just outside the line of its former walls.

On Starosadsky pereulok the beige-and-brown Gothic-style **Lutheran Church** ❹ (*Lyuteransky sobor*) is located at No. 7/10. Built in 1812 and then rebuilt between 1903 and 1905, it was the venue of a charity organ concert by Franz Liszt in 1843. Interestingly, the clock from the destroyed tower of this church adorns the former KGB building on Lubyanka Square.

Beyond the Yauza

The last leg of the Boulevard Ring slopes gently down to the southeast from ulitsa Pokrovka to the Yauza

Foreign Literature Library, a one-stop foreign culture shop housing the American Centre, British Council and French Cultural Centre (1 Nikoloyamskaya ulitsa).

Taganka

At the top of the hill (follow Yauzas-kaya ulitsa) is Taganskaya ploschchad, commonly called 'Taganka' and named for the craftsmen who made *tagan*, iron stands that held cooking cauldrons. 'Taganka' is a word rich in associations for Russians. From 1804 to the 1950s, one of Moscow's most infamous prisons was located not far from here. The prison and the trials of Russians have been immortalised in dozens of folk songs still sung today by students and anyone sitting around the table with a guitar and an urge for liberty (and sentimentality).

In the 1960s, the spirit of Taganka was continued at the capital's most popular theatre, Yuri Lyubimov's **Theatre on Taganka** . The most freedom-loving personality of the

Performance at the Taganka Theatre.

Andrei Rublev statue, Andronikov Monastery.

theatre was the famous Vladimir Vysotsky (1938–80), a hard-drinking, hard-loving, raspy-voiced songwriter, singer and actor, whose songs were passed around the country on boot-legged tapes. When he died of a heart attack during the 1980 Moscow Olympics, over 10,000 people flocked to the theatre from all over the country. He's still a celebrated figure in Russia and the former Soviet Union.

In the square across from the theatre is the pretty brick and white **Church of St Nicholas on Bolvanka**, built in 1697–1712. Behind it is the early Baroque **Church of the Dormition of the Holy Mother of God in Gonchari**, built in 1654.

Museum of Vysotsky ❼

Address: 3 Nizhny Tagansky tupik
Tel: 495-915 7578
Opening Hrs: Tue–Sat 11am–6pm
Entrance Fee: charge
Transport: Taganskaya

Not far from the Theatre on Taganka, there is a small Museum to Vysotsky (*Tsentrmuzey V.M. Vysotskovo*), just before you reach the square via Yauska ulitsa, with memorabilia, documents and photographs of his life in theatre, film and with his family.

Andrey Rublyov Museum ❽

Address: 10 Andronevskaya ulitsa; www.rublev-museum.ru
Tel: 495-678 1467
Opening Hrs: Sat–Tue 11am–6pm, Thu 2–9pm; closed last Fri of the month
Entrance Fee: admission and photo charges
Transport: Taganskaya

Bolshaya Kommunisticheskaya ulitsa ends at Andronevskaya ploschad, which is dominated by the robin's-egg-blue **Church of St Sergius of Radonezh in Rogozhkaya** settlement, built in the 18th and 19th centuries. Across the roundabout to the east is a square with a statue of Andrey Rublyov before the **Saviour-Andronikov Monastery** which is home to the icon-packed **Andrey Rublyov Central Museum of Old Russian Art and Culture**. Built in 1360, it is the oldest fortress-monastery extant in Moscow. Its thick white walls and towers topped by tent roofs (built in the 17th century) conceal a peaceful cloister, now dominated by two churches.

The three-tiered, airy **Church of the Archangel of Michael** was built in the 17th and 18th centuries; it was finished with funds provided by the first wife of Peter the Great, Evdokiya Lophukhina, and serves as a crypt for the Lopukin family.

Moscow's oldest stone church stands in the centre of the monastery, the **Cathedral of the Icon of the Saviour Not Made by Hands** (*Sobor Spasa Nerukotvornovo Obraza*). Built in the early 1400s with frescoes (now lost) by Andrey Rublyov, who served and was interred in this monastery, the church was rebuilt to its original appearance. The museum displays a rich collection of icons, including the 13th-century Icon of the Saviour Not Made by Hands that once graced the Cathedral.

The walls of Andronikov Monastery.

Monument to Peter the Great.

BEYOND THE RIVER

Outside Moscow's walled city, the 'Merchant Kings' made the area south of the river their home. They used their riches to build numerous churches and to found the Tretyakov Gallery, the world's finest collection of Russian art.

The tongue of land to the south of the Moscow River is called Zamoskvoreche ('Beyond the Moscow River'). This low, boggy land was filled with the royal family's gardens and small settlements of sheep-herders, minters and smithies. Representatives of the Golden Horde lived along the road that now bears the name ulitsa Bolshaya Ordynka which the princes took south to pay tribute to the Tatar khans. By the 16th century it had become the home of Ivan the Terrible's feared oprichniki. Later, musketeers, translators and Cossacks were billeted here to protect this vulnerable route from the south.

All that is left of these settlements are street names although there is still a mosque on Bolshaya Tatarskaya ulitsa where the Golden Horde Tatars once lived. After the mutiny of the musketeers, Peter the Great cleared the area of armed men, and it became empty and neglected. In the 19th century merchants bought cheap land for their factories and homes, eventually taking over Zamoskvoreche and transforming it into a 'separate country' of 'Merchant Kings'. One of these was Pavel Tretyakov, who built the Tretyakov Gallery to house his considerable collection of Russian art. The area is also renowned for its churches, mostly

built by rich merchants, in gratitude for their good fortune or in atonement for their sins. They are set on quiet lanes lined with the merchant homes that weave among the four main thoroughfares of Zamoskvoreche: Pyatnitskaya, Bolshaya Ordynka, Polyanka and Yakimanka.

Bog Island

To combat flooding, the Drainage Canal (Vodootvodny kanal) was cut in 1783, creating a long island called the Bog Island (*Bolotny ostrov*). It is

Main Attractions

Red October Chocolate Factory
Monument to Peter the Great and the 300th Anniversary of the Russian Navy
Church of the Martyr George the Victorious in Yendova
Tretyakov Gallery
New Tretyakov Gallery
Church of St Nicholas in Pyzhakh

Map

Page 186

The State Tretyakov Gallery.

joined to the 'mainland' of the city by one foot and four road bridges. The Great Stone Bridge ends by the Kremlin's Borovitsky Gates. It was built in 1645 and has been renovated at least six times, most recently in 1938. The next crossing (off Red Square) is the Great Moscow River Bridge, built in 1872 and rebuilt in 1938 – it was on this bridge that Russian opposition politician Boris Nemtsov was shot dead in 2015. Entering the island via these bridges gives great views of the Kremlin.

Bog Square

Over the Great Stone Bridge to the east is a park, **Bog Square ❶** (*Bolotnaya ploshchad*) where in 1774 Yemelian Pugachev, a Cossack from the Don River who had organised an uprising, was beheaded and quartered. Today there is a statue of the Realist painter Ilya Repin (1844–1940) in the square, and a statuary group called *Children Are the Victims*

'Children Are the Victims of Adults' Vices', by Ilya Repin, in Bog Square.

of Adults' Vices by the émigré artist Mikhail Shemyakin.

West of the wide thoroughfare off the Great Stone Bridge is one of

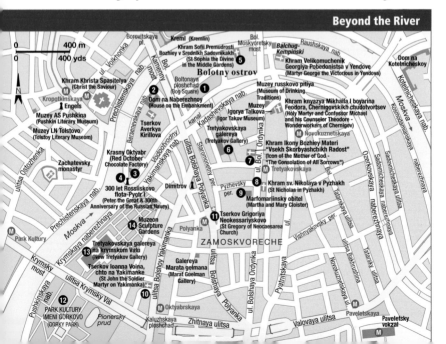

Moscow's most famous apartment houses, Government House; or the **House on the Embankment ❷** (*Dom na Naberezhnoy*). Commissioned in the late 1920s for high Communist Party officials, it has more than 500 apartments and 24 entrances. Once home to hundreds of ministers; under Stalin's purges its residents began to disappear: over 700 officials and their families were arrested, executed or exiled. The house was immortalised in Yuri Trifonov's 1976 novel *The House on the Embankment.*

On the west side of the apartment house is the former **Red October Chocolate Factory ❸** (*Krasny Oktyabr;* 4 Bersenevskaya naberezh-naya). Built by the young Berliner Theodore Einem and his partner Julius Heuss, in the mid-19th century, the factory is now an artists' community.

To the west of the Red October factory is Zurab Tsereteli's most controversial statue, the enormous **Monument to Peter the Great and the 300th Anniversary of the Russian Navy ❹**. Rumour has it that the sculpture was meant to be

of Christopher Columbus but was changed to Peter the Great when New York City refused it. Cross the Tsereteli-designed footbridge to see the Cathedral of Christ the Saviour (see page 129), another Tsereteli commission.

Sophia Embankment

The river bank between the Great Stone and Moscow River bridges is the Sophia Embankment, named after the church at No. 32. The house at No. 14 was built by architect Vasily Zalessky in 1893 and was famed for its Gothic interiors by Shekhtel. It was given to the British for their embassy in 1931, a decision Stalin rued: it annoyed him to see the Union flag from the Kremlin. In 2000 a new embassy opened and the mansion is now home to the British Ambassador. At No. 32 is the **Church of St Sophia the Divine in the Middle Gardens ❺** (*Khram Softi Premudrosti Bozhiey v Srednikh Sadovnikakh*), tucked behind a grand bell tower that houses a small church. The pale-pink, ornamented tower was built in 1868; the stone church, decorated with *kokoshniki,*

Buildings on Sophia Embankment.

delicate tiles and brickwork rising up to five cupolas of dark-green tiles, dates from 1682.

Balchug

If you continue along the Sophia Embankment, just past the Moscow River Bridge is an area called Balchug, now home to the elegant Balchug-Kempinski Hotel. The word *balchug* meant 'market' (which existed here centuries ago) or 'mud' (which has existed here since time immemorial). Behind the hotel, on ulitsa Nizhnikh Sadovnikakh, is the dark-red 1653 **Church of the Martyr George the Victorious in Yendova** (*Khram Velikomuchenik Georgiya Pobedonitsa v Yendove*). The church is stunning, with a pyramid of *kokoshniki* rising to five domes and decorative stone-work around the windows. The bell tower collapsed during a flood and was rebuilt in 1806 in a boxy clas-sical style. The wooden cross com-memorates the victims of the Gulag

The Balchug-Kempinski Hotel.

Ride, 1832, by Karl Brylluv, on display at the Tretyakov Gallery.

at Solovky Monastery, with which the church is associated. The church is open for services.

Tretyakov Gallery ❻

Address: Lavrushinsky pereulok 10; www.tretyakovgallery.ru
Tel: 495-629 4435
Opening Hrs: Tue–Sun 10am–6pm, Thu–Fri until 9pm
Entrance Fee: charge
Transport: Okhotny Ryad, Aleksandrovsky Sad

By far the biggest attraction on the south bank of the Moskva River is one of the greatest collections of Russian art in the country. The fully renovated Tretyakov Gallery (*Tretyakovskaya Galereya*) spans 1,000 years of Russian art, from early icons to 20th-century works. The building itself is in the Russian style – an urban interpreta-tion of a boyar's mansion built in 1900 to house the collection accumu-lated by the brothers Pavel and Sergei

Tretyakov in the late 19th century. The two men, who had made their fortunes in textiles, later donated their collection and palace to the state.

Most people begin their visit on the gallery's ground floor, where you'll find the remarkable icon collection including the Byzantine *Mother of God of Vladimir* and Andrey Rublyov's 15th-century *The Trinity*. You'll find 17th- and 18th-century portraits upstairs, along with treasures of Russian realism and grand historical canvases. The Tretyakov collection is designed to be seen chronologically, starting on the upper floor (signs in English point the way). Hall numbers above the doors refer to the rooms after the doorway, not the room you are in; English maps and an audioguide are available.

Beyond the gallery

At No. 21 ulitsa Bolshaya Ordynka, on the left just before Tretyakovskaya metro station, are the former Dolgov Mansion and, across the street at No. 20, the round yellow church built for this merchant family. The **Church of the Icon of the Mother of God 'The Consolation of All Sorrows'** ❼ (*Khram ikony Bozhiey Materi 'Vsekh Skorbyashchikh Radost'*) was the work

of Bazhenov, but all that remains of his original church after a fire is the bell tower (1790). Rebuilt in 1833 in the Empire style by Bové, it was closed from 1933 to 1948, but the interiors remained intact, including the church's icons.

On the right at No. 27a/28 is the delightful white stone **Church of St Nicholas in Pyzhakh** ❽ (*Khram sv. Nikolaya v Pyzhakh*), built in the late 17th century by the musketeer regiment of Bogdan Pyzhov. The tent bell tower, ornamented with carving, cornices and recessed arches, is considered one of the finest in Moscow.

Across the street at No. 34 (accessed through a wrought-iron gate) is the **Martha and Mary Cloister** ❾ (*Marfomariinsky obitel*), founded by the Grand Duchess Yelizaveta after her husband, Grand Duke Sergey, the uncle of Tsar Nicholas II, was killed by a terrorist bomb in 1905. She became a nun and used her vast fortune to build the cloister, which

Icon on display at the Tretyakov Gallery.

LOOKING AT ICONS

Icons were painted by a group of artists overseen by one master, who usually painted the faces, according to set patterns: proscribed ways of depicting the Mother of God or Saviour that had names, such as 'Tenderness' or 'In Thee Rejoiceth'. They are painted in 'reverse perspective' or from several points of view, and the images appear rather flat, with the most important figures largest. They depict time as simultaneous, not sequential. The impact of an icon is in the balance between this ritualised depiction and its emotional power. Some icons, called 'miracle-working', are believed to have the power to heal or answer prayers.

TIP

The redeveloped
Krymskaya Embankment
is a pleasant place for a
stroll, with market stalls,
artist pavilions and
fountains. Cycle lanes
have replaced the busy
road that used to run
along this section of the
river, and the small
artificial hills sculpted
into the landscape are
used for skating, skiing
and sledging in winter.

cared for the sick, elderly and poor. It was closed after the Revolution and used as a city clinic and artrestoration studio. Although the cloister is again functioning, the city has yet to move the clinic, and the glorious **Church of the Intercession of the Mother of God** remains in the grip of the restoration studio. The church was built in 1908–12 by Aleksey Shchusev (who later went on to build Lenin's mausoleum). It ingeniously combines elements of the Novgorod and Pskov schools of church building with *style moderne*. Interior frescoes painted by Mikhail Nesterov remain inaccessible.

Bolshaya Yakimanka

After crossing the Small Stone Bridge over the Drainage Canal, the road from Borovitskaya ploshchad splits – ulitsa Bolshaya Polyanka runs to the east and ulitsa Bolshaya Yakimanka leads to the west. In the centre is a statue to the first leader of the People's Republic of Bulgaria, Georgi Dimitrov (after whom Yakimanka was named from 1957 to 1993).

Yakimanka is a conflation of Joaquim and Anna, parents of the Virgin Mary, after whom a church here was named. Successive rounds of reconstruction have turned it into a joyless street for walking, lined with elite apartment buildings and the President Hotel. The former Igumov Mansion on the north side was designed by Nikolay Pozdeev from Yaroslavl for the manufacturer Nikolay Igumov. It is now the residence of the French Ambassador; the new embassy is next door.

Across the street is the **Church of St John the Soldier Martyr on Yakimanka** ❿ (*Tserkov Ioanna Voina na Yakimanke*). It was built on Peter the Great's initiative and based on his own sketch. It honours the victory over the Swedes in Poltava. Completed in 1712, it is a fine example of Baroque. Inside is the *Icon of the Saviour* that once graced the Saviour Gates to the Kremlin. The intersection with the Garden Ring is called Kaluzhskaya ploshchad. It though most Muscovites call it Oktyabrskaya after the metro station under the square. Once a huge market, the square is surrounded by state office buildings. A right along the Garden Ring leads to the New

Relaxing in Gorky Park.

Church of St. Gregory of Neocaesarea.

Tretyakov Gallery (see page 188) and Gorky Park (see page 191).

Bolshaya Polyanka

Bolshaya Polyanka (Great Meadow) has retained a few more charms than ulitsa Bolshaya Yakimanka, but it has also suffered from ill-conceived building booms. Still, the striking **Church of St Gregory of Neocaesarea** ⓫ (*Tserkov Grigoriya Neokessariyskovo*) at No. 29a is worth a glance. Commonly called the Red Church, it was commissioned by the spiritual advisor to Tsar Aleksey in 1668–79 and built by Kremlin masters, including icon painters from the Ushakov school; the Tsar attended the dedication ceremony. Its decorative rows of *kokoshniki*, rising to five cupolas, tent bell tower and ornate white stone ornamentation brighten an otherwise dull stretch of roadway.

Krymsky Val

Another way to reach Zamoskvoreche from the centre of the city is to follow the Garden Ring Road past Park Kultury metro station and Krymsky Most to ulitsa Krymsky Val, southeast of Bog Island. This once marked the fortifications of the city on the route that led south to Crimea (*Krym* in Russian), and is now associated with **Gorky Park** ⓬ (*Park Kultury imeni Gorkovo*) on the right over the bridge and the New Tretyakov Gallery on the left. The famous park has undergone a major transformation in recent years, from seedy fun fair packed with illegal kiosks and death-trap fairground rides to eco-friendly recreational zone for Muscovites who want to breathe fresh air as they jog and walk their dogs.

The **New Tretyakov Gallery** ⓭ (*Novaya Tretyakovskaya Galereya*; Krymsky Val 10; Tue–Sun 10am–6pm, Thu–Fri until 9pm), on the northern side of ulitsa Krymsky Val houses the Tretyakov Museum's collection of 20th-century art, including many excellent avant-garde paintings by Vasily Kandinsky, Marc Chagall and Kazimir Malevich. The **Muzeon Sculpture Gardens** ⓮ next door (daily 9am–8pm) displays more than 600 statues, including Soviet monuments pulled down in 1991.

Kandinsky on display at the New Tretyakov Gallery.

Grand Palace, Tsaritsyno.

PARKS AND PALACES

Russia's nobility lavished incredible time and effort on their country estates. Many now lie within a bus or metro ride of the city centre and make an excellent excursion – from the Vernisazh market and the ceramic collection at Kuskovo to the wooden buildings at Kolomenskoye and the the restored grandeur of Tsaritsyno.

Just as today Muscovites clog the highways out of the city in the great Friday afternoon dacha exodus, centuries ago Russia's tsars and noble families rode out of Moscow to spend the summer at country palaces dedicated to art, theatre and the delights of nature. This 'estate culture' is a separate chapter in Russian history: the greatest artists and architects of their day created magnificent palaces, pavilions and gardens where their patrons held week-long parties with dancing, theatre performances and endless meals in candlelit, silk-lined halls, and where romance was encouraged in the moonlit gardens.

Izmailovsky and Vernisazh

One of the city's oldest parks is the 332-hectare (820-acre) **Izmailovsky Park ❶** (17 Narodny prospekt; daily 10am–11pm, market best on Sat and Sun; Izmailovsky Park metro, often called Partizanskaya), best known for its Vernisazh market.

The estate belonged to the Romanov family from the 16th century, but was most popular after 1663, when Tsar Aleksey built a wooden palace, church, theatre and glass factory. He turned the land into an

experimental agricultural station with windmill, vineyards, menagerie and 20 well-stocked fish ponds.

Since the 1990s, Izmailovsky has been a weekend Mecca for shoppers at **Vernisazh ❷** (Izmailovskoye schosse 73zh; daily 9am–6pm). Once an enormous, disorganised flea market selling everything from Lada parts to pre-Revolutionary china, it is now organised into rows of booths under fake Russian wooden towers and turrets, with shashlyk stands, bio-toilets and trained bears at the

Main Attractions
Vernisazh
Kuskovo
Kolomenskoye
Tsaritsyno

Map
Page 194

The entrance to Vernisazh Market, Izmailovsky Park.

main entrance. Excellent bargains can be discovered past the touristy booths near the entrance: table linen in bright colours, jewellery of amber and Russian semiprecious stones, thick angora sweaters and shawls, quilts and silk scarves, ceramics from Uzbekistan and an ever-changing assortment of handicrafts. The second tier has a fabulous rug market where you can still find carpets from the Caucasus coloured with natural dyes.

The upper level also has several rows of antiques and icons, where you can occasionally see serious collectors examining museum-quality items. Given the laws on exporting antiques, it's better just to look at this section and move on to the art exhibition and brightly coloured quilts flapping in the breeze. Remember to haggle.

To reach the old Izmailovsky estate, veer to the right, instead of following the path from the metro station to the Vernisazh, and then head in the direction of the market area,

Relaxing in Izmailovsky Park during summer.

on the outside of the fence. On your right you'll see a pond with an island (reached by a small bridge) with what remains of the Romanov estate where Peter the Great spent much of his childhood. It was on the pond here that he learned to sail.

Here the **Church of the Intercession** ❸ (*Pokrovsky sobor*), completed in 1679, is a good example of Moscow Baroque, with five black 'scaled' domes and gables brightly ornamented with tiles. On its right are the brick remains of the Bridge Tower. On the other side of the estate is the white stone Ceremonial Gate, a main entrance flanked by two smaller gates and topped by a tent spire. If the architecture fails to impress you, just enjoy the 17th-century oasis of the little island.

Kuskovo and the Ceramics Museum

Vying with several other estates around Moscow for the title of the

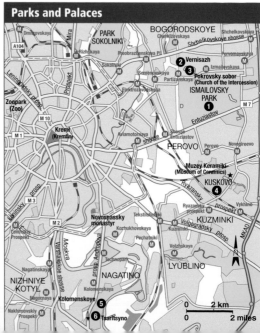

Parks and Palaces

The Italian House at Kuskovo.

'Russian Versailles' is **Kuskovo ❹** (2 ulitsa Yunosti 2; tel: 495-375 3131; www.kuskovo.ru; Wed–Sun 10am–6pm; closed last Wed of the month; Ryazansky prospekt metro; from the city centre exit from the front of the train and take bus nos 133 or 208 six stops to the estate). Kuskovo was built by Count Pyotr Sheremetev (see page 200) in the late 18th century as a summer palace with French-style gardens.

After Pyotr's death, his son Nikolay focused his efforts on rebuilding their estate at Ostankino (see page 176), and Kuskovo faded from the social life of the city. But in its heyday all Russia's nobility, including Catherine the Great, enjoyed its 'countless delights and pleasures.'

Today it is renowned as one of the best-preserved of Moscow's estate palaces, with an excellent collection of ceramics and porcelain – and as a classical music venue both in summer and winter.

The estate has more than 20 buildings artfully placed among the gardens, including a **Dutch House**, the **Italian House**, **Hermitage** and the **Church of the Archangel Michael** (1738) – the oldest building on the grounds. Several of the buildings are accessible to the public, including the main palace, the grotto and the orangery, which houses the Ceramics Museum.

The palace was built by two serf architects, Argunov and Mironov, under Karl Blank in the neoclassical style with elements of Baroque. The interior rooms open to the public include a ballroom, several sitting rooms and the bedroom – all have silk wallpaper, enormous glittering chandeliers, parquet floors and lush frescoes depicting scenes from myths and antiquity. The grotto is the most interesting structure on the estate. Built in 1761 by Argunov, it is designed to look like a Baroque, highly stylised underwater cave.

The orangery (1761–83) consists of a central pavilion flanked by airy glass galleries and small side pavilions. The central pavilion was used for concerts and dances, accompanied by musicians in the balcony.

The orangery at Kuskovo.

Now a **Ceramics Museum**, it displays china, porcelain and pottery from all over the world, with a particularly fine collection of Russian pieces from the 18th century.

Russian folk art at Kolomenskoye

You can explore four centuries of Russian art and history, see Russian folk crafts and traditions, and enjoy fairs and folk festivals on most weekends at **Kolomenskoye ❺** (39 prospekt Andropova; www.mgomz.com; tel: 495-232 6190; park compound daily Apr–Oct 8am–10pm, Nov–Mar 8am–9pm; museums Tue–Sun 11am–7pm; separate admission charges for the main museum, Peter the Great's cabin and the water tower can be purchased inside the compound in any ticket booth; Kolomenskoye metro). On the south side of the city overlooking the Moscow River, this is one of the oldest inhabited parts of greater Moscow, with settlement dating back more than 2,500 years. As a summer residence of the early Russian grand princes and tsars, it dates from the 14th century.

Ivan the Terrible had a palace here, and in the 17th century Tsar Aleksey built a wooden fantasy dubbed the Eighth Wonder of the World. It had an asymmetrical maze of 270 rooms and a front gate tower flanked by mechanical lions that 'roared'. When it became dilapidated, Catherine the Great had it torn down and replaced by a four-storey palace, which was destroyed by the French in 1812. The final imperial palace, built by Alexander I, has also not survived.

In the Soviet period Kolomenskoye became a compound for wooden architecture and stone monuments brought from across Russia. The few old churches and buildings that remain are set on a glorious hillside high above the Moscow River, with paths leading into ravines and woods and a spring reputed to have healing properties.

Touring the royal estate

Inside the main gate on the left is the **Church of the Icon of the Mother of God of Kazan** (*Tserkov Kazanskoy ikony Bozhiey materi*), believed to

Kolomenskoye, the reconstruction of Tsar Alexei Mikhailovich's wooden palace.

have been built by Tsar Mikhail in 1644, with domes of deep lapis and dotted with gold stars. In the small centre chapel, somewhat cramped by two enormous frescoed pillars, there is a copy of *The Mother of God of Kazan* icon, which miraculously helped the Russians rout the Polish invaders in 1612.

Beyond the church is the **Front Gate Museum**, once the main entrance to the estate, and the brew house (*Sytny dom*), both of which house the **Treasures of Kolomenskoye Museum**. The brew house has an excellent collection of woodcarvings (the altar doors are astonishing in their ornamentation), tiles, ecclesiastical vestments and icons.

The second floor displays everyday objects, clothing and a tile fireplace (1899) by the artist Mikhail Vrubel that depicts the folk tale of Prince Volga and the peasant Mikula, in which the prince comes to appreciate the unsung labourer's work. The highlight of the museum is the exact model (scaled 40/1) that Catherine the Great had made of Tsar Aleksey's fantastic wooden palace.

Just before the Front Gate Museum is a simple round stone podium called the **Petition Stone** in English, but more exactly translated as the 'browbeating stone'. When petitioners came to the tsar, they 'beat their brows' against the stone in deference (and presumably to ensure a positive response to their request). Behind the brew house is the **Stone Maiden**, an 11th- or 12th-century gravestone from a Polovtsian burial ground. The stones are near a grove of oaks, reputedly planted by Peter the Great.

Church of the Ascension

The masterpiece of Kolomenskoye is the magnificent **Church of the Ascension** (*Tserkov Vozneseniya Gospodnya*), on Unesco's World Heritage list and a rival of St Basil's on Red Square in its beauty. It was built in 1532 by Tsar Vasily III as a votive church for the birth of a male heir (to become Ivan the Terrible). The church is a massive conical sliver of stone, with decorative rows of gables over the bays leading up to an octagonal drum and a tent-shaped spire

Church of the Ascension.

soaring 62 metres (203ft) above the river bank. Galleries round its base anchor it to the ground.

The church seems to borrow from Russian wooden architecture but includes elements of Western Gothic and Renaissance styles. There is some evidence that it was built by Pietro Solario, an Italian master who worked in the Kremlin. The interior of the church is surprisingly small. To support the towering spire the whitewashed walls are up to 3 metres (10ft) thick, and the only lighting comes from the narrow windows in the octagonal drum and tent. There was no traditional sanctuary, but there was an iconostasis, and the walls may have originally been decorated with geometric designs.

On the gallery facing the river are remains of a stone throne, where, according to legend, Ivan the Terrible would sit to survey the river and countryside.

Gates at Tsaritsyno.

Wooden buildings

Several wooden structures were moved here from the northern part of Russia, including the gateway tower from the 18th-century Nikolo-Korelsky monastery, a mead brewery from the town of Preobrazhenkoye and a stockade tower from Bratsk. On the path leading to the stockade is the massive **Boris Stone**, a 12th-century property marker carved with the cross and the inscription, 'Lord, protect your servant Boris.'

Another delight on the estate is the **cabin of Peter the Great**, where the tsar stayed while he was in the northern city of Arkhangelsk to supervise the building of the Novodvinsk fortress. As you crouch down to step into the low-ceilinged rooms, note the white tape on the wall opposite marking Peter the Great's height (2 metres/6ft, 7in) and pity his two-month stay in what must have been extremely cramped conditions. The four-room cabin is simple and rustic, with hewn log walls, heavily carved furniture and benches and brightly coloured tile stoves.

Inside the Church of the Ascension.

Past the stockade tower is a path that leads down to a gully and then up a steep incline through the woods to the 16th-century **Church of the Beheading of St John the Baptist** (*Tserkov Useknoveniya glavi Ioanna Predteche*), which may have been built by the same architects who designed St Basil's in Red Square.

Tsaritsyno

One of the strangest of Moscow's urban estates is **Tsaritsyno ❻** (1 ulitsa Dolskaya; www.tsaritsyno-museum. ru; tel: 499-725 7287; museums Tue–Fri 11am–6pm, Sat until 8pm; tickets to the Small Palace, Opera House and the 2nd and 3rd Cavalier Pavilions purchased at the Opera House; Orekhovo or Tsaritsyno metro).

The village here, called Black Mud, was owned by several noble families until Catherine the Great took a fancy to it and bought it in 1775, renaming it 'the tsarina's village.' She commissioned Vasily Bazhenov to design the estate buildings and approved his plans for neo-Gothic palaces and pavilions.

Ten years later she returned, spent two hours surveying the buildings and demanded that they be torn down because 'it would be impossible to live in them.' For the past two centuries historians have speculated why she disliked the original buildings, citing everything from the decorative elements, which are suggestive of Masonic symbols, to the small, low-ceilinged rooms, lack of grand halls and impractical service and kitchen quarters. She commissioned Matvey Kazakov to redo the main palace, and before it was completed, lost interest altogether.

A 19th-century writer noted that the palace 'reminds you of a huge crypt on a bier, surrounded by gigantic monks holding candles.' In 2005 Moscow City Hall 'traded' the former Lenin Museum, owned by the city, for Tsaritsyno, owned by the federal government, and restorers have been renovating the palace according to Kazakov's revised blueprints ever since.

Several of the Bazhenov pavilions have been restored. The two Cavalier pavilions (*Kavelerskie korpusy*) opposite the palace display permanent exhibitions about the estate and Catherine; the one closest to the Patterned Bridge screens a fascinating video reconstruction of the original Bazhenov structures.

Along a lane to the right of the palace (as one faces it) are the reconstructed **Small Palace** (*Malydvorets*) and Opera House (*Opemy dom*), lovely light structures which display various temporary exhibitions. The pale-green **Church of the Icon of the Mother of God 'Life-Bearing Source'**, which predated Catherine's purchase of the land (1722–60), is open for services.

The fun of Tsaritsyno is simply strolling among the ruins, along the brick and stone bridges covered with stars, crosses and other Gothic ornamentation, and enjoying the smells of the woods and the fresh air of the meadows.

The rennovated Grand Bridge at Tsaritsyno Park.

AT HOME WITH THE COUNTS SHEREMETEV

The Sheremetev's Ostankino and Kuskovo estates were key in the rise of Moscow's estate culture and essential to the growth of the arts.

The huge inequalities in Russian society, which led in part to the 1917 Revolution, are clearly seen in the large estates of Moscow's nobility, its princes, boyars and royal favourites, who acquired property and land at the expense of the bonded serf peasantry. Some of the estates that can be seen around Moscow were modest mansions or artistic communities. Others were vast enterprises with palaces, churches, pavilions, formal gardens, monuments, grottoes and even theatres; these estates, which were fully occupied in summer, played an important role in the developing cultural life of the city. Undoubtedly the most extravagant of them all belonged to the Sheremetev family.

The original benefactor of the family estates was Field Marshal Count Boris Sheremetev, who had received his grant of land from Peter the Great for bloody work against the Tatars and against the Swedes in the Baltic States. He also discovered in Latvia a 17-year-old serving girl called Martha who later became Peter the Great's wife, changing her name to Catherine. Boris' son, Pyotr, enlarged the estate at Kuskovo (see page 195) in an attempt to make it the Versailles of Russia. The well-preserved interior gives an excellent impression of the cultural pretensions of the high nobility during the reign of Catherine the Great.

Abramstevo Museum.

The Ballroom at Seremetev Palace, constructed from 1769-77 and designed by Karl Blank (1728-1793).

The Dutch House at Kuskovo.

A horse-drawn carriage at Kuskovo Palace.

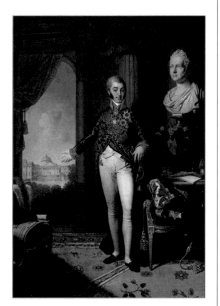

Portrait of Nikolai Sheremetev

OSTANKINO'S DRAMATIC SECRET

Ostankino Palace.

The dowry of Pyotr Sheremetev's wife included the estate at Ostankino (see page 176), and it was here in 1792 that their son Nikolay undertook the construction of a much larger residence. He had inherited his father's passion for the theatre, had travelled widely in Europe and had performed in theatre and dance productions. Said to be twice as rich as any other noble Russian, he set up his own troupe of serfs, comprising 200 actors, singers and musicians, making Ostankino a 'pantheon of the arts'. One eight-year-old girl who joined the troupe was to become the brilliant actress Praskovia Zhemchugova. It was for her that Nikolay is said to have moved the theatre at Kuskovo to Ostankino, opening in 1795 with an opera of *The Capture of Ismail*. In 1801, when she was found to have tuberculosis, Nikolay secretly married her. Nikolay's 'serf countess' was the scandal of high society, although such informal liaisons were common.

Resotoring a Delft vase from the Kuskovo Estate.

Traditional wooden house, Suzdal.

Trinity Lavra of St. Sergius, Sergiyev Posad.

DAY TRIPS FROM MOSCOW

Major religious centres and delightful country estates are within striking distance of the city; on a day trip you can easily take in a stunning monastery or the museum-home of Tchaikovsky or Tolstoy. The finest towns of the Golden Ring, including Vladimir and Suzdal, are better appreciated with an overnight stay.

There is more than enough in Moscow to keep you busy, but many might say you'll never truly understand the Russian character without exploring the treasure-laden countryside beyond the city limits that all Muscovites – rich businessmen or widowed pensioners alike – retreat to as often as possible. All the following destinations can all be done in a day, but they will be full days. Picnics and patience are well rewarded when you are dependent on rural Russia's tourist infrastructure, which is functionally adequate but often basic.

Sergeev Posad Monastery ❶

Many travellers regard the white walls and gold domes rising above the town of Sergeev Posad as one of the finest sights in Russia. These herald the **Holy Trinity Monastery of St Sergius** (*Sviato-Troitskaya Sergeeva Lavra*; www.musobl.divo.ru; tel: 496-540 5356; suburban train from Yaroslavsky station and then a 20-minute walk up the hill to the monastery).

On a summer day the monastery is filled with unhurried activity: pilgrims paying reverence to the holy relics, young priests and their families enjoying the gardens, monks strolling along the tidy paths. But

the monastery hasn't been frozen in time: you can see monks chatting on mobile phones and trainers peaking out from under seminarians' robes.

The monastery was founded in the 14th century by St Sergius of Radonezh. Born Varfolomey Kirillovich in 1314 to a wealthy boyar family, he began a life of prayer in the forest, soon drawing followers. After taking monastic vows, he became the *hegumen* (abbot) of the monastery he founded, which soon became the

Main Attractions
Sergeev Posad Monastery
Abramtsevo manor house
Church of the Intercession
  on the Nerl
Suzdal
Tchaikovsky Museum
Yasnaya Polyana

Map
Page 207

Suzdal at dusk.

Tourists under the Tsar Bell at Trinity Lavra of St. Sergius.

Inside one of the cathedrals in the Trinity Monastery of St. Sergius.

leading religious centre in Russia. His diplomatic missions to Russia's principalities ensured the 'gathering of the Rus' that led, it is claimed by the Russians, to the formation of the Russian state.

In 1550, after several Tatar raids, the monastery's first stone walls were built, and in 1618 these were raised to 10–14 metres (33–46ft), with towers on the kilometre-long walls. After the Revolution the monastery was closed and many of its treasures plundered. Partially reopened in 1946 and made a museum, it was returned to the church in 1988.

Today there are about 300 monks, a divinity academy (the successor of the Russian-Greek-Latin Academy founded in 1687), a seminary and schools for choir masters and icon painters. The monastery is a *lavra*, an honorary title denoting special importance and service, conferred by Empress Yelizaveta in 1744.

Inside the monastery

You enter the monastery through the **Beautiful** or **Holy Gates**, with scenes from the life of St Sergius, and under the Gate Church of St John the Baptist, built in 1693. To the left is the faceted and brightly painted Refectory (*Trapeznaya*), from 1692.

Next to the Refectory against the south wall is the 1778 Palace of Metropolitans, which served as the residence of metropolitans and patriarchs from 1946 until 1988, when it was moved to Daniilovsky Monastery in Moscow. Standing on the small square between the Refectory and the Palace of Metropolitans, you are surrounded by five magnificent churches and chapels under the great turquoise-and-white bell tower (built 1740–70).

Rising 88 metres (290ft) in five tiers, the bell tower has 42 bells, including the largest in Russia (75 tons). In front of it is the delightful Baroque **Chapel over the Well** (*Nadkladeznaya chasovnya*), built over a spring that erupted in 1644 during renovations to the Cathedral of the Dormition. Next to it the spring burbles under the **Canopy Over the Cross** (*Sen nad krestom*), with delicate columns and rich frescoes.

The monastery's oldest church is the **Trinity Cathedral** (*Troitsky sobor*), in front of the Palace of Metropolitans. Built in 1425 to replace a wooden church over the grave of St Sergius, it is rather austere, with a single helmet cupola and little ornamentation; only the side chapel to Nikon, the abbot who succeeded St Sergius, adds a decorative note. The sense of height is achieved by a slight inward thrust of the walls as they rise. But the interior has perhaps the finest frescoes and icons in all Russia. The monk and brilliant icon painter Andrey Rublyov was asked to return to the monastery where he once served, and here he painted the *Old Testament Trinity*, considered the greatest masterpiece of icon-painting in Russia. The original is in the Tretyakov Gallery (see page 188), but a copy and other icons by Rublyov and Daniil the Black fill the small church. In the Cathedral are the relics of St Sergius, and on most days there is a long line of pilgrims waiting to view them.

Closer to the entrance gates stands the **Church of the Holy Spirit** (*Dukovskaya tserkov*), built in 1476 by architects from Pskov. Its three narrow bays rise up to the single cupola above the bell tower. The interior is the final resting place of several of the monastery's most revered abbots.

The largest church is the magnificent **Cathedral of the Dormition**, built in 1559–85 to replicate the church of the same name in the Kremlin. This church is considerably larger, with four azure-blue cupolas decorated with gold stars around the central gold cupola. Inside is an enormous five-tiered iconostasis with 76 icons; the icons and frescoes were painted in 1684.

Two other churches on the monastery grounds are worth noting: the small Baroque masterpiece of the **Church of the Smolensk Icon of Mother of God** (*Tserkov Smolenskoy*

Belltower, Sergiev Posa.

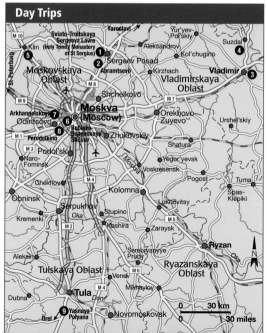

ikony Bozhiey Materi), built in 1745, and the 17th-century tent-spired **Church of SS Zosima and Savvaty** (*Khram prepodobnikh Zosimy i Savvatiya Solovetskikh*) that is part of the hospital wing.

The monastery **Museum** (*Riznitsa*) has an extraordinary collection of ecclesiastical vestments, vessels, gold-and-jewel-encrusted Bible covers, embroidery and imperial gifts to the monks. In the Tsar's Apartments is the monastery's teaching museum of icons.

Abramtsevo manor house

The first art colony in Russia was set up at **Abramtsevo ❷** (www.abramt sevo.net; tel: 495-993 0033; buildings Wed–Sun 10am–6pm, park Wed–Sun 10am–8pm; charge; suburban train from Yaroslavsky station to the Abramtsevo stop, exit and cross the tracks, turn left on the paved road to the museum). It was founded by railway magnate and patron of the arts Savva Mamontov as a place to create, experiment and live close to

Church of the Saviour Not Made by Hands, Abramtsevo.

Statue of Prince Vladimir Monomakh.

nature surrounded by the inspiration of folk art. In 1870 he bought the manor house of the writer Sergey Aksakov near Sergeev Posad, and invited Ilya Repin, Valentin Serov, Mikhail Vrubel, Konstantin Korovin, Mikhail Nesterov, Viktor Vasnetsov, Yelena and Vasily Polenov, and other artists and their families to spend summers here.

Mamontov left untouched much of Aksakov's manor house, which Chekhov used as the model for the decaying country estate in *The Cherry Orchard*. Inside, note the copy of the portrait *A Girl with Peaches* that Serov painted of Mamontov's daughter.

Today you can visit most of the buildings on the estate. Especially lovely is the fairy-tale *teremok* of wood that Ivan Ropet built as a bathhouse. Decorated with intricate carvings, a barrelled gable and a sharply pitched roof, the cosy interior is filled invitingly with wooden furniture.

The pride of the estate is the small **Church of the Saviour Not Made by Hands** that was built and decorated by the entire artistic circle in the style of Pskov and Novgorod churches. The icons were painted by Repin, Nesterov, Apollinary Vasnetsov and Polenov. Viktor Vasnetsov designed the mosaic floor and Vrubel built the ceramic stove.

To keep the children happy, the two Vasnetsov brothers built the charming **Hut on Chicken Legs**. This is the house of the witch Baba Yaga in Russian fairy tales (see page 59), which could turn on its legs when children ventured too close. The house is a sheer delight.

The Golden Ring

In the 1960s Soviet tourist agencies began to call the best-preserved of Russia's historic cities near Moscow the Golden Ring. The name stuck and now these towns around Moscow are some of the most popular destinations for foreign tourists in the country. They were all important principalities or trading centres in the centuries before Russia existed as a state, and but for the whims of fate (and various Tatar invasions), any of them might have become the capital of this vast land. An overnight trip to Vladimir, or to the 'White Monuments' of both Vladimir and Suzdal, can be a welcome break from Moscow's frenzied pace.

Vladimir

For centuries the political and cultural centre of the Russian lands was the city of **Vladimir** ❸, about 200km (120 miles) to the east and slightly to the north of Moscow. Founded by the Kievan leader Vladimir Monomakh in 1108, it was the most powerful principality until the Tatars burned it to the ground in 1238. Vladimir Monomakh's son, Yuri Dolgoruky, went on to found a small fortress in Moscow, and Yuri's sons Andrey Bogoliubsky ('Godloving') and

Vsevolod III (called 'Of the Great Nest' having sired 12 sons) built some of the finest churches of the medieval period.

Start your tour at the **Golden Gates**, built in 1152–64 and modelled on Kiev's walls (which were, in turn, modelled on the walls of Constantinople). They are rather squat, but still majestic, combining a defence tower, triumphal arch and gateway church in one small structure. The **Museum** in the Gates has a diorama of the Tatar attack that gives a vivid sense of the city's bygone beauty and terrible destruction. Further along the earthen ramparts is the **Water Tower Museum**, with an exhibition of Old Vladimir.

The centrepiece of the city is **Cathedral Square**, on a high hill overlooking the Klyasma River. Here you can see the **Cathedral of Dormition** that was the model for the church of the same name in the Moscow Kremlin. It was built in 1158–89 and, after a fire, cleverly rebuilt to be much wider and higher. All the grand princes were crowned here until the 15th century. Some of the icons and frescoes were painted

Golden gate at night, Vladimir.

by Andrey Rublyov and Daniil the Black; the original iconostasis was discovered in a nearby village and is now kept in the Tretyakov Gallery (see page 188), but the frescoes of the Last Judgement under the choir gallery and in the south gallery were created by these masters (1408).

The small **Cathedral of St Dmitry** is both a masterpiece of early Russian architecture and a mystery. Built in 1194–7, it is structurally austere, with three bays and a single helmet dome. But it is lavishly ornamented with a band arcading of saints and a profusion of bas-relief that puzzles specialists. They have been able to identify some of the Biblical and historical figures represented but not the meaning of all the fantastical beasts and figures.

About 10km (6 miles) to the northeast of the city is the village of **Bogoliubovo**, where Prince Andrey once had his palace and administrative buildings. The princely settlement is gone, but what has remained is the jewel in the crown of Russian medieval architecture, the **Church of the Intercession on the Nerl**. Accessible only by a stroll across an enormous field, the delicately proportioned white church stands peacefully on the banks of the narrow Nerl River, reflected in the still waters. Built in one year (1165) when the river was on the other side of the structure, it stood on a high place faced by stone with stairs leading from the water to the church. Here the bas-reliefs are less profuse and more subtle than on the Cathedral of St Dmitry; the 20 women's faces still seem to offer intercession and protection to all who come here.

Suzdal

The 'White Monuments' of Vladimir and **Suzdal ❹**, 35km (25 miles) to the north, are Unesco-protected World Heritage sites. Suzdal is a neat and tidy town with white-walled monasteries and carved and brightly painted wooden houses with geraniums on the windowsills. Meandering paths and brooks cross fields scented with apple blossoms in spring and as peaceful as a down duvet in winter, when the town's churches and houses lie covered by pristine snow. You may be tempted to rush about the town trying to take in all 200 sights, but try

Convent of the Intercession, Suzdal.

Lenin Street, Suzdal.

section of the town, you can shop at the stone trading arcade and marvel at the 'summer' and 'winter' churches remarkably preserved throughout the area. The summer churches were loftier and lighter, but freezing in the winter; next to them smaller churches were built with thick walls that maintained the warmth of the congregation. Fine examples are the summer **Church of St Lazarus** and winter **Church of St Antipus**. Be sure to visit the 18th-century **Likhonin merchant house**, recreated down to the bast shoes by the stove, and the lovely **Posad House**, the only surviving 17th-century dwelling in the town.

Across a wooden footbridge from the kremlin is the **Museum of Wooden Architecture**, where several wooden structures from different parts of the country have been reconstructed and placed next to Suzdal's existing buildings. Purist

instead to succumb to the slow pace and give yourself a full day or two for peaceful and aimless wandering.

Suzdal was the centre of the principality until Prince Andrey moved it to Vladimir. Today there is hardly a single street that isn't graced by a church or lovely house, but the main sights are largely centred around the **kremlin**, the trading settlement (the *posad* area), the Museum of Wooden Architecture, and monasteries. The stone walls that once surrounded the **kremlin** were dismantled in the 18th century, but the earthen ramparts and moats are still visible.

The highlights of the former fortress are the **Cathedral of the Nativity of the Mother of God** (built 1222–5 and rebuilt several times since, with five blue domes dotted with gold stars and a particularly impressive portal); the **Metropolitan's Palace**, with its pillar-free 'cross chamber' surpassing in size and grandeur even the Moscow Kremlin's chamber; and the **Historical Museum**. In the *posad*

Boat trip, Suzdal.

Frescoes at the Monastery of Saint Euthymius.

Monument to Tchaikovsky at the Tchaikovsky Museum, Klin.

preservationists may grumble (the jumble of windmills, churches, houses and barns is far from a typical Russian village), but it's a delight to walk among them and look inside during the summer months to see what life was like for common folk in the 18th and 19th centuries.

Suzdal has two monasteries and two convents that are once again active, in whole or in part. The most interesting is the **Saviour-St Euphemius Monastery**, a fortress-monastery founded in 1352 on the high bank of the Kamenka River. Part of the monastery was made into a prison under Catherine the Great, and the prison wing contains reconstructed cells. The monasteries, churches and museums, including a nice collection of folk art, are open to visitors. And the view of the river and the white-walled **Convent of the Intercession** across a field on the other side is one of the most peaceful and serene in Russia.

Tchaikovsky country

The gentle hills, meandering rivers, woods and fields of **Klin ❺** (about 90km/60 miles northwest of

Moscow) have inspired many artists who had estates in the area, including Tchaikovsky. First mentioned in the chronicles in 1190, Klin was a flourishing way station between the principalities of Tver and Moscow. It was virtually destroyed under the reign of Ivan the Terrible, when his private security police, the *oprichniki,* went on a rampage against his purported enemies, and it was briefly occupied by the German army in World War II. Today the built-up city has few charms except for the excellent Klinskoye beer, smoked hams and sausages.

Pyotr Tchaikovsky lived in three homes in and around Klin. After his death, his brother turned the last of these (where the composer lived between 1892 and 1893) into the **Tchaikovsky Museum** (*Dom-muzey P. I. Tchaikovskovo*; 48 ulitsa Tchaikovskovo; tel: 496-242 1050; Fri–Tue 10am–5pm; closed last Mon of the month; charge; English tours available by appointment; 1.5 hours on bus No. 437 from Rechnoy Vokzal metro). The large, pale-blue wooden house with white trim is filled with souvenirs from Tchaikovsky's travels

THE DACHA

'Dacha', from the verb 'to give', originally meant a plot of land given to someone for service to the Empire. Over the years the dacha became a fixture of Russian life: even before the Revolution, middle-class families would spend the summer at a country house to enjoy swimming, mushroom- and berry-picking, bicycle trips and walks. During the Soviet period, the standard 600 sq-metre plot was usually made into an enormous vegetable garden to grow easily stored root vegetables, and cucumbers and tomatoes for pickling. While many dachas remain a source of self-sufficiency that families can fall back on during times of crisis, today some dacha settlements have almost become gated communities for the rich.

and archives, and his main living areas have been preserved.

The airy living room is dominated by a Becker grand piano that is played twice a year, on his birthday (7 May) and on his memorial day (6 November). On 7 May, the honour goes to the winner of the Tchaikovsky Competition. The first laureate to play was Van Cliburn, who won the competition in 1958.

The heavily ornamented and panelled library and cosy bedroom, with Tchaikovsky's small slippers, are open to visitors, as are the gardens where he would stroll with his dogs every morning. In spring they are scented by the composer's favourite flowers – lilies of the valley. The concert hall built onto the house in the 1960s holds regular concerts. The house was under renovation at the time of writing and it wasn't clear when it would reopen.

The smartest dachas

During the Soviet period the countryside to the west of the city was traditionally the locale for Party dachas: gated communities with stone or wooden houses, large yards and any modern convenience you could think of. There is no industry in these parts, so the rivers and fields are still pristine, and the roads are well tended to handle the traffic of official cars shuttling between state compounds and the city. The most exclusive area is along the **Rublyovo-Uspenskoye Shosse** ❻, a meandering two-lane highway that grinds to a halt twice a day when President Putin leaves or returns to his residence near the Moscow River.

In the 1990s Rublevo-Uspenskoye shosse became the hottest real estate in town. Residents privatised their spacious official dachas and sold them to New Russians; developers snapped up fallow collective farm lands and started building 'cottage' communities, 'cottage' being the Russian word for a four-storey stone house with turrets and towers, a six-car garage, swimming pool and tennis courts. Services

A modern dacha near Moscow.

followed: upscale shopping malls, chic restaurants, health clubs and, for a short time, the single most expensive farmer's market in the world.

State Folk Museum

Fitting perfectly into the Rublyovo-Uspenskoye atmosphere of ostentatious country living is the estate of **Arkhangelskoye** ❼ (*Gosudarstvenny Muzey-usadba Arkhangeskoye;* Illinskoye shosse; www.arkhangelskoe.ru; tel: 495-363 1375; museum Wed–Sun 10.30am–5pm, park Wed–Sun 10am–8pm; Tushinkskaya metro, then bus No. 549 to Arkhangelskoye stop or minibus No. 151 to Sanatorium stop).

This lovely land on a high bank of the Moscow River was owned by the princely Golitsyn family, but in 1810 it was bought by Nikolay Yusupov, said to be richer than the tsar himself. Nikolay invested hundreds of thousands of roubles to create his version of the Russian Versailles. He asked Rastrelli to design the palace, laid out French-style gardens filled with pavilions and statuary, particularly lions, and built a 400-seat theatre and a number of cottage factories to provide glassware and china for the family.

He filled the house with his enormous library and an extraordinary art collection that included Velazquez, Raphael and David – the corner rooms had eight sides to display his art better. This pleasure estate was always filled with guests at week-long celebrations. It was also one of the sites for coronation celebrations; here Nicholas II and Alexandra were feted.

After a generation of neglect, it was restored by Zinaida Yusupova in the late 19th and early 20th centuries. Although she had two sons (one of whom, Felix, murdered Rasputin in his St Petersburg palace), she willed the estate to the Russian Empire to be turned into a museum. Alas, her will was carried out by the Soviet government, which in 1937 dismantled some park buildings, including faux ruins, in order to build a sanatorium in the grounds.

The art exhibitions are displayed in two of the estate buildings, and the beautiful park grounds are a delight to explore. The tiny Tea House (*Chainy domik*) is a masterpiece of

Lion statue at Arkhangelskoye.

Memorial to Pasternak.

since the 1930s Peredelkino's wooden houses tucked behind fences along quiet narrow lanes have been home to some of the USSR's and Russia's finest writers.

Pasternak's dacha

The poet and novelist Boris Pasternak (1890–1960) lived here from the 1930s until his death. He is best known in the West for his novel *Dr Zhivago*, which was published abroad in an Italian translation in 1957. Pasternak was awarded the Nobel Prize in 1958, but was forced by the Soviet government to refuse it. In 1986 his dacha was made into the **Pasternak Dacha Museum** (*Dommuzey B.L. Pasternaka*; 3 ulitsa Pavlenko, Peredelkino; www.pasternak museum.ru; tel: 495-934 5175; Tue–Wed 10am–4pm, Thu–Fri 10am–5pm, Sat–Sun 10am–6pm; closed last Tue of the month). Its oval two-storey porch launches out into the yard as

classical estate architecture, as is the Yusupov Family Chapel and Crypt, designed as a copy of St Petersburg's Kazan Cathedral on a small scale. Walk through the woods to the white Church of Archangel Michael (*Tserkov Mikhaila Arkhangela*), built in 1667: nestled in tall trees, its myriad *kokoshniki* gables rise to three 'scaled' cupolas. Next to it is the grave of Zinaida's sister Tatiana, who died of typhus and was buried by the church beneath an angel monument.

Writers' village

The village of **Peredelkino** ❽ has existed since the 17th century, but only appeared on the cultural map in 1934 when Maxim Gorky suggested building a dacha community for writers here. The poet Yevgeny Yevtushenko, a long-time Peredelkino resident, suggests that Stalin agreed in order to keep a closer eye on the intelligentsia. Whatever the reason,

Pasternak Dacha Museum.

The Transfiguration of the Saviour Cathedral.

if the house were a ship about to sail into the fields. These fields, little changed, are the view Pasternak saw from his book-lined bedroom-study on the upper floor. The museum also exhibits the lower-floor main room, with walls filled with paintings by the poet's father, the painter Leonid Pasternak.

The Chukoysky dacha

Another extraordinary family of writers lived near Pasternak on ulitsa Serafimovicha: Korney Chukovsky (1882–1969) and his daughter Lydia (1907–96). A famed writer of children's books and verse, critic, translator and linguist, Korney Chukovsky endured periods of official disfavour during the Soviet era, but miraculously escaped arrest during the purges. His daughter, Lydia Chukovskaya, spent time in jail for anti-Bolshevist activities. She is best known for her memoirs and critical essays. Both father and

daughter took a final political risk in the 1960s when they let the dissident writer Alexander Solzhenitsyn live at their Peredelkino house before he was forced into exile abroad.

The house and children's library built by Korney Chukovsky next door have been lovingly preserved by Lydia's daughter as the **Chukovsky Dacha Museum** (*Dom-muzey K.I. Chukovskovo*; 3 ulitsa Serafimovicha; tel: 495-593 2670; Tue–Sun 10am–6pm; charge, call ahead for admission). The light rooms are filled with elegant pre-Revolutionary furniture, paintings, photos and mementoes of the family's literary life, spanning nearly a century from the Silver Age to the post-Soviet period.

Near Peredelkino train station is the charming salmon-coloured 17th-century **Transfiguration of the Saviour Cathedral** (*Khram Spaso-Preobrazheniya*), part of the Patriarch's Court. The Patriarch's summer residence is next to it. Pasternak, Chukovsky and the poet Arseny Tarkovsky (father of the film-maker Andrey Tarkovsky) are buried in its lovely hillside cemetery.

Tolstoy's family home

In 1828 Leo Tolstoy was born at the estate of **Yasnaya Polyana**  (*Gosudarstvenny memorialny i prirodny zapovednik Muzey-usadba L.N. Tolstovo Yasnaya Polyana*; Tula oblast; www.ypmuseum.ru; tel: 487-517 6073; daily 10am–3.30pm; Tolstoy House closed last Tue of the month, Kuzminsky House closed last Wed of the month; charge; English-language tours by appointment).

He lived here for much of his life, writing his most acclaimed works, *War and Peace* and *Anna Karenina*, raising his enormous family, and beginning to put into practice his theories of social equality and simple Christian piety. The estate belonged to Tolstoy's mother's family, the Volkonskys. His grandfather, prince

Nikolay Volkonsky, built a comfortable wooden house at the end of a long, shady drive *(Preshpek)*, a French park (called The Wedges), an English park (called the Lower Park) and a stone house (Kuzminsky House), which now displays Tolstoy's literary legacy and temporary exhibits.

After Tolstoy's death, his wife Sofia twice petitioned Nicholas II to make the estate a national preserve, but was refused. It was finally made a museum in 1921.

During World War II the German army occupied the house for 45 days, but the entire contents of the house had been evacuated in 110 crates to Tomsk before their invasion. In the 1990s Vladimir Tolstoy, the great-grandson of the writer, assumed directorship of the estate and museum, and turned it into a centre for Russian culture.

Thanks to Sofia Tolstoy's meticulous preservation of her husband's legacy, the comfortable house does not seem like a museum at all: it's as if the family just stepped out to hunt for mushrooms and will be back before lunch. Virtually the entire Volkonsky House is open to visitors, from the spacious hall on the upper floor where the family met for meals and entertained such distinguished literary guests as Anton Chekhov and Ivan Turgenev, to the 'room under the eaves' that once served as Tolstoy's study.

Tolstoy's last study, where he worked for about 15 years, is exactly the way he left it, with books, photos and paintings, and a turtle bell he used to call his secretary. The sofa in this room belonged to his ancestors: the writer himself was born on it, as were his brother and sister, eight of his 13 children, and several grandchildren. The contrast between Tolstoy's ascetic bedroom, with a narrow bed and simple furniture, and his wife's more luxurious sitting room and bedroom, filled with over-stuffed chairs and knick-knacks, gives a good visual sense of the contrast between the spouses.

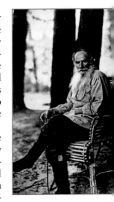

Tolstoy in Yasnaya Polyana in 1908.

Tolstoy's house at Yasnaya Polyana.

INSIGHT GUIDES TRAVEL TIPS
MOSCOW

TRANSPORT

GETTING THERE AND GETTING AROUND

GETTING THERE

By Air

Many international airlines connect Moscow with the rest of the world. Flights take around 9 hours from New York, 4 hours from London or Paris, 3 hours from Frankfurt, 2 hours from Stockholm, 6 hours from Delhi and 8 hours from Beijing.

British Airways and Aeroflot offer daily flights from London Heathrow. Numerous European carriers offer connections between British cities (and Dublin) to Moscow via their hub cities.

If you're coming from North America the only direct routes are from New York, Seattle, Washington DC, Los Angeles and Toronto with Delta, Air Canada or Aeroflot. There are no direct flights to Moscow from Australia or New Zealand.

Moscow has several air terminals, each servicing domestic and international locations. Moscow's most modern international airport is Domodedovo in the south of the city, though even here there can be overcrowding and long queues in summer. Sheremetevo and Vnukovo are the city's other airports, handling domestic and a handful of inter-national flights.

Domodedovo
www.domodedovo.ru
Sheremetyevo
www.svo.aero
Vnukovo
www.vnukovo.ru

By Rail

Within European Russia railways are the most important means of transport. Railways connect the largest Russian, Belorussian and Ukrainian cities (Moscow, St Petersburg, Kiev and Minsk) with many Western European capitals – there are direct trains to cities such as Warsaw, Berlin and Budapest.

A popular rail route between the west and Russia is the Helsinki–St Petersburg line, which takes 8 hours. Helsinki–Moscow by standard train takes almost 17 hours. Surprisingly modern, high-speed trains run between Moscow and St Petersburg.

The Trans-Siberian rail route can be used to access Moscow from the east; there are several trains every week from Beijing and Vladivostok. The 5- or 7-day journey demands an adventurous spirit and a willingness to spend a week on the train contemplating the endless Siberian landscapes.

AIR SAFETY

Air safety has improved in the last 15 years in Russia but is still poor when it comes to small domestic airlines. Aeroflot and other large airlines adhere to international standards, others may not or their fleets may be so old that planes do not have the safety features that modern planes do.

Railway stations

Of the nine railway stations in Moscow, the most important are:

Belorussky vokzal, ploshchad Tverskaya Zastava; trains for Western Europe, Poland, Belarus and Lithuania.

Kievsky vokzal, ploshchad Kievskovo Vokzala; trains to Ukraine, Budapest, Prague and Bucharest.

Leningradsky vokzal, Komsomolskaya ploshchad 3; trains to Helsinki, Tallinn, Novgorod, Murmansk, Tver and St Petersburg.

Rizhsky vokzal, Rizhskaya ploshchad; trains for Riga, Latvia.

Yaroslavsky vokzal, Komsomolskaya ploshchad 5, for the Trans-Siberian Express, Siberia and the Far East.

GETTING AROUND

To/from the Airport

Domodedovo – Aeroexpress trains leave from Paveletsky vokzal every 30 minutes. Sheremetyevo – Aeroexpress trains leave Belorussky vokzal every 30 minutes. Vnukovo – Aeroexpress trains leave from Kievsky vokzal every hour.

Orientation

Moscow's geography is organised in a series of concentric circles, which – like the rings of a tree – reflect the city's stages of growth around the Kremlin in the centre. The city is bisected by the Moscow River, which winds through the city along with its tributaries. The old walls of Kitaigorod once enclosed areas around Red Square down to the river. This division is now marked by Teatralny proezd and Lubyanka, Staraya and Novaya ploshchads.

The first ring built after Kitaigorod was the White City, a protected residential district whose walls stretched in an arch along

METRO TICKETS

Tickets for the metro are sold at the cash desks inside the stations. Tickets can be bought for 1, 2, 5, 10 or 20 journeys. There are also monthly passes available. A ticket is good for one journey, no matter how far you travel. Given the inexpensive nature of tickets on the metro you may find it is worth buying a pass for 20 journeys at the beginning of your stay. Even though you may not use all of this, it will save you queuing for a ticket each time you travel. During peak periods, buying a ticket from the *kacca* can take just as long as a journey to your destination.

what is now the Boulevard Ring. This road, congested with traffic but with a boulevard of trees and gardens in the centre, was laid in the late 18th century when the White City walls were demolished. The final historic ring of the city is the Garden Ring, which replaced the old earthen ramparts of medieval times after the War of 1812. This is now little more than a massive motorway, but still marks the end of Moscow's city centre.

Outside the Garden Ring there are a few neighbourhoods of note. Krasnaya Presnaya is the area between the Moscow River and the Garden Ring to the west. Cross the Moscow River here to get to Fili. To the south lie Sparrow Hills and Moscow State University.

The big 'tongue' which lies to the south of the Moscow River opposite the Kremlin is known as Zamoskvoreche (beyond the Moscow River) and has always been a separate entity to Moscow's walled city. East of Zamoskvoreche and south of the Yauza River is the area of Taganka.

Two more ring roads now encircle the city: the Third Transport Ring within the city and the Moscow Ring Road (known by the Russian abbreviation MKAD), which marks the outer limits of the city proper.

Public Transport

Metro

The quickest and most convenient form of transport in Moscow is the metro, which links the city centre with the suburbs and carries 9.7 million passengers a day.

Construction started before World War II, and the system is still expanding. At the last count there were 12 lines, 200 stations and 333km (207 miles) of track. Not only is the service efficient but, from an architectural point of view, the stations are tourist attractions in their own right (see page 120).

The metro runs from 6am to 1am, and there are trains at approximately 3-minute intervals. The fares increase sharply every few months, but still remain very cheap for foreigners (one journey costs about 70 US cents).

As efficient as the system is, it does have its quirks. Many stations have several exits, which are located hundreds of metres away from one another. Luckily all exits are labelled with the streets and main attractions that are above you. However, most of these signs are still only in Russian.

To add to the confusion, when lines meet, the 'stations' for each line have a different name.

Boarding a plane at Domodedovo Airport.

TRANSPORT

A – Z

LANGUAGE

The bilingual maps in all train carriages are of enormous benefit.

Commuter trains

Commuter trains (*Elektrichki*) serve Moscow's satellite towns. At train terminals serving long-distance locations, tickets are sold at the *Prigorodnie Kassi*. Tickets are sold according to the intended destination.

Trams, trolleybuses and buses

All of these forms of transport run from 5.30/6am to 1am, depending on the route. Tickets can be bought singly or in 'books' in the underpasses next to metro stations. Some buses have a system of mechanised entry (you place the ticket in the slot and the gate opens), which can considerably slow journey times at rush hours. On some trams/ trolleybuses you pay the conductor. On others you pay the driver, passing the money through the hole in the glass, even while the bus is in motion. Failure to pay after one stop may lead to an encounter with the Moscow Travel Inspectors, burly guys who travel in pairs looking for fare dodgers (known as *zayts* – or 'hares' – in Russian) to fine.

Taxis

There are two types of taxi: registered taxis are for personal use and run day and night; taxi-buses or *marshrutnye taxis* (small, fast

mini vans) operate the same routes from 9am to 9pm from metro or mainline stations.

Marshrutnye can be flagged down anywhere on route. They don't take standing passengers, but they do get plenty of squashed ones. Only pay the flat fare that is marked on the window.

Moscow's registered taxis are usually yellow with a narrow chequered band round the sides. Most taxis are metered but there is no official tariff and fares vary considerably, so agree a price beforehand. It is always safer to get a hotel to book a cab for you.

Driving

Car rental

Several car-rental companies operate in Moscow, but you may feel most comfortable with the familiar Western companies which can be found at airports. Hiring a car in Russia isn't recommended.

Petrol stations

Petrol stations are located all over the city. On the outskirts they are found on main roads, but near the centre they tend to be hidden on side streets.

Rules of the road

Rules of the road and road signs correspond in general to international standards. The basic rules, however, are worth mentioning. Traffic drives on the right.
Don't drive after drinking or under the influence of drugs or medication.
Drivers must have an international driving licence and documents verifying their right to drive the car. These papers must be in Russian and can be issued by Russian travel agents.
Vehicles, except for those rented from official travel agencies, must carry the national registration code and have a national licence plate.
The use of the horn is prohibited within city limits except in emer-

gencies.
The use of seat belts for the driver and front-seat passenger is compulsory.
The speed limit in populated areas (marked by blue-coloured signs indicating 'town') is 60kph (37mph); on most arterial roads the limit is 90kph (55mph). On highways different limits apply and these are shown on road signs.

On Foot

Despite Moscow's size, within the Garden Ring it is quite possible to get around on foot, especially if you break your journeys up into 'chunks'. Bicycling is not really an option; there are no cycle lanes in Moscow, and cyclists, while becoming more common, are still rare.

Russian drivers are particularly reckless, and one should take great care when crossing the road.

Taxi.

TRANSPORT

A – Z

AN ALPHABETICAL SUMMARY OF PRACTICAL INFORMATION

A

Admission charges

You will still occasionally find dual pricing (one price for locals, another for foreigners) at Russian museums and galleries. The difference can be big. International student discount cards are occasionally accepted as proof of identity where there is a system of student discounts. However, the cashiers sometimes only recognise those issued by Russian educational authorities.

B

Budgeting for your trip

Although Moscow has a real dearth of cheap, budget hotels, it is still worth hunting around for hotel rooms. Moscow is expensive but not prohibitively so, and when you look at the low average wage it's clear that a lot of people get by in the Russian capital with not much money at all.

If you choose to stay in luxury five-star hotels, eat in expensive restaurants, take taxis provided by your hotel, etc, you are not going to get much change out of US$700 a day. However, by staying in cheaper hotels or hostels,

eating in self-service cafeterias and using the metro it is possible to get by on US$50–100 a day, per person, depending on what you do on a particular day.

Public transport is very cheap (see page 221). One unwelcome expense is the hefty photography charge many museums, the Kremlin and most churches slap onto ticket prices.

C

Climate

Moscow has a continental climate, with cold, snowy winters and warm, humid summers. The first snowfall usually occurs in early November, and in most years the city is snow-covered until mid-to-late March. In midwinter daytime temperatures are typically between –10 and –5°C (14–23°F), with the odd milder day around freezing point. Occasional Siberian spells bring temperatures below –20°C (–4F). Spring is fairly short-lived, with large swings in temperature and some rainy weather. By the middle of June the weather is more settled, and by mid-August most days are warm or hot (typically 22–26°C/72–79°F) although heat waves do occur, when it can be over 32°C (90°F) for days on

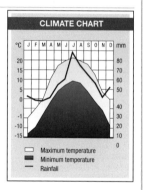

CLIMATE CHART

°C | J F M A M J J A S O N D | mm

- Maximum temperature
- Minimum temperature
- Rainfall

end. North winds can also bring some very cool summer days, below 15°C (59°F). Rain is not uncommon in summer. Autumn tends to be cool and dry, as the days shorten from late August until the colder weather arrives in late October and the long winter starts again.

When to visit

Moscow offers two distinctive seasons for visitors. For those wanting to experience a real Russian winter – cold, but very beautiful – the middle of January to end of February is the best time to stay. The summers in Moscow are too hot and dusty for most – the driest and most sweltering period is between June and early September. Two periods worth avoid-

A – Z

LANGUAGE

ing are the beginning of May, when much of the city shuts down to take advantage of the month's two national holidays (the 1st and 9th), and New Year and Orthodox Christmas (7th January), when Russians also take a long break.

What to wear

Unless you are planning to attend a formal event, smart casual tends to do it in Moscow. Dressing to blend in with the D&G and Chanel crowd will make you look ridiculous, as will purposefully dressing down to look inconspicuous. When packing for a winter trip, remember that temperatures can reach −29°C (−20°F), and you should bring gloves, a good winter coat and thick waterproof shoes/boots.

Crime and Safety

Taking into account the size of Moscow, average salaries and general atmosphere in society, the Russian capital is not as dangerous for visitors as might be expected. However, while there is no need to become excessively cautious, taking the obvious precautions that you would in any large city (wearing a money belt, etc) should help to ensure a trouble-free visit. If you are robbed you will probably require a police report to claim compensation from your insurance company.

Try not to draw attention to yourself, especially late at night on the metro. There have been a number of attacks on foreigners of African, Middle Eastern or Asian descent over the years, and travellers should be particularly alert at night on public transport.

Apart from this, the only problem likely to be encountered is the police. Although it is forbidden for ordinary police officers to stop and check registration documents on the street, the police may well continue to do so, counting on the average tourist's ignorance of the law and lack of

Russian language skills. Even if your papers are in order they will more than likely 'find' a problem and demand an on-the-spot 'fine'. For the non-Russian speaker there is little that can be done about this. The best option is to refuse stubbornly, pleading incomprehension, but if 'officers' persist, ask to be taken to the nearest police station – this usually does the trick.

Customs Regulations

When you arrive in the country, you must fill out a customs declaration for any cash over US$10,000. In this case, be sure to use the Red Channel at the airport and have the customs officer stamp your declaration. You are allowed to bring in personal property you do not intend to offer for sale on the territory of the Russian Federation. It's a good idea to keep receipts for expensive gifts and souvenirs to avoid interminable questions at customs.

The only time some foreigners get caught out by Russia's customs laws is when they try to take anything out of the country which looks old. Anything manufactured or printed over 50 years ago is considered an object of cultural significance and may be confiscated. If you are unsure about something you have bought, the Ministry of Culture (ulitsa Akademika Korolyova 21; tel: 499-391 4212) should be able to confirm whether an item can be exported. There are also restrictions on tobacco, alcohol and caviar.

D

Disabled Travellers

Russia is a difficult place for people with disabilities, with many disabled Russians spending virtually their entire lives indoors. There are almost no facilities for the disabled (the metro, for example, would be virtually impossible

to navigate in a wheelchair). For this reason, it is recommended that travellers with disabilities do not come to Moscow alone and think very hard about coming even if accompanied by an able-bodied person.

E

Electricity

Electrical supply is 220v. Sockets require a continental-type two-pin plug. Take adaptors with you as they are not available in Russia.

Embassies and Consulates

Embassies in Moscow

Most countries are represented in Moscow. Below is a list of some of the main embassies.
Australia
Podkolokolny pereulok 10A/2
Tel: 495-956 6070
Canada
Starokonyushny pereulok 23
Tel: 495-105 6000
Ireland
Grokholsky pereulok 5
Tel: 495-937 5911
New Zealand
Povarskaya ulitsa 44
Tel: 495-956 3579
South Africa
Granatny pereulok 1, bldg 9
Tel: 495-540 1177
UK
Smolenskaya Naberezhnaya 10
Tel: 495-956 7200
US
Bolshaya Devyatinsky pereulok 8
Tel: 495-728 5000

Entry Requirements

Today the best way to get a visa is to go through a specialist visa agency in your own country. The process otherwise takes a long time and involves a lot of paperwork. In the UK, Real Russia (www.realrussia.co.uk) is a very professional outfit. Note that applicants in the UK must visit the

Russian embassy visa application centre to provide fingerprints. In the US, Visa HQ (www.visahq.com) are the people to turn to.

There are essentially three types of visa: tourist visas valid for a maximum of 30 days, business visas valid for up to a year and transit visas valid for 72 hours. The only time you won't need a visa to enter Russia is if you are a passenger arriving on a cruise ship in St Petersburg.

When you arrive in the country, you will have to fill out a migration card, usually provided on board the plane. You must keep the stamped migration card with your passport and surrender it upon leaving the country.

You are obliged to have your passport and visa registered within seven working days of arrival and every time you move to another town. Taking weekends into account, this in theory gives you 9 days in which to register. Hotels will do this for you. If you are staying with a friend he or she can, in theory, register you at the post office. It is sensible to carry your passport and visa at all times while you are in Russia as the police have the right to check your identity at will. However the police do not have the right to fine you if you are unregistered. They must hand you over to the immigration authorities who should open an official case against you. This is rarely done.

Etiquette

Russians expect you to take off your shoes when entering a private flat and whistling indoors is considered unlucky. Uniquely, museum guests are often asked to wear felt slippers *(tapochki)* when touring museums. It helps keep wooden floors clean and shiny. These days conversations about Russia's foreign policy in Ukraine and Syria should probably be avoided with strangers, and with friends if you wish to keep them.

In Russia, eye contact does not have to be established between

customer and shop assistant/ ticket seller for the transaction to begin – this can be disconcerting for Westerners. The Russians also have a saying – 'A smile without reason is a sign of stupidity' (it rhymes in Russian), so what you consider a friendly smile can be interpreted in quite a different way by strangers in public situations.

Women visiting Russia should be aware that men in Russia are a lot more 'old-fashioned' than men in the West, and should not be surprised if a male companion holds open doors, offers his hand when getting off buses, etc. Men are also, usually, expected to foot the bill in restaurants on dates.

Emergency Numbers

All Russian cities have the same emergency telephone numbers for the individual emergency services, which can be dialled free of charge from public telephones. There is also a single emergency number: 112. Officials responding to these calls speak very little English, so a minimal knowledge of Russian may be needed to make yourself understood.
Fire *(Pozharnaya okhrana).* 101
Police *(Politsiya):* 102
Ambulance *(Skoraya pomoshch):* 103
Gas emergency *(Sluzhba gaza):* 104

G

Gay and Lesbian Travellers

Russia was always a conservative society and the hostility towards 'alternative lifestyles' that Putin's regime has created has made things even worse. Open hostility is rare, but public displays of affection between members of the same sex might at best evoke ridicule, at worst lead to arrest. There is a gay scene in Moscow but it's kept very low key for obvious reasons.

H

Health and Medical Care

Water

Although the water is not as bad as in St Petersburg, it is still not a particularly good idea to drink it straight from the tap in Moscow. That said, it is OK in small doses (brushing teeth, etc), and can be used for cooking. Cheap mineral and drinking water is available everywhere.

Medical Services

No vaccinations are required for visits to Russia, but immunisation aginst tetanus and diphtheria are recommended. It is also advisable to be inoculated against Hepatitis A.

It is a good idea to take your own medicines, although there are pharmacies selling foreign medicines where you can find most things you need. Emergency medical services for tourists are free of charge, but you will have to pay for drugs and in-patient treatment, so health insurance is strongly recommended. Doctors at the major hotels speak foreign languages. The following hospitals offer Western levels of service, but charge accordingly:
MEDSI International Clinic
Grokholsky pereulok 1
Tel: 495-290 9386
International SOS Clinic
Grokholsky pereulok 31, 10th floor
Tel: 495-937 5760
European Medical Centre
Spiridonsky pereulok 5
Tel: 495-933 6655

Dentists

Dentists are available at the American (MEDSI) and European Medical Centres (see above).
European Dental Centre
6/1, 1-y Nikoloschepovsky pereulok; tel: 495-933 0002 (24 hours); Smolenskaya metro

Pharmacies

36.6 (www.366.ru) is a chain of good Western-style pharmacies in Moscow. It has branches throughout the city, mostly open Mon–Sat 10am–8pm, including: GUM (Red Square), 9 ulitsa Tverskaya and 5/1 Teatralny proezd.

I

Identity Papers

According to Russian law, everyone should carry their passport (Russians have an internal one) at all times. Foreigners also need to carry their registration receipts and possibly used plane and railway tickets, too! Some visitors choose to carry photocopies, fearing their documents may be stolen, and indeed it is extremely difficult to replace a lost or stolen visa. The best idea is to make copies of all your documents and leave them in the hotel. If you are stopped by the police and they find a problem with your papers, ask to be taken to the nearest police station. Never pay a fine on the spot as this is just the cops looking for a bit of cash from a foreigner.

Internet

Wi-fi is ubiquitous across Moscow and you are never far away from a café or bar where Wi-fi is laid on free of charge and rare is the hotel that doesn't provide web connection. Speeds are normally high. When using a smartphone, get a local SIM card (see page 227) as roaming charges in Russia are astronomical.

L

Left Luggage

There are places to leave luggage – *Kamer; khraneniya* – in train terminals and airports. This is also the name used for baggage checks in many museums.

M

Maps

Although in the USSR it was extremely hard to get hold of accurate maps, today they are available everywhere, and you can probably pick one up in your hotel.

Media

Newspapers

News-stands in major hotels as well as foreign-owned supermarkets in the big cities have current English-language magazines and newspapers.

In Moscow, *The Moscow Times* (www.moscowtimes.ru) takes a rare critical view of the Kremlin and is a good read.

Russian-language Press

The Russian media has changed since Vladimir Putin came to office in 2000. The major television stations (the main source of news for Russians) are strongly managed by the State and do not provide a diversity of information and opinion. However, the print media, internet and to some extent radio have a certain degree of independence, although they reach a far smaller portion of the population. Tabloids and glossies are very popular; the Russian edition of *Cosmopolitan* is the magazine's second biggest seller. For an entertaining taste of the absurd propaganda Russians are exposed to on a daily basis but in English log onto www.english.pravda.ru.

Television

Most large hotels provide cable or satellite television with a full array of English-language news and entertainment stations, and in the major cities there are also sports bars and other venues that broadcast English-language programming.

Money

Currency

The rouble is divided into 100 kopeks. There are 5, 10, 50, 100, 500 and 1,000 rouble banknotes. Coins are 1, 2 and 5 roubles, as well as 1, 5, 10 and 50 kopeks.

Currency Exchange

These can be found all over the city, including in hotels. Most deal exclusively in cash and major credit cards (eg Amex, Visa), but not usually traveller's cheques; to change these, try a bank.

Credit Cards

Most tourist-related businesses accept major credit cards: American Express, Diners Club, Visa and MasterCard. ATMs (called *bankomat*) are more widespread than in most Western cities. Some issue roubles and dollars/euros.

Tipping

The tipping etiquette in Russia is confused. Some guidebooks recommend adding 10 percent to the bill but most serving staff would be bewildered by such an amount. Rounding up the bill is now common, but the general rule is only tip if you are actually satisfied with the service.

O

Opening Hours

Most stores in Russia open from 10am to 8pm, though in the centre of major cities it is not difficult to find 24-hour convenience food stores and chemists. Lunch breaks are more or less a thing of the past, though don't be surprised if you encounter a locked door between 1pm and 3pm, especially outside of the city centre. Banks are normally open 9am to 6pm weekdays and in some cases Saturdays, too. Restaurants are generally open between 11am and 11pm.

TRANSPORT

P

Photography

Generally speaking, taking photographs in galleries, museums and exhibitions is permitted though usually for a hefty fee; visitors should take care not to take photographs of military installations or anything else that might be seen as a threat to security. This could in theory include railway stations, bridges, factories and tunnels. Innocent photographers are still sometimes detained in Russia for taking photos on and around train stations, though this normally happens well away from Moscow.

Postal Services

Post offices open Mon–Sat 9am–6pm; they often close at midday for an hour, and are closed on Sundays. Some post offices, however, open only from 9am–3pm or 2–8pm. The mail service in Russia provides an increasing variety and standard of services, including fax, courier, mail and sometimes internet. Not all post offices accept international mail bigger than a standard letter. International postal delivery can be slow – it may take two or three weeks for a letter from Moscow to reach Western Europe and sometimes even a month or more to reach the US. Theft of postal items is now rare.

Main post offices *(Glavpochshtamt):* 26 ulitsa Myasnitskaya, open 24 hours, and 7 Tverskaya ulitsa, open Mon–Fri 9.30am–6pm.

Public Holidays

1–5 January New Year holidays
7 January Orthodox Christmas Day
23 February Defence of the Motherland
8 March Women's Day
1 May Labour Day

9 May Victory Day
12 June Independence Day
4 November Unity Day

Public Toilets

There are fee-charging chemical toilets outside most metro stations. They are generally clean. Failing this, nip into one of the city's ubiquitous McDonalds.

R

Religious Services

Most churches are open for services. The main Sunday service usually starts around 9am.

S

Student Travellers

Many places (museums, etc) in Russia only recognise Russian student ID cards, although a lot depends on the cashier. Russia doesn't have any particularly good deals for students. Students are, the Russian view seems to be, foreigners, and little distinction is made between them and their wealthier compatriots.

T

Telephones

The mobile phone signal in Moscow covers the entire city. Local SIM cards are cheap, but you'll have to get a local to buy one for you as you must have a resident's permit to do so. Calls are relatively cheap.

The main type of public phone box uses plastic cards, available in units of 5, 10, 20 or 50 at metro stations and kiosks. Insert the card and dial the number. When your call is answered press the # button to complete the connection.

International phone fees as charged by hotels are exorbitant. Most travellers to Russia now rely on Skype calls.

Calling from Abroad

To call Moscow from abroad you must dial the country code, 7, followed by 495 (or 499), the area code(s) for Moscow. Unless you have a special discount plan you will find calling Russia very expensive.

Calling Abroad

For international calls, dial 8 +10 + the country code, followed by the area code (minus the initial 0) and finally the number.
Australia 61
UK 44
US and Canada 1

Time Zone

GMT plus 3 hours.

Tourist Information

Surprisingly Moscow has no tourist office, although www.moscow.info, a tourism website sponsored by the city government, has information on sights, listings and travel services.

Tour Operators

Today the city has dozens of tour operators offering all sorts of services, from hotel reservations and home stays to tickets for cultural events and trips around the Golden Ring.
Patriarshy Dom
Tel: 495-795 0927; www.toursinrussia.com
Capital Tours
Tel: 495-232 2442; www.capitaltours.ru

W

Weights and Measures

Russia uses the metric system of weights and measures.

A – Z

LANGUAGE

LANGUAGE

UNDERSTANDING THE LANGUAGE

LINGUISTIC HISTORY

Russian belongs to the Slavonic branch of the Indo-European family of languages. English, German, French, Spanish and Hindi are its relatives.

It is important when speaking Russian that you reproduce the accent (marked here before each stressed vowel with the sign ') correctly to be understood well.

Historically Russian can be called a comparatively young language. The evolution of the language to its present form on the basis of the spoken language of Eastern Slavs and the Church-Slavonic written language is thought to have occurred between the 11th and 14th centuries.

Modern Russian has absorbed a considerable number of foreign words. Very few tourists will be puzzled by Russian words such as *telefon*, *televizor*, *teatr*, *otel*, *restoran*, *kafe*, *taxi*, *metro*, *aeroport*.

What intimidates people making their first acquaintance with Russian is the Cyrillic alphabet. In fact the alphabet can be remembered easily after a few repetitions and the difference with the Latin alphabet is only minimal. An understanding of the Russian alphabet permits one to make out the names of the streets and the shop signs.

The Russian (or Cyrillic) alphabet was created by two brothers, philosophers and public figures Constantine (St Cyril) and Methodius, both born in Solun (now Thessaloniki in Greece). Their purpose was to facilitate the spread of Greek liturgical books to Slavonic speaking countries. Today the Cyrillic alphabet with different modifications is used in the Ukrainian, Belarusian, Bulgarian and Serbian languages, among others.

TRANSLITERATION

There are four systems of transliteration of Russian words into English (see *The Transliteration of Modern Russian for English Language Publications* by J.T. Shaw, the University of Wisconsin Press, 1967). If necessary, the systems can be combined so that one letter or a group of letters is transliterated according to one system and the other according to another. To transliterate some Russian letters, English letter combinations are used: ж = zh, х = kh, ц = ts, ч = ch, ш = sh, щ = shch, ю = yu, я = ya, ё = yo.

The Russian letter combination кс is transliterated both as *ks* and as *x*. Russian letters are transliterated (with a few exceptions) in a similar way: й, ы = y, е, ё = e.

To transliterate the Russian soft sign between the consonants or where there is no consonant after the vowel, the apostrophe is

LANGUAGE CENTRES

A relatively inexpensive way to visit Russia is through institutes that run Russian language courses. Among these are the Lomonosov and Lumumba universities, the Pushkin Institute of Russian Language in Moscow, the University of St Petersburg and other universities and linguistic co-operatives. The Shevchenko University in Kiev, Ukraine, is another option. They are all able to arrange visas and inexpensive accommodation during the study period.

To communicate directly with the universities you should contact the cultural attaché of the Russian embassy or consulate.

When selecting courses, care should be taken to ensure that the teaching is on a professional level. It is also worth contacting the Russian departments of universities at home. Many are now running short (one- or two-week) overseas study tours (which include flights, accommodation and transport within Russia and tuition fees) for the general public.

used, or the soft sign is ignored, as before vowels. The transliteration of nominal inflections has a number of peculiarities: ый, ий = y, ие, ье = ie, ия = ia.

If the traditional English spelling in names differs from their letter-by-letter transliteration they are mostly translated in their English form: Moscow (city), but river Moskva.

The genitive inflections in the names of streets and other objects are translated according to their pronunciation, not their spelling: площадь Горького, (ploshchad' Gór'kogo) = ploshchad Gorkovo in this book. The transliteration in this section shows the way to pronounce Russian words and therefore does not correspond exactly with their spelling.

The city maps and their captions use Russian words and abbreviations: ul. (úlitsa) means street; per. (pereúlok) – lane; prosp. (prospékt) – avenue; pl. (plóshchadь) – square; alléya – alley; bulvár – boulevard; magistrál – main line; proézd – passage; shossé – highway; spusk – slope.

The Russian system of writing out house numbers is as follows prosp. Kalinina 28 (28 Kalinin Avenue).

USEFUL WORDS AND PHRASES

Numbers

1 adín один
2 dva два
3 tri три
4 chityri четыре
5 pyat' пять
6 shes't' шесть
7 sem семь
8 vósim восемь
9 d'évit девять
10 d'ésit десять
11 adínatsat' одиннадцать
12 dvinátsat' двенадцать
13 trinátsat' тринадцать
14 chityrnatsat' четырнадцать
15 pitnátsat' пятнадцать
16 shysnátsat' шестнадцать
17 simnátsat' семнадцать
18 vasimnátsat' восемнадцать
19 divitnátsat' девятнадцать
20 dvátsat' двадцать
21 dvatsat' adin двадцать один
30 trítsat' тридцать
40 sórak сорок
50 pidisyat пятьдесят
60 shyz'disyat шестьдесят
70 s'émdisyat семьдесят
80 vósimdisyat восемьдесят
90 divinósta девяносто
100 sto сто
200 dv'és'ti двести
300 trísta триста
400 chityrista четыреста
500 pitsót пятьсот
600 shyssót шестьсот
700 simsót семьсот
800 vasimsót восемьсот
900 divitsót девятьсот
1,000 tysicha тысяча
2,000 dve tysichi две тысяч и
10,000 d'ésit' tysich десятьтысяч
100,000 sto tysich сто тысяч
1,000,000 milión миллион
1,000,000,000 miliárd миллиард

Pronouns

I/we ya/my я/мы
You ty (singular, informal)/vy (plural, or formal singular) ты/вы
He/she/they on/aná/aní он/она/они
My/mine moj (object masculine)/mayá (object feminine)/mayó (neutral or without marking the gender)/maí (plural) мой/моя/моё/мои
Our/ours nash/násha/náshe/náshy (resp.) наш/наша/наше/наши
Your/yours tvoj etc. (see My)/vash etc. (see Our) твой/ваш
His/her, hers/their, theirs jivó/jiyó/ikh его/её/их
Who? khto? Кто?
What? shto? Что?

Greetings and Acquaintance

Hello!
zdrástvuti (neutral, and often accompanied by shaking hands, but this is not necessary) Здравствуйте!
zdrástvuj (to one person, informal) Здравствуй!
alo! (by telephone only) Алло!

The first two columns show the printed letter in Russian upper and lower case. The third column demonstrates how the Russian letters sound; the final letters in bold are the name of the letter in Russian.

А а **a**, archaeology **a**
Б б **b**, buddy **be**
В в **v**, vow **v**
Г г **g**, glad **ge**
Д д **d**, dot (the tip of the tongue close to the teeth, not the alveoli) **de**
Е е **e**, get **ye**
Ё ё **yo**, yoke **yo**
Ж ж **zh**, composure **zhe**
З з **z**, zest **ze**
И и **i**, ink **i**
Й й **j**, yes **jot**
К к **k**, kind **ka**
Л л **l**, life (but a bit harder) **el'**
М м **m**, memory **em**
Н н **n**, nut **en**
О о **o**, optimum **o**
П п **p**, party **pe**
Р р **r** (rumbling – as in Italian, the tip of the tongue is vibrating) **er**
С с **s**, sound **es**
Т т **t**, title (the tip of the tongue close to the teeth) **te**
У у **u**, nook **u**
Ф ф **f**, flower **ef**
Х х **kh**, hawk **ha**
Ц ц **ts**, (pronounced conjointly) **tse**
Ч ч **ch**, charter **che**
Ш ш **sh**, shy **sha**
Щ щ **shch**, (pronounced conjointly) **shcha**
ъ (the hard sign)
Ы ы **y** (pronounced with the same position of a tongue as when pronouncing G, К) **y**
ь (the soft sign)
Э э **e**, ensign **e**
Ю ю **yu**, you **yu**
Я я **ya**, yard **ya**

priv'ét! (informal) Привет!
Good afternoon/Good evening
dóbry den'/dobry véchir Добрый день/Добрый вечер
Good morning/Good night
dobrae útra/dobraj nóchi (= Sleep

well) Доброе утро/Доброй ночи
Goodbye
dasvidán'ye (neutral) До свиданья
ciao! (informal) Чао!
paká! (informal, literally 'until')
Пока!
Good luck to you! *shchislíva!*
Счастливо!
What is your name? *kak vas
(tibya) zavút?/kak váshe ímya
ótchistva?* (the second is formal)
Как вас (тебя) зовут?/Как ваше
имя и отчество?
My name is.../I am... *minya
zavut.../ya...* Меня зовут.../Я...
It's a pleasure *óchin' priyatna*
Очень приятно
Good/excellent *kharashó/
atlichno* хорошо/отлично
Do you speak English? *vy gava-
ríti pa anglíski?* Вы говорите
по-английски?
**I don't understand/I didn't
understand** *ya ni panimáyu/ya ni
pónyal* Я не понимаю/Я не понял
Repeat, please *pavtaríti pazhál-
sta* Повторите, пожалуйста
What do you call this? *kak éta
nazyvaitsa?* Как это называется?
How do you say...? *kak ska-
zat...?* Как вы сказаиь...?
Please/Thank you (very much)
pazhálsta/(bal'shóe) spasíba
Пожалуйста/(бальшоэ) спасибо
Excuse me *izviníti* Извините

Getting Around

Where is the...? *gd'e
(nakhóditsa)...?* Где
находится...?
beach *plyazh* ...пляж
bathroom *tualet* ...туацет
bus station *aftóbusnaya stánt-
syja/aftavakzál* ...автобусная
станция/автовокзал
bus stop *astanófka aftóbusa* ...
остановка автобуса
airport *airapórt* ...аэропорт
railway station *vakzál/stántsyja*
(in small towns) ...вокзал/станция
post office *póchta* ...почта
police station *...milítsyja* ...
милиция
ticket office *bil'étnaya kássa* ...
билетная касса
market place *rynak/bazár* ...
рынок/базар
embassy/consulate *pasól'stva/*

kónsul'stva ...посольство/
консульство
Where is there a...? *gd'e
z'd'es'...?* Где здесь...?
currency exchange *abm'én
val'úty* ...обмен валюты
pharmacy *apt'éka* ...аптека
(good) hotel *(kharóshyj) atél'/
(kharoshaya) gastínitsa* ...
(хороший)отель/(хорошая)
гостиница
restaurant *ristarán* ...ресторан
bar *bar* ...бар
taxi stand *stayanka taxi* ...
стоянка такси
subway station *mitró* ...метро
service station *aftazaprávach-
naya stantsyja/aftasárvis* ...
автозаправочная станция
news-stand *gaz'étnyj kiosk* ...
газетный киоск
public telephone *tilifón* ...
телефон
supermarket *univirsám* ...
универсам
department store *univirmák* ...
универмаг
hairdresser *parikmákhirskaya* ...
парикмахерская
jeweller *yuvilírnyj magazine* ...
ювелирный магазин
hospital *bal'nítsa* ...больница
Do you have...? *u vas jes't'...?* У
вас есть...?
I (don't) want... *ya (ni) khachyu...*
Я (не) хочу...
I want to buy... *ya khachyu
kupít'...* Я хочу купить...
Where can I buy... *gd'e ya magú
kupít'...* Где я могу купить...
cigarettes *sigaréty* ...сигареты
wine *vinó* ...вино
film *fotoplyonku* ...фотоплёнку
a ticket for... *bilét na... ...билет
на...
this *éta* ...это
postcards/envelopes *atkrytki/
kanv'érty* ...открытки/конверты
a pen/a pencil *rúchku/
karandásh* ...ручку/карандаш
soap/shampoo *myla/shampún'*
...мыло/шампунь
aspirin *aspirn* ...аспирин
I need... *mn'e núzhna...* Мне
нужно...
I need a doctor/a mechanic
mn'e núzhyn dóktar/aftamikhánik
Мне нужен доктор/автомеханик
I need help *mn'e nuzhná*

TERMS OF ADDRESS

Modern Russian has no established and universally used
forms of salutation. The old
revolutionary form *tavárishch*
(comrade), still used among
some party members, lacks
popularity among the rest of
the population. Alternatives
include: *Izviníti, skazhíte
pozhálsta...* (Excuse me, tell
me, please...) or *Izviníti,
mózhna sprasít...*) or *I ozhálst*
(Excuse me, can I ask you...).

If you want to sound original
and show your understanding
of the history of courteous
forms of greeting, you can
address a man as *gospodin*
(sir), and a woman as *gos-
pozha* (madam). These are
very formal honorifics, used
with a person's last name.

If you know the name of the
father of the person you are
talking to, the best and the
most neutral way of address-
ing them is to use their first
name and patronymic, formed
by adding -*ich* to their father's
name if it is a man, and -*orna* if
it is a woman.

You will hear the common
parlance forms *Maladói
chelavék!* (Young man!) and
Dévushka! (Girl!) directed
towards a person of any age,
and also *Zhénshchina!*
(Woman!) to women on the
bus, in the shop or at the market. These forms should be
avoided in conversation.

pómashch' Мне нужна помощь
Car/plane/trains/ship
mashyna/samal'yot/póist/karábl'
машына/самолёт/поезд/корабль
A ticket to... *bil'ét do...* билет
до...
How can I get to... *kak ya magu
dabrátsa do...* Как я могу
добраться до...
Please, take me to... *pazhalsta
atvizíti minya...* Пожалуйста,
отвезите меня...
What is this place called? *kak
nazyváitsa eta m'ésta?* Как

называется это место?
Where are we? *gd'e my?* Где мы?
Stop here *astanavíti z'd'es'*
Остановите здесь
Please wait *padazhdíti pazhalsta*
Подождите, пожалуйста
**When does the train [plane]
leave?** *kagdá atpravl'yaitsa póist
[samal'yot]?* Когда отправляется
поезд (самолёт)?
Where does this bus go? *kudá
id'yot état aftóbus?* Куда идёт
этот автобус?

Shopping

How much does it cost? *skól'ka
eta stóit?* Сколько это стоит?
That's very expensive *eta óchin'
dóraga* Это очень дорого
A lot, many/A little, few *mnóga/
mála* много/мало
It (doesn't) fits me *eta mn'e (ni)
padkhódit* Это мне (не) подходит

At the Hotel

I have a reservation *u minya
zakázana m'esta* У меня
заказановнецто
I want to make a reservation *ya
khachyu zakazát' m'esta* Я хочу
заказать место
A single (double) room
*adnam'éstnuyu (dvukhmestnuyu)
kómnatu* одноместную
(двухместную) комнату
I want to see the room *ya
khachyu pasmatrét' nómer* Я
хочу посмотреть номер
Key/suitcase/bag *klyuch/chi-
madán/súmka* ключ/чемодан/
сумка

Eating Out

Waiter/menu *afitsyánt/minyu*
официант/меню
I'd like a table for... people
bud'tye dobri stolik na... Будьте
добры, столик на...
Do you have...? *yest' li u vas* Есть
ли у вас...?
a set menu/a children's menu
*komplyeksniye obyedi/dyetskoye
myenyu* комплексные обеды/
детское меню
What do you recommend? *chto
vi posovyetuyetye* Уто вы

посоветуете?

I want to order... *ya khachyu
zakazat'...* Я хочу заказать
Breakfast/lunch/supper *záftrak/
ab'ét/úzhyn* Завтрак/обед/ужин
the house speciality *firminnaya
blyuda* фирменное блюдо
Mineral water/juice *minirál'naya
vadá/sok* минерал'ная вода/сок
Coffee/tea/beer *kófe/chai/píva*
кофе/чай/пиво
**What do you have to drink (alco-
holic)?** *shto u vas jes't' vypit'?*
Что у вас есть выпить?
Ice/fruit/dessert *marózhynaya/
frúkty/disért* мороженое/
фрукты/дессерт
Salt/pepper/sugar *sol'/périts/
sákhar* соль/перец/сахар
**Beef/pork/chicken/fish/
shrimp** *gavyadina/svinína/
kúritsa/ryba/kriv'étki* говядина/
свинина/курица/рыба/креветки
Vegetables/rice/potatoes
óvashchi/ris/kartófil' овоши/рис/
картофель
Bread/butter/eggs *khleb/
másla/yajtsa* хлеб/масло/яйца
Fork/knife/spoon *vilku/nozh/
lozhku* вилку/нож/ложку
The food is cold *yeda kholodnaya*
Еда холодная
The bill, please *shchyot pazhalsta* Счёт, пожалуйста
Is service included? *chayeviye
vklyuchyeni* Чаевые включены?
We'd like to pay separately *mi
budyem platit' porozn'* Мы будем
платить порознь
Delicious/Not so good *fkúsna/
ták sibe* вкусно/так себе
I want my change, please *zdá-
chu pazhalsta* Сдачу,
пожалуйста

Money

Do you accept credit cards? *vy
prinimáiti kridítnyi kártachki?* Вы
принимаете кредитные
карточки?
What is the exchange rate?
kakój kurs? Какой курс?

Time

What time is it? *katóryj chas?*
Который час?

Just a moment, please *adnú
minútachku* Одну минуточку
How long does it take? *skól'ka
vrémini eta zanimáit?* Сколько
времени это занимает?
Hour/day/week/month *chas/
den'/nid'élya/m'ésits* час/день/
неделя/месяц
At what time? *f kakóe vrémya?* В
какое время?
Yesterday/today/tomorrow
fchirá/sivód'nya/záftra вчера/
сегодня/завтра
Sunday *vaskris'én'je*
воскресенье
Monday *panid'él'nik*
понедельник
Tuesday *ftórnik* вторник
Wednesday *sridá* среда
Thursday *chitv'érk* четверг
Friday *pyatnitsa* пятница
Saturday *subóta* суббота
The weekend *vykhadnyi dni*
выходные дни

Signs and Inscriptions

вход/выход/входа нет *fkhot/
vykhat/fkhóda n'et* **Entrance/
exit/no entrance**
туалет/уборная *tual'ét/ubórnaya*
Lavatory
Ж (З)/М (М) *dlya zhén'shchin/
dlya mushchín* **Ladies/gentle-
men**
медпункт *medpúnkt* **Medical
services**
справочное бюро *správachnae
bzuro* **Information**
вода для питья *vadá dlya pit'ya*
Drinking water
вокзал *vakzál* **Terminal/railway
station**
открыто/закрыто *atkryta/zakryta*
Open/closed
продукты/гастроном *pradúkty/
gastranóm* **Grocery**
булочная/кондитерская *búlach-
naya/kan'dítirskaya* **Bakery/con-
fectionery**
закусочная/столовая *zakúsach-
naya/stalóvaya* **Refreshment
room/canteen**
самообслуживание
samaaslúzhivan'je **Self-service**
баня/прачечная/химчистка
bánya/práchichnaya/khimchístka
**Bathhouse/laundry/dry
cleaning**

FURTHER READING

HISTORY

The Blackwell Encyclopaedia of the Russian Revolution, edited by H. Shukman.
Catherine the Great, by J.T. Alexander.
Comrades 1917 – Russia in Revolution, by Brian Moynahan.
A History of the Soviet Union, by G.A. Hosking.
A History of Twentieth Century Russia, by Robert Service.
The Icon and the Axe, by James Billington.
The Last Tsar, by Edvard Radzinsky.
The Making of Modern Russia, by L. Kochan and R. Abraham.
A People's Tragedy, by Orlando Figes.
Nicholas II: Emperor of all the Russians, by Dominic Lieven.
Paul I of Russia, by Roderick E. McGrew.
Peter the Great: His Life and Work, by Robert K. Massie.
Soviet Colossus: History of the USSR, by Michael Kort.
Stalin, Man of Contradiction, by K.N. Cameron.
Stalinism and After: Road to Gorbachev, by Alec Nove.

LITERATURE

And Quiet Flows the Don and **The Don Flows Home to the Sea**, by Mikhail Sholokhov.
Anthology, by Daniil Kharms.
Blue Lard, by Vladimir Sorokin.
Crime and Punishment, The Brothers Karamazov, The Devils, by Fyodor Dostoyevsky.
Dead Souls Diary of a Madman and Other Stories, by Nikolai Gogol.

Doctor Zhivago, by Boris Pasternak.
Eugene Onegin, by Alexander Pushkin.
Fathers and Sons, On The Eve, A Hero of Our Time, by Mikhail Lermontov.
Lady with Lapdog and Other Stories, by Anton Chekhov.
The Life of Insects, by Victor Pelevin.
The Master and Margarita, by Mikhail Bulgakov.
The Penguin Book of Russian Short Stories, edited by David Richards.
Red Cavalry and Other Stories, by Isaac Babel.
Sportsman's Sketches, by Ivan Turgenev.
We, by Evgeny Zamyatin.
War and Peace, Anna Karenina and **The Death of Ivan Ilyich and Other Stories**, by Leo Tolstoy.

POLITICS

Glasnost in Action, by A. Nove.
Lenin's Tomb, by David Remnick.
The Other Russia, by Michael Glenny and Norman Stone.
Voices of Glasnost, by S. Cohen and K. van den Heuvel.

BIOGRAPHY/MEMOIRS

The Gulag Archipelago, by Alexander Solzhenitsyn.
The House by the Dvina, by Eugenie Fraser.
In the Beginning, by Irina Ratushinskaya.
The Making of Andrei Sakharov, by G. Bailey.
Ten Days that Shook the World, by John Reed.

ART

History of Russian Painting, by A. Bird.
The Irony Tower, by Andrew Solomon.
The Kremlin and its Treasures, by Rodimzeva, Rachmanov and Raimann.
New Worlds: Russian Art and Society 1900–3, by D. Elliott.
Russian Art of the Avant-Garde, by J.E. Bowlt.
Street Art of the Revolution, Tolstoy, V.I. Bibikova and C. Cooke.

TRAVEL

Travel and Natural History
Among the Russians, by Colin Thubron.
The Big Red Train Ride, by Eric Newby.
Caucasian Journey, by Negley Farson.
Epics of Everyday Life, by Susan Richards.
First Russia, Then Tibet, by Robert Byron.
The Food and Cooking of Russia, by Lesley Chamberlain.
Imperial Splendour, by George Galitzine.
Journey into Russia, by Laurens van der Post.
The Natural History of the USSR, by Algirdas Kynstautas.
The Nature of Russia, by John Massey Stewart.
The New Russians, by Hedrick Smith.
Portrait of the Soviet Union, by Fitzroy Maclean.
Sailing to Leningrad, by Roger Foxall.
The Trans–Siberian Rail Guide, by Robert Strauss.

MOSCOW STREET ATLAS

The key map shows the area of Moscow covered by the atlas
section. An index of street names and places of interest
shown on the maps can be found on the following pages.
For each entry there is a page number and grid reference

Map Legend

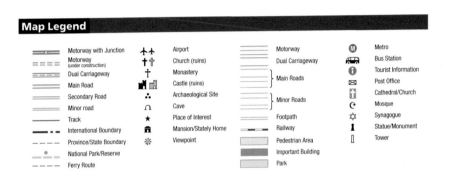

Motorway with Junction	✈ ✈ Airport	Motorway	Ⓜ	Metro
Motorway (under construction)	✝ ✝ Church (ruins)	Dual Carriageway	🚌	Bus Station
Dual Carriageway	✝ Monastery	Main Roads	❶	Tourist Information
Main Road	🏰 Castle (ruins)		✉	Post Office
Secondary Road	∴ Archaeological Site	Minor Roads	✝	Cathedral/Church
Minor road	∩ Cave		☾	Mosque
Track	★ Place of Interest	Footpath	✡	Synagogue
International Boundary	🏛 Mansion/Stately Home	Railway	🗿	Statue/Monument
Province/State Boundary	⁂ Viewpoint	Pedestrian Area	⯗	Tower
National Park/Reserve		Important Building		
Ferry Route		Park		

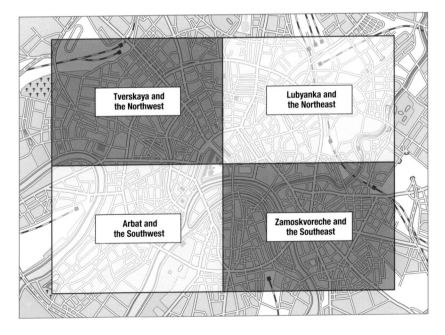

Tverskaya and
the Northwest

Lubyanka and
the Northeast

Arbat and
the Southwest

Zamoskvoreche and
the Southeast

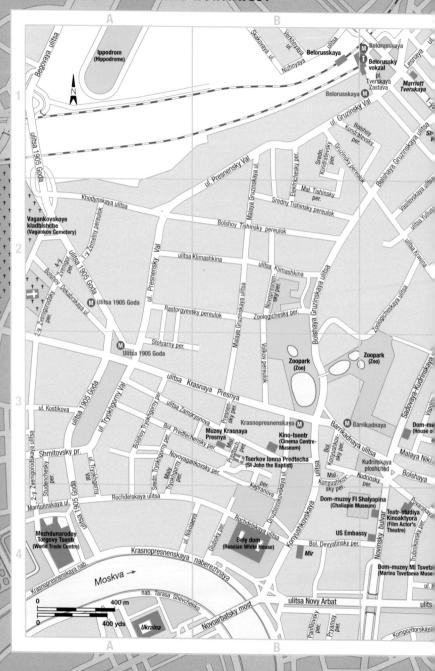

Ippodrom
(Hippodrome)

Belorusskaya

M Belorussky
vokzal
pl.
Tverskaya
Zastava

Marriott
Tverskaya

Belorusskaya **M**

ul. Gruzinsky Val

Skakovaya ul.

Verkhnaya ul.

Nizhnyaya

Bolshoy
Kondratevsky
per.

Sredn.
Kondratevsky
per.

Elektrichesky per.

Mal. Tishinsky
per.

Bolshaya Gruzinskaya ulitsa

Vasilyevskaya ulitsa

ulitsa Krasina

Lesnaya

Sh

Begovaya ulitsa

ulitsa 1905 Goda

ul. Presnensky Val

Khodynskaya ulitsa

Vagankovskoye
kladbishche
(Vagankov Cemetery)

4-y Zemelny pereulok

ulitsa 1905 Goda

Bolshoy Dekabrsky
per.

2-y Zvenigorodsky
per.

M Ulitsa 1905 Goda

M Ulitsa 1905 Goda

Stolyarny per.

Sredny Tishinsky pereulok

Bolshoy Tishinsky pereulok

ul. Presnensky Val

ulitsa Klimashkina

ulitsa Klimashkina

Malaya Gruzinskaya ulitsa

Novopresnen-
sky per.

Bolshaya Gruzinskaya ulitsa

Zoologichesky ulitsa

Rastorgyevsky pereulok

Zoologichesky per.

Volkov pereulok

Zoopark
(Zoo)

Zoopark
(Zoo)

Sadovaya-Kudrinskaya

ulitsa Krasnaya Presnya

ul. Kostikova

ulitsa 1905 Goda

Shmitovsky pr.

2-y Zvenigorodsky ulitsa

Studenchesky
per.

Mantulinskaya ul.

ulitsa 1905 Goda

ul. Tryokhgorny Val

Bolshoy Tryokhgorny per.

ulitsa Zamoryonova

Sredn. Tryokhgorny
per.

Mely
Tryokhgorny
per.

Novovagankovsky per.

Rochdelskaya ulitsa

ul. Nikolaeva

Presnen-
sky per.

Maly
Predtech.
per.

Bol. Predtechensky per.

Krasnopresnenskaya **M**

Muzey Krasnaya
Presnya

Kino-tsentr
(Cinema Centre-
Museum)

Tserkov Ionna Predtecha
(St John the Baptist)

M Barrikadnaya

Barrikadnaya ulitsa

Bol.
Konyushkov-
sky per.

Mal.
Konyushkov-
sky per.

Kudrinsky
per.

Kudrinskaya
ploshchad

Konyushkovskaya

per.
Kapranova

Druzhinnikovskaya ulitsa

Rochdelskaya ulitsa

Glubovky per.

Dom-m
(House o

Malaya Niki

Bolshaya

Dom-muzey FI Shalyapina
(Chaliapin Museum)

Teatr-studiya
Kinoaktyora
(Film Actor's
Theatre)

US Embassy

Novinsky bulvar

Povarskaya

Trubnikovsky per.

Mezhdunarodny
Torgovy Tsentr
(World Trade Centre)

Krasnopresnenskaya naberezhnaya

Bely dom
(Russian White House)

Mir

Bol. Devyatinsky per.

Dom-muzey MI Tsveta
(Marina Tsvetaeva Muse

ul.

Krasnopresnenskaya nab.

Moskva →

nab. Tarasa Shevchenko

ulitsa Novy Arbat

ulits

0   400 m

0   400 yds

Novoarbatsky most

Ukraina

Panfilovsky
per.

Pryamoy
per.

Kompozitorskaya

D

E

AAFadeevu

Alexandra Nevskovo ulitsa

Chayanova

Dolgorukovskaya ulitsa

Krasnoproletarskaya ulitsa

1-y Samotyochny per.

2-y Samotyochny per.

Samotyochnaya ulitsa

ulitsa

Olimpiysky prospekt

Fadeeva

Kosoy per.

**Muzey dekorativno prikladnovo I narodnovo iskusstva
(Museum of Decorative and Applied Art and Folk Art)**

Delegatskaya ulitsa

2-y Volkonsky per.

1-y Volkonsky per.

**Gosudarstvenny akademichesky tsentralny teatr kukol
(Obrazstov Puppet Theatre)**

Sadovaya-Samotyochnaya ulitsa

Oruzheyny pereulok

Sadovaya-Trufalnaya ulitsa

ulitsa Malaya Dmitrovka

ul. Karetny Ryad

Likhov per.

Bolshoy Karetny per.

Tsvetnoy Bulvar

Tsvetnoy bulvar

Teatr miniatyur

SAD ERMITAZH

Karetny per.

Sredn. Karetny per.

**Moskovsky tsirk im. Nikulina
(Moscow Circus)**

Triumfalnaya ploshad

Mayakovsky

Mayakovskaya

Teatr Sfera

Teatr Ermitazh

Vorotnikovsky per.

Uspensky per.

2-y Kolobovsky per.

1-y Kolobovsky per.

3-y Kolobovsky per.

Trubnaya

Trubnaya ploshad

Peking

**Kontsertny zal imeni Pl. Chaykovskovo
Tchaikovsky Concert Hall**

**SAD AKVARIUM PARK
(AQUARIUM PARK)**

Bol. Sadovaya ul.

Starolimennovsky

Degtyarny per.

Staropimenovsky

Marriott Grandhotel

**Muzey Unikalnykk Kukol
(Museum of Unique Dolls)**

Tverskaya ulitsa

Nastasinsky per.

Bol. Putinkovsky

FN Petrovu

Teatr Lenkom

Tserkov Rozhdeniya Bogoroditsy v Putinkakh

Strastnoy bulvar

Petrovka

Vysoko petrovsky monastyr

Krapivensky per.

Petrovsky bulvar

ulitsa Gasheka

Brestskaya ulitsa

3-ya Tverskaya-Yamskaya ulitsa
2-ya Tverskaya-Yamskaya ulitsa
4-ya Tverskaya-Yamskaya per.
Tverskaya-Yamskaya ulitsa
1-ya Tverskaya-Yamskaya ulitsa

Blagoveshchensky per.

Mamonovsky per.

**Moskovsky muzey Sovremenovo iskusstva
(Museum of Contemporary Art)**

Bol. Sadovaya ul.

Krylov

**Muzey sovremennoy istorii Rossii
(Museum of Contemporary History of Russia)**

Mal. Palashevsky per.

Tverskaya ulitsa

Izvestiya

Pushkinskaya

Pushkinskaya

AS Pushkin

Chekhovskaya

Kozitsky per.

**Moskovsky muzey Sovremenovo iskusstva
(Museum of Contemporary Art)**

Petrovsky per.

Rakhmanovsky per.

Nizhn. Kiselny per.

Sandunovskie bani

Sandunovsky per.

**Patriarshie prudy
(Patriarch's Ponds)**

Yeliseev's

Tsentralny

Sytinsky per.

B. Gnezdnikovsky per.

Glinishchevsky per.

ul. Petrovka

Budapest

Neglinnaya ulitsa

ulitsa Rozhdestvenka

Spiridonyevsky per.

Maly Gnezdnikovsky per.

Muzykalny teatr im. Stanislavskovo i Namirovicha-Danchenko

Marriott Royal

Petrovsky Passazh

Mal. Bronnaya ulitsa

Malaya Bronnaya ul.

Bogoslovsky per.

Bolshaya Bronnaya ul.

Tverskoy bulvar

Tverskaya ulitsa

Tverskoy per.

Strolesnikov per.

Dmitrovsky per.

ul. Kuznetsky Most

TsUM

Pushechnaya ul.

Savoy

Marco Polo Presnya

Spiridonovka ul.

**Sinagoga Lyubavicheskikh khasidov
(Lubavitch Synagogue)**

Maly Kozikhinsky per.

Shvedsky tup.

Leontyevsky per.

Dolgoruky

**Pravitelstvo Moskvy
(Mayor's Office)**

**MKhAT
(Moscow Arts Theatre)**

Kamergersky per.

**Bolshoy teatr
(Bolshoy Theatre)**

**Maly teatr
(Maly Theatre)**

Chekhova per.

Spiridonovka per.

TTeatr na Malaya Bronnaya

**Dom-muzey MN Yermolovoy
(Maria Yermolova Home)**

Muzey MKhAT

**Dom Soyuzov
(Hall of Unions)**

Teatralnaya

Teatralny pr.

Metropll

**Muzey-kvartiry AM Gorkovo
(Maxim Gorky Museum)**

pl. Nikitskie vorota

**Dom-muzey KS Stanislavskovo
(Stanislavsky Museum)**

Kazetny pereulok

**Gosudarstvennaya duma
(State Duma)**

Okhotny Ryad

ul. Okhotny Ryad

Teatralnaya pl.

Teatralnaya

Old Wall

Nikolskaya ul.

skaya ulitsa

Tserkov Bolshovo Vozneseniya

Tserkov Feodora Studita

Bolshaya Nikitskaya ulitsa

**Moskovskaya konservatoriya im. Pl Chaikovskovo
(Moscow Tchaikovsky Conservatory)**

Bryusov per.

Gazetny per.

National

Moskva

Revolutsii

Ploshad Revolutsii

Skaternly per.

Khlebny per.

Stoleshny per.

**Gosudarstvenny muzey Vostoka
(Museum of Oriental Art)**

Sredn. Kislovsky per.

Nikitskaya ulitsa

Zoologichesky muzey

MGU Moskovsky universitat

**Muzey V. I. Lenina
(former Lenin Museum)**

Manezhnaya ploshad

Zhukov

Zaikonospassky monastyr

**Kazansky sobor
(Kazan Cathedral)**

Mal. Rzhevsky per.

Mal. Kislovsky per.

Bol. Kislovsky per.

Romanov per.

Mogila Neizvestnovo Soldata

Manezhnaya pl.

**Gosudarstvenny istorichesky muzey
(State Historical Museum)**

Krasnaya ploshad

GUM

Povarskaya ulitsa

ul. M. Molchanovka

Nizh. Kislovsky per.

Mokhovaya ulitsa

ALEKSANDROVSKY SAD

**Dom-muzey MYu Lermontova
(Lermontov Museum)**

**Dom Yevropy
(House of Europe)**

**Muzey arkhitektury im AV Shcheva
(Shchusev Museum of Architecture)**

Manege

Biblioteka im. Lénina

**Kreml
(Kremlin)**

Mavzoley V. I. Lenina

Minin & Pozharsky

Molchanovka

y Arbat

**Dom Knigi
(House of Books)**

**Tserkov Simeon Stolpnika
(Siméon the Stylite)**

Arbatsky vorota ploshad

Arbatskaya

ulitsa Vozdvizhenka

**Rossiiskaya Gosudarstvennaya Biblioteka im. Lenina
(State Lenin Library)**

Aleksandrovsky Sad

Manezhnaya ploshad

**Sobor Vasiliya Blazhennovo
(St Basil's)**

D · E

Leningradsky vokzal

V. I. Lenina

anchyovskaya

Komsomolskaya

Yaroslavsky vokzal

Komsomolskaya ploshchad

Krasnoprudnaya ul.

Komsomolskaya

Nizhnyaya Krasnoselskaya ulitsa

Olkhovskaya ulitsa

Baumanskaya ulitsa

radskaya

Kazansky vokzal

Ryazansky proezd

Olkhovsky tup.

Olkhovsky per.

Olkhovskaya ulitsa

Bakuninskaya ulitsa

rskaya ulitsa

Yuzhny pr.

Novoryazanskaya ulitsa

Bogoyavlensky Kafedralny Sobor v Yelokhove (Epiphany in Yelokhovo)

ulitsa

Baumanskaya

ul. Fridrikha Engelsa

Kalanch. tup.

Ryazansky per.

Basmanny pereulok

jed. numero Basmanny

Novoryazanskaya ulitsa

Spartakovskaya ulitsa

Pletesnkov.

Baumanskaya ulitsa

Ladozhskaya ulitsa

Poslannikov per.

MYu Lermontov

Basmannaya

ulitsa

ul. A.Lukyanova

Staraya Basmannaya ulitsa

Dobroslobodskaya ul.

Lefortovsky per.

sky per.

Aptekarsky pereulok

Starokirochny per.

voya

Basmanny tupik

Tokmakov pereulok

Denisovsky pereulok

Gardnerov- sky per.

Baumanskaya ulitsa

2-ya Baumanskaya ulitsa

Khomutovsky tupik

Dobroslobodskaya ul.

Bolshoy Demidovsky

Brigadirsky per.

per.

rava-Chernogryazskaya ulitsa

Mashkova ulitsa

Gorokhovsky pereulok

Maly Demidovsky per.

Novokirochny per.

Tekhnichesky per.

artira tsova aznetsov Museum)

ulitsa

Kazakova

ulitsa Kazakova

ulitsa Radio

ulitsa Radio

tsa Pokrovka

Maly Kazyonny pereulok

Zemlyanov Val

Sadov. tup.

Puteysky tup.

Nizhny Susalny per.

Yelizavetinsky pereulok

Bol. Kazyonny per.

Kurskaya

naberezhnaya Akademika Tupoleva

Yauza

Yakovoapostolsky per.

Kurskaya

Krasnokazarmennaya nab.

Lyalin pereulok

Kursky vokzal

PARK IM. 1 MAY

Samokatnaya

ulitsa

Slobodskoy per.

pereulok

Chkalovskaya

Mruzovsky per.

naberezhnaya

Volochaevskaya ulitsa

per. Obukha

rontsovo Pole

ulitsa Zemlyanov Val

Verkh. Syromyatnich.

Melnitsky per.

2-y Syromat- nicheskiy per.

3-Y Syrom. per.

4-y Syrom. per.

Maly Poluyaroslavsky pereulok

Bol. Poluyaroslavsky per.

Syromyatnichesky pr.

Nizhnyaya Syromyatnicheskaya ul.

Syromyatnichesky

Zolotorozhskaya nab.

Syrogaanovsky

Zolotorozhsky

proezd

D · E

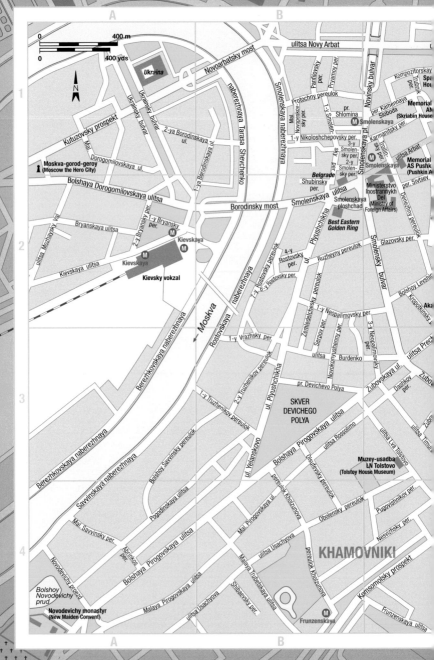

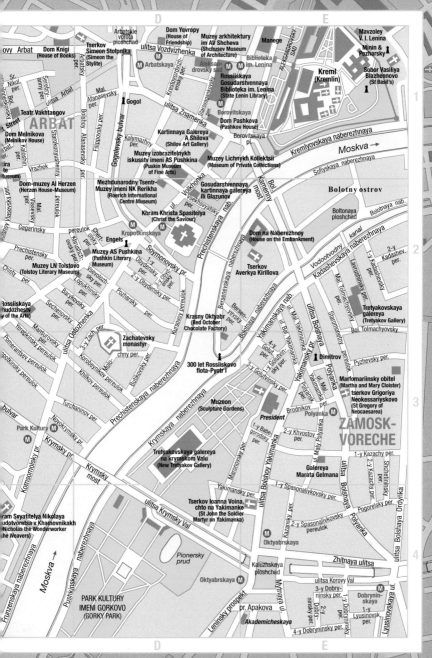

ovy Arbat
Dom Knigi
(House of Books)

Tserkov Simeon Stolpnika
(Simeon the Stylite)

Ⓜ Arbatskaya

Sr. Nikol. per.
Serebryanny per.
ulitsa Arbat
Bol. Afanasyevsky per.
Mal. Afanasyevsky per.

Teatr Vakhtangov
ARBAT

Dom Melnikova
(Melnikov House)
Arbat.
ira Museum)

Bolshoy Afanasyevsky per.
Krestovozdvizhensky per.
Starokonyushenny per.
Filippovsky per.
Gogolevsky bulvar

‡ Gogol

ulitsa Znamenka

Dom-muzey AI Herzen
(Herzen House-Museum)

Mal. Vlasyevsky per.
Gagarinsky per.
Kolymazhny per.

Kartinnaya Galereya A Shilova
(Shilov Art Gallery)

Muzey izobrazitelnykh iskusstv imeni AS Pushkina
(Puskin Museum of Fine Arts)

Chert. olsky per.
pereulok
Kholstovy per.
Starovagankovsky per.
Volkhonka ul.
Vsekhsvyatsky per.

Mezhdunarodny Tsentr-Muzey imeni NK Rerikha
(Roerich International Centre Museum)

Gosudarstvennaya kartinnaya galereya Ili Glazunova

Dom Yevrópy
(House of Friendship)

ulitsa Vozdvizhenka

Ⓜ Aleksan-drovsky sad

Borovitskaya

Dom Pashkova
(Pashkov House)

Borovitskaya pl.

Muzey arkhitektury im AV Shcheva
(Shchusev Museum of Architecture)

Manege

Rossiiskaya Gosudarstvennaya Biblioteka im. Lenina
(State Lenin Library)

Muzey Lichnykh Kollektsii
(Museum of Private Collections)

Biblioteka im. Lenina

ALEKSANDROVSKY SAD

Kreml
(Kremlin)

Mavzoley V. I. Lenina

Minin & Pozharsky

Sobor Vasiliya Blazhennovo
(St Basil's)

Kremlyovskaya naberezhnaya

Moskva →

Sofiyskaya naberezhnaya

Bolotny ostrov

Boltonaya ploshchad

Bolotnaya nab.

Ⓜ Kropotkinskaya

Khram Khrista Spasitelya
(Christ the Saviour)

‡ Engels

Muzey AS Pushkina
(Pushkin Literary Museum)

Muzey LN Tolstovo
(Tolstoy Literary Museum)

Rossiiskaya udozhestv
y of the Arts)

Prechistensky per.
Chisty per.

Soymonovsky pr.
Prechistenskaya nab.

Obydensky per.
2-y Obydensky per.
Vsevolozh-sky per.
Lopukhinsky per.
Pozharsky per.
Kursovoy pereulok

Dom na Naberezhnoy
(House on the Embankment)

Tserkov Averkya Kirillova

Bersen-yevsky per.
Bersenevskaya naberezhnaya

Krasny Oktyabr
(Red October Chocolate Factory)

Bersenevskaya nab.

Vodootvodny kanal

Kadashevskaya naberezhnaya

Mal. Tolmachovsky per.
Lavrushinsky per.

Tretyakovskaya galereya
(Tretyakov Gallery)

Bol. Tolmachovsky

2-y Kadashev. per.

Baryovsky per.
Sechenovsky per.
Mansurovsky per.
Yeropkinsky pereulok
Pomerantsev pereulok
opotkinsky pereulok

Zachatevsky monastyr

chny per.

Korobeynikov pereulok
Khilkov pereulok

Turchaninov per.

Butikovsky per.

Molo.

300 let Rossiiskovo flota-Pyotr I

Yakimanskaya nab.

Bol. Yakimanka
Mal. Yakimanka

4-y Golut. per.
3-y Golutvin-sky per.

‡ Dimitrov

Pyzhevsky per.

Marfomariinsky obitel
(Martha and Mary Cloister)

tserkov Grigoriya Neokessariyskovo
(St Gregory of Neocaesarea)

bulvar

Ⓜ Park Kultury

Novokrymsky per.

Muzeon
(Sculpture Gardens)

Brodnikov per.

Ⓜ Polyanka

ZAMOSK-VORECHE

Ⓜ Krymsky pr.

Komsomolsky pr.

ulitsa Ostozhenka

Krymskaya naberezhnaya
Prechistenskaya naberezhnaya

Krymsky most

President

1-y Babe-gorodsky per.
2-y Khvostov. per.

ulitsa Bolshoy Yakimanka

ul. Bol. Polyanka
ul. Mal. Polyanka
Mal. Polyanka per.

Galereya Marata Gelmana

ulitsa Bolshaya Ordynka

1-y Kazachy per.
2-y Kazachy per.

Shchetininsky per.

Tretyakovskaya galereya na krymskom Valu
(New Tretyakov Gallery)

Maronovsky per.

1-y Spasonalivkovsky per.

Pogorelsky per.

ulitsa Koroy Val

ulitsa Krymsky Val

Tserkov Ioanna Voina, chto na Yakimanke
(St John the Soldier Martyr on Yakimanka)

Yakimansky per.

Kazansky per.

2-y Spasonalivkovsky pereulok

ram Svyatitelya Nikolaya udotvoretsa v Khamovnikakh Nicholas the Wonderworker he Weavers)

Frunzenskaya naberezhnaya

Pushkinskaya naberezhnaya

Moskva →

Pionersky prud

**PARK KULTURY IMENI GORKOVO
(GORKY PARK)**

Kaluzhskaya ploshchad

Ⓜ Oktyabrskaya

Ⓜ Oktyabrskaya

Mytnaya ul.

pr. Apakova

Leninsky prospekt

Leninsky prospekt

Zhitnaya ulitsa

ulitsa Koroy Val

3-y Dobry-ninsky per.
2-y Dobryninsky per.
1-y Dobryninsky per.
4-y Dobryninsky per.

1-y Lyusinovsk. per.

Lyusinovskaya ul.
Bolshaya Ordynka

Ⓜ Dobryninskaya

Akademicheskaya

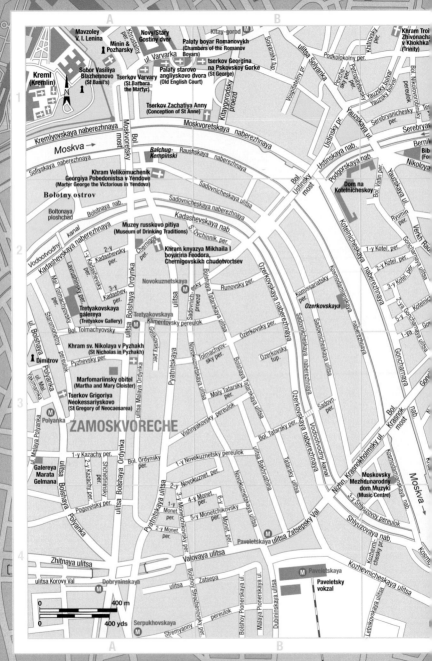

Mavzoley V. I. Lenina

Minin & Pozharsky

Novy/Stary Gostiny dvor

ul. Varvarka

Palaty boyar Romanovykh (Chambers of the Romanov Boyars)

Tserkov Georgina na Pskovskoy Gorke (St George)

Khram Troi Zhivonacha v Khokhka (Trinity)

Kitay-gorod

Khrustaly per.

Soyansky pr.

ulitsa Solyanka

Podkolokolny per.

Pevche-sky pr.

Petroverigsky per.

Khitrov per.

Bol. Nikolovorob. pereulok

Yauzsky bulvar

Yauzsky blvd.

Serebryanichesky

Serebrya

Sobor Vasiliya Blazhennovo (St Basil's)

Tserkov Varvary (St Barbara the Martyr)

Palaty starovo angliyskovo dvora (Old English Court)

Kreml (Kremlin)

Tserkov Zachatiya Anny (Conception of St Anne)

Kitaygorodsky proezd

Kitaygorodsky proezd

Vospitalny pr.

Ustinsky pr.

Berni

Bib (Fo

Nikolaya

Kremlyovskaya naberezhnaya

Moskva →

Moskvoretsky most

Bol. Ustinsky most

Moskvoretskaya naberezhnaya

Ustinskaya nab.

Yauzskaya ul.

Sofiyskaya naberezhnaya

Balchug-Kempinski

Raushskaya naberezhnaya

Bol. Ustinsky most

Podgorskaya nab.

Bol. Ustinsky most

Ryumin per.

Verkh Radi

Khram Velikomuchenik Georgiya Pobedonistsa v Yendove (Martyr George the Victorious in Yendova)

Bolotny ostrov

Sadovnicheskaya ulitsa

Dom na Kotelnicheskoy

Kotelnicheskaya naberezhnaya

Bol. Yalin nab.

Boltonaya ploshchad

Bolotnaya nab.

Sadovnicheskaya naberezhnaya

Vodootvodny kanal

Kadashevskaya naberezhnaya

Kadashevskaya nab.

Muzey russkovo pitiya (Museum of Drinking Traditions)

Ovchinnik per.

Chernigov pest.

1-y Kotel. per.

2-y Kotel. per.

2-ta Goncharna ulitsa

Kotelnie

Mal. Tolmachevsky per.

2-y Kadashevsky per.

1-y Kadashevsky per.

Lavrushinsky per.

Khram knyazya Mikhaila I boyarina Feodora, Chernigovskikh chudotvortsev

Bolshaya Tatarskaya ulitsa

Ozerkovskaya naberezhnaya

Sadovnicheskaya naberezhnaya

Komissariatsky

2-y Kotel. per.

3-y Kotel. per.

Goncharnaya

3-y Kadashev per.

Novokuznetskaya ulitsa

Runovsky per.

Ozerkovskaya

Staromonetny pereulok

Tretyakovskaya galereya (Tretyakov Gallery)

Bol. Tolmachevsky

Tretyakovskaya

Klimentovsky pereulok

Sadovnichesky proezd

Ozerkovsky per.

Ozerkovsky per.

Ozerkovsky per.

Ozerkovskaya naberezhnaya

ulitsa Bolshaya Ordynka

Khram sv. Nikolaya v Pyzhakh (St Nicholas in Pyzhakh)

Pyzhevsky per.

Ordynsky tup.

Tolmachev-sky per.

Ozerkovsky tup.

Dimitrov

ul. Bol. Polyanka

ul. Mal. Yakimanka

Marfomariinsky obitel (Martha and Mary Cloister)

Pyatnitskaya ulitsa

Maly Tatarsky per.

Sadovn. nab.

Tserkov Grigoriya Neokessariyskovo (St Gregory of Neocaesarea)

Bol. Tatarsky per.

Vodootvodny kanal

Sadovn.

ZAMOSKVORECHE

Vishnyakovsky pereulok

Tatarsky per.

Nizhn. Krasnokholmsky most

Bol. Krasnok nab.

Bol. Krasnok most

Polyanka

1-y Kazachy per.

Bol. Ordynsky per.

1-y Novokuznetsky pereulok

ulitsa Bakhrushina

Novokuznetskaya ulitsa

Kosmodamianskaya naberezhnaya

Moskva →

Galereya Marata Gelmana

Shchetininsky per.

2-y Kazachy per.

Bol. Ordynka ulitsa

2-y Novokuznet. per.

Moskovsky Mezhdunarodny dom Muzyki (Music Centre)

ulitsa Malaya Polyanka

Pogoretsky per.

Pyatnitskaya ulitsa

1-y Monet. per.

2-y Monetchikovsky per.

3-y Monet. per.

4-y Monet per.

5-y Monetchikovsky

6-y Monet. per.

Tatarsky per.

Kozhevni-chesky per.

Shlyuzovaya nab.

3-y Shlyuzovov pereulok

Shlyuzovaya nab.

Paveletskaya ulitsa Zatsepsky Val

Kosmodamianskaya

Kozhevnicheskaya ulitsa

Zhitnaya ulitsa

ulitsa Korovy Val

Dobryninskaya

Valovaya ulitsa

ulitsa Bolshoy Zatsepa

Dubininskaya ulitsa

Bolshoy Pionerskaya ul.

Malaya Pionerskaya ulitsa

Paveletskaya

Paveletsky vokzal

Letnikovskaya ulitsa

0 _____ 400 m

0 _____ 400 yds

Serpukhovskaya

Stremyanny per.

STREET INDEX

ART AND PHOTO CREDITS

INDEX

ABOUT THIS BOOK

INSIGHT GUIDES

MOSCOW

Editors: Rachel Lawrence and Tom Fleming
Author: Marc Di Duca
Head of Production: Rebeka Davies
Pictures: Tom Smyth
Cartography: original cartography Stephen Ramsay, updated by Carte

Distribution

UK, Ireland and Europe
Apa Publications (UK) Ltd
sales@insightguides.com

United States and Canada
Ingram Publisher Services
ips@ingramcontent.com

Australia and New Zealand
Woodslane
info@woodslane.com.au

Southeast Asia
Apa Publications (SN) Pte
singaporeoffice@insightguides.com

Hong Kong, Taiwan and China
Apa Publications (HK) Ltd
hongkongoffice@insightguides.com

Worldwide
Apa Publications (UK) Ltd
sales@insightguides.com

Special Sales, Content Licensing and CoPublishing
Insight Guides can be purchased in bulk quantities at discounted prices. We can create special editions, personalised jackets and corporate imprints tailored to your needs. sales@insightguides.com; www.insightguides.biz

Printing
CTPS-China

What makes an Insight Guide different? Since our first book pioneered the use of creative, full-colour photography in travel guides in 1970, we have aimed to provide not only reliable information but also the key to a real understanding of a destination and its people.

Now, when the internet can supply inexhaustible (but not always reliable) facts, our books marry text and pictures to provide that more elusive quality: knowledge. To achieve this, they rely on the authority of local expert authors.

This new edition of City Guide Moscow was commissioned and copyedited by **Rachel Lawrence** and **Tom Fleming**. It was updated by **Marc Di Duca**, who has been criss-crossing the former Communist world for more than 25 years. He is the author of several guides to Russia, a confident Russian speaker and makes regular visits to the country.

This edition builds on the previous work of **Michele A. Berdy**, an American-born columnist for the *Moscow Times*, **Carl Shreck**, a colleague of Berdy at the *Moscow Times*, and leading scholar **William Craft Brumfield**.

The Travel Tips section was expertly put together by **Marc Di Duca**, **Brian Driotcour** and **Marc Bennetts**. The vivid photography of Richard Nowitz appears throughout the book.

The book was proofread by **Kathryn Glendenning** and the index was compiled by **Penny Phenix**.

SEND US YOUR THOUGHTS

We do our best to ensure the information in our books is as accurate and up-to-date as possible. The books are updated on a regular basis using local contacts, who painstakingly add, amend, and correct as required. However, some details (such as telephone numbers and opening times) are liable to change, and we are ultimately reliant on our readers to put us in the picture.

We welcome your feedback, especially your experience of using the book "on the road". Maybe we recommended a hotel that you liked (or another that you didn't), or you came across a great bar or new attraction that we missed.

We will acknowledge all contributions, and we'll offer an Insight Guide to the best letters received.

Please write to us at:
Insight Guides
PO Box 7910, London SE1 1WE
Or email us at:
hello@insightguides.com